# ─ I Will ─
# ARISE
# and Go Now

## Reflections on the Meaning of Places & People

# I Will ARISE and Go Now

## Reflections on the Meaning of Places & People

Herbert O'Driscoll

Morehouse Publishing
NEW YORK

Unless otherwise noted, the Scripture quotations contained herein are from the New Revised Standard Version Bible, copyright © 1989 by the Division of Christian Education of the National Council of Churches of Christ in the U.S.A. Used by permission. All rights reserved.

Morehouse Publishing, 19 East 34th Street, New York, NY 10016
Morehouse Publishing is an imprint of Church Publishing Incorporated.
www.churchpublishing.org

Cover photo courtesy of the O'Driscoll family
Cover design by Jennifer Kopec, 2Pug Design
Typeset by Rose Design

Library of Congress Cataloging-in-Publication Data

Names: O'Driscoll, Herbert, author.
Title: I will arise and go now : reflections on the meaning of places and people in a life / Herbert O'Driscoll.
Identifiers: LCCN 2020045362 (print) | LCCN 2020045363 (ebook) | ISBN 9781640653351 (paperback) | ISBN 9781640653368 (epub)
Subjects: LCSH: O'Driscoll, Herbert. | Church of Ireland--Clergy--Biography. | Anglican Church of Canada--Clergy--Biography. | Anglican Communion--Clergy--Biography.
Classification: LCC BX5595.O36 A3 2021 (print) | LCC BX5595.O36 (ebook) | DDC 283.092 [B]--dc23
LC record available at https://lccn.loc.gov/2020045362
LC ebook record available at https://lccn.loc.gov/2020045363

## DEDICATION

For Paula, whose song sets the world aright;
and for Deirdre, Erin, Moira, and Niall:
four wonderful adults who once were our children.

# Contents

# Acknowledgments

Memoir is only made possible by those who live in our memories, and so my first thanks go to the great company of those who abide in mine and appear in these pages.

After them come those friends who in various ways made this book possible. My thanks to Ian Alexander, who devoted countless hours to reading, selecting, and editing my texts, and made available to me his wide experience in the world of media and publishing. To Helen Barron, who guided me to the gates of Church Publishing, and to Heather Pearson and Nancy Bryan, who opened them to me. To Joan Roberts, whose administrative skills and caring disposition enriched the pilgrimages formed by the then College of Preachers, making them a pleasure for so many. To Marcus Losack, who guided me in Celtic lands I had not known in my youth, and to Richard LeSueur, friend and colleague, who rescued me from the realm of retirement and gave me a role as preacher in his parish and later as travelling commentator and storyteller with his organization, Pilgrim Routes.

# About Memory, Gratitude, This Book, and Its Title

In one sense, this book is a simple retelling of scenes from the sequence of my life. Born in Ireland in 1928, I followed in the footsteps of countless fellow countrymen and women before me and set sail across the Atlantic in 1954, returning briefly the following year to be married, and then settling permanently in Canada. This vast and lovely land would be our home for most of the rest of our lives, welcoming into its bosom our children, grandchildren, and great-grandchildren, and serving as home base for wide-ranging travels.

The first section of the book, "Old Country," is a collection of things remembered from childhood and student years, lived mainly in the small city of Cork in the south of Ireland, and punctuated by long summers on my grandfather's farm in Donaguile, County Kilkenny.

The second part, "New World," tells stories from my years of active ministry in Canada, the United States, and, on occasion, other parts of the world Church.

The last portion, entitled "To Be a Pilgrim," recalls experiences from those years (largely in what some might loosely call "retirement") during which I had the privilege to lead many groups of fellow-pilgrims on trips to the Middle East, Ireland, and Great Britain.

One could say it has been a relatively unadventurous life, but it is one in which I have been given gifts of love and friendship, and opportunities to learn and grow, far beyond my counting or deserving.

So in another sense, these pages allow me to revisit in memory the times when, and places where, I was given something of lasting, permanent value—an image, an idea, an insight—and the people who gave them to me, or in whose company I shared them.

"Remember me," writes Christina Rossetti, "remember me when I have gone away, gone far away into the silent land." I'm sure that there is in all memoir something of that most human wish to both remember, and to be remembered.

I note my own interest in those of my family who lived before me. I find myself wishing I had asked them more questions about their lives, and learned the stories behind old photographs that show in the vigor and attractiveness of youth those whom I knew only as elderly. I hope that those who come after me might be grateful that I kept the door of time open wide enough to give them a pathway back, should they wish it.

I have read enough biography and autobiography to know that there is something fascinating about the living of another human life. I would like to think that there are things in my own life that might attract the interest of others, even if only to spark in them a recollection of similar escapades and experiences of their own.

Those of us who were born between the two world wars of the twentieth century, and have lived on into the first quarter of the twenty-first, have witnessed a transformation of human experience seldom, if ever, equaled in world history. That might seem to render the recent past irrelevant, and yet the very opposite seems to be the case. Popular history, historical fiction, and memoir have all become immensely widely read genres.

It is as if to be whirled into an unpredictable and frightening future makes us all the more interested in a very different, yet still familiar, world where those who nurtured and loved and formed us were themselves formed. After all, the world's great literature teaches us that in every age, the experiences of human life, and our responses to them, can be understood and shared in common across centuries, if not millennia. If this be true, how much more may it be true of the recent past?

The memories that matter live on as much in the heart as in the head. Think of your own deepest memories: the ones that bring with them feelings, longings, delight, a sigh or a tear, a tightness in the chest, a lump in the throat. I'm willing to wager that for you, as for me, they are connected with specific times and specific places, with a room or a landscape, with a season and its weather, and always, always with the voice and the face and the name of a person. So it is with these memories of mine.

A few words about the title of this book. You may have recognized it the moment you saw it. One day when W. B. Yeats was living in London but wishing very much to be back in the west of Ireland, he was sitting at a restaurant table—shall we imagine it to be one of the ubiquitous Lyons tea rooms of those days? Suddenly, he reaches for pen and paper and begins to scribble rapidly, before the idea is gone.

If I know anything about how these things happen, I'm sure that the bustle of the restaurant faded, the traffic outside the windows disappeared, and Yeats was wafted away to a small wooded island near the shore of a lake in County Sligo. His pen darts across the page, and for the first time the world sees the line: "I will arise and go now, and go to Innisfree."

Or did it?

Is it possible that the original hastily scrawled line in the notebook on that tea-stained, crumb-dotted table was not quite as it finally became? If I know anything about how a poem forms in the mind, I think it's quite possible that Yeats may have written half a dozen opening lines before he settled on the one that we have today, the one that takes us as surely as it took its author from the thundering traffic of crowded London to the beloved, quiet little treed island of Innisfree in Lough Gill.

That love and those memories were formed early on. Yeats's family moved first to London when he was only two, but he spent long summers with his mother's parents in Sligo. The countryside beneath the looming slopes of Ben Bulben is the world of the poet's childhood, and of his lifelong imagination, and the source of many of his best-known poems.

So it is for many of us. The years of childhood and adolescence are when life is most generous in giving us a rich treasure house of memories and images that can be stored up for use in later life.

On a May day just over three years ago, I found myself with a group of friends on a small craft moving slowly under grey skies across the calm waters of Lough Gill toward Innisfree. As we circled slowly around the island, listening to the elderly owner of the boat reciting Yeats's lines, it occurred to me that I had found the title for this collection of memories which I had been jotting down for some time.

These pages take us not merely to Innisfree, but to many places that I have been fortunate enough to visit in a long life, with much travel. Some of them were visited in childhood and youth. Others were shared with my wife, Paula, and, in later years, our family. Still others with friends on pilgrimages hither and yon. What they all have in common is that in that particular place, at that particular time, with those particular people, I learned or discovered or experienced something that I later realized had been life-forming, and that has stayed in mind and heart: what we sometimes call an epiphany.

For that, one can only be grateful. You will discover that gratitude is another theme running through this book. Frequently, I have been moved to record my recollections of an incident, as a way of saying "thank you" for it—often to a specific individual, whether encountered in the flesh or through the conversation that takes place between writer and reader—at other times to the hand of fate or God that caused something important to happen, whether one realized its significance at that moment, or only much later.

Johann (Meister) Eckhart, Dominican theologian and mystic in the Rhine Valley in that dark and terrible early fourteenth century, wrote, "If you were to say only one prayer in your whole life, and that prayer were 'thank you,' that would suffice." Such is my prayer.

So, let's you and I arise and go now . . .

Herbert O'Driscoll
Victoria, BC
Nativity of the BVM
September 2020

PART ONE

# Old Country

The author's parents: Terence James O'Driscoll and Anne Copley.

# CHAPTER ONE

# The City

*T*he Norse mariners who in the ninth century came upon the entrance to what is today known as Cork Harbor must have been awed by its size. As they crossed its vast expanse, they would have found the mouth of the river that feeds into it, today called the Lee. As they proceeded slowly upriver, their eyes would have been peeled for wealthy monastic settlements, ripe for plunder. At some stage, they would have reached the point where the river divides into two channels. Between them lies an extent of marshy ground. Here the Norsemen began a small settlement.

The local people would have told them that the name of the area was "Corcoc," meaning a marsh. Many centuries later, an English ear would hear this Gaelic word and translate it into a single syllable, "Cork," the name of the small but vibrant Irish city where I was born and grew up.

## 1. A CITIZEN OF NO MEAN CITY
### Cork City between the Wars

The apostle Paul used those words to describe his native city of Tarsus. I echo his sentiment about *my* native city of Cork. Alas, however, there has always been something about it that has invited humorous mockery. Even the word "Corkonians" that names its citizens has something of a derisive sound about it.

A Christmas pantomime I was taken to at a tender age featured a buxom dame played by a very funny man named Jimmy O'Dea. That night in the Opera House he threw off a line that my mother would often quote at home. "Cork's own town and the divil's own people."

She would say this when she knew that her three boys were up to some form of what she called "divilment."

There has always been an ongoing rivalry between Cork and the capital, Dublin. From time to time Cork voices have claimed that the *real* capital of Ireland should be on the banks of the river Lee, not the Liffey. Only a few days ago, as I was writing this memoir, I saw the cover of a tourist magazine referring to Cork as "The Real Capital."

I was in university before I realized the darker history behind this. In the brutal civil war that had brought the Irish Republic into being only six years before I was born, Cork City and the northern parts of the county saw some of the fiercest fighting. In 1920, the heart of the city was burned by British forces. Some voices claimed that Cork had earned the right to be named the capital. However, it was not to be.

My parents met in the mid-1920s and married in 1927. They enjoyed some good years as part of the first adult generation in the newly independent republic. The economy was depressed, but there was a sense of relief and hope now that the War of Independence was over. Early photographs show Mother in her probationary nurse's uniform, while Dad appears in a smart Norfolk jacket and fishing leggings, standing with a friend on the bank of a small river. I came along the year after their wedding, followed four years later by my brother Terry and six years after that by our youngest brother, Percy.

Some years before meeting my mother, my father had joined a national bakery as one of its travelling salesmen. The job took him over the southwestern quadrant of the country at a time when hostilities still raged and life could be dangerous. Eventually, he was made manager of the office in Cork and remained so for the rest of his working life. Since he was responsible for the distribution of products over the whole country, he would face further challenges during the Second World War, striving to serve customers when petrol was severely rationed and trains ran on peat fuel rather than coal.

These are the houses we lived in: first, the big house on Grattan Hill where Terry and I were born, then the new house at 6 St. Anne's Drive. Only three years later, Dad suffered a minor heart attack and the doctor, with the slender knowledge and resources of those days, told him he could not live where he had to climb two hilly streets as he walked home from work each evening. So we rented for a while on the south side of the city, on the Douglas Road. My memory is of a pleasant, large old house where we occupied the ground floor. However, for me the move necessitated a change of school and of church choir, which was difficult.

My most vivid memory of this fleeting chapter is having to make my way on dark winter evenings to the back door of St. Nicholas' Church, passing on the way an ancient family tomb that had holes in its ivy-covered door. To the imagination of a nine-year-old, it was quite a fraught moment, as I hurried toward the lighted window of the choir room.

As it turned out, we spent only a year there before a conversation between my father and his oldest brother, my Uncle Jack, resulted in a move back north of the river to 3 Magnolia Terrace on Mahony's Avenue. This meant a return to everything familiar in my young life: school, church, choir, Wolf Cubs, Scouts, Boys Brigade, Sunday school, all ecstatically recovered once again.

Television was still in the future. Radio was our source of information and popular culture. Dad was a radio buff, forever fiddling with valves and knobs and wires. That technical interest he did not succeed in passing on to us, but he did ensure that we would be news junkies for the rest of our lives.

And, of course, there were the movies, just entering their first golden age. We would stand in line for the cinema for hours. I remember the first film I ever saw. One Saturday, Dad suggested that he and I should go to the Coliseum to see *The Texas Rangers*. One scene remains in my memory, the very last. A Ranger has died. All the other Rangers are lined up on their horses. Background music. They all begin to sing "Should old acquaintance be forgot . . ." I'm quite sure that for good measure the sun was setting. I wept copiously. It was the beginning of a lifelong love affair with the silver screen.

Later, as the war ended, our teenage social lives were enriched by a new milk bar, a wondrous shining emporium hitherto unknown in Ireland. Replete with bright lights, chrome tables, coffee and juice dispensers, and ice creams with exotic names, it became the mecca for our generation.

Somewhere in all the fragments of earlier memories is that of my first bicycle. Even now, the images come flooding back. I overhear two friends in Sunday school saying that they had just been given bicycles. I raise the subject at home. Some weeks pass. Then, one Saturday, Dad says we are going downtown. There comes the wondrous moment when Mr. Crowley wheels out my very own bicycle. It shines with a radiance forever remembered. Its axles gleam, its gears hum with lubricating oil, its spokes shimmer as the wheels turn. It's a day when a boy's world enlarges and new horizons beckon.

## 2. THE PAST AS ANOTHER COUNTRY
### Childhood in Cork, 1928–1940

To understand the cultural formation of my generation in the Irish Republic in the years just before, during, and after the Second World War, one needs to have some idea of the patterns of piety and worship and self-understanding that characterized the Church of Ireland at that time. In 2020 this may sound very strange, but the fact is that the church was all-pervasive in our lives, just as it was for our Roman Catholic neighbors.

Just as for them, the evening Angelus rang solemnly for us, punctuating our days in a way we found comforting, rather than intrusive. Just as they did, we celebrated the lives of major saints and the feast days of our Lord's mother. Just as in their schools the timetable was interspersed with daily periods of religious instruction such as catechism, often conducted by the parish priest, so it was with us during the regular visits of the rector or the curate.

At the same time, an implacable boundary existed with regard to fraternization after the passing of early childhood. Marriage across that boundary was forbidden and, if by any mischance it occurred, was regarded with a deep sense of grief and betrayal. The reason for this can be summed up in two words: *Ne Temere*, the Latin document which had to be signed by the non–Roman Catholic partner, assigning to the Catholic partner all rights of religious formation of any children born to the marriage.

Because this will be so difficult to understand for subsequent generations living in a very different culture, I need to point out two things. The first is that the Church of Ireland, which is the Irish province of the Anglican Communion, existed as part of a tiny 4 percent minority in the population, along with all other denominations except Roman Catholic. Thus, identity was supremely important.

Secondly, the place of the church in people's lives in those days was utterly different from what it is today. The church was not something you *went to*; it was, in many ways, something you *lived in*. For us, the church formed the total context of our growing years, not only for worship and faith development, but for all of our education and much of our social life. The Church of Ireland offered much to its children and youth. Large Sunday schools with, for the most part, dedicated and knowledgeable teachers were available in almost all parishes. For boys, membership in the parish choir was more than encouraged; it was strongly and insistently expected.

Perhaps a look at a typical Sunday in my early life and that of my two brothers might show the pattern and the richness of it. Sunday school began at 10 a.m., an hour before church service at 11. Attendance at both was mandatory. Sunday afternoon at 3 o'clock there was another service designed for children. Evening Prayer was at 7 p.m., needing choirboys (choir practice having already taken place for boys on Wednesday afternoon after school). After that would come separate Boys Brigade and Girls Brigade bible classes at 8:15 p.m.

Because such a Sunday would today be unthinkable, I think I need to say that neither in myself nor among any of my friends do I recall the least resentment about it. It was just taken for granted. I suspect that this was largely because there were almost no exceptions to participation. We were all there, girls and boys, and we all knew each other. As well, during the week there would be meetings of Boys and Girls Brigade, Boy Scouts and Girl Guides, Wolf Cubs and Brownies that involved gymnastics and games, not to mention a good collection of light reading appropriate for our ages. In later young adult years, there would be regular parish dances, again within the buildings of the church. In summertime there would be group bicycling trips.

On the edge of the city there was a large, well-kept sports field which hosted field hockey games, tennis tournaments, and track and field days for Church of Ireland youth and young adults. Within the city stood the large Church of Ireland Centre, where the Diocesan Synod and many other meetings took place, but where there were also amenities for youth: a good library, two full-sized billiard tables, and table tennis equipment.

For most of us, our thirteenth year meant we were sent off to one of the many boarding schools that functioned under the auspices of the various Christian denominations. There we would remain for at least four years, when it was assumed that many of us would go on to university, most likely Trinity College Dublin: a foundation of Queen Elizabeth the First and an institution which the Roman Catholic Church in Ireland forbade its young people to attend. (Interestingly, this prohibition did not prevent many *English* Roman Catholics studying there.)

I hope I have succeeded in showing that unless one rejected what the church offered (which very few at the time did), it was possible to live a full, active, youthful life within it. Our church community was a world within a larger world. Mind you, we also participated in that larger world around us. The Carnegie Municipal Library, the Opera House, that milk bar I've already mentioned—owned, incidentally, by an enterprising Church of Ireland family—not to mention the seductive dream world of the cinema, all attracted us—probably, as I look back, to the slight concern of our families.

I realize now that we were moving outward into a world that even in our small land was on the cusp of great change. Let this, then, be a partial portrait of a past time and place, one with many features that we recognize today needed to change, but one that also held for us, in the innocence of youth, its joys and pleasures, its follies and adventures—not to mention, for some of us, the seeds of a lifelong Christian faith.

## 3. THE SHOEMAKER'S SON
### Grattan's Hill, Cork, 1934

Mr. McCarthy's shoe-mending business was in the tiny front room of his house, only a short walk from my home. When I was sent to take in shoes for mending, I would look over the half door and place them on the small shelf just inside. Mr. McCarthy would give a gruff greeting and continue with his work. He was a stocky man who always wore a cap and a black leather apron and had his shirt sleeves rolled up.

Beside him on the bench sat his son Brendan. Seeing him filled me with fearful curiosity. Even a child could sense that he was in some strange way distant, his movements slow. I never once heard him utter a sound. As I look back now, I think he would have been about twenty and was developmentally challenged in some way. In that long-ago society there were precious few medical or psychological resources for such as Brendan.

There came a day when I took a pair of my father's shoes in for repair and was surprised to see Mr. McCarthy sitting alone at the work bench. At the place where Brendan had always sat and worked along-side his father, there were no tools and no shoes waiting to be repaired. As a child I did not ask where Brendan was.

Eventually word passed through the neighborhood that Brendan had been taken to Mount Melleray. To a child, that news held a mysterious and rather frightening quality. Brendan's going had been so sudden that my mind played fearfully with the thought that I myself might also be taken by unknown hands and spirited away through imagined great gates that would close behind me forever, taking me to where I would never again play, never again see my parents, never again be free. All I knew about Mount Melleray was that it was a large monastery on a hilltop—at least my mind placed it on a hilltop—in the neighboring county of Waterford. The order of monks which owned it were the Trappists. The very word sent a chill through a small boy.

Life went on. Years passed. We left the neighborhood and went to live elsewhere. I came to a greater understanding of what, unknown to a small boy, had happened to Brendan. In a way hard to comprehend today, the Catholic Church in the Ireland of my childhood was not simply one aspect of life as it would be—for good or for ill—today. In those days, the church had a vast and powerful life of its own. It did not see itself as a part of society, so much as it saw society as a child to be nurtured and guided and, when necessary, corrected and disciplined.

If a youth such as Brendan had needs to which society could not respond, if the father of that youth had come cap in hand to the local parish priest on his son's behalf, that request would enter into unseen channels of authority and would receive consideration by faces and voices unseen and unknown. A decision would be taken, the half door into the McCarthy home would be opened, and Brendan would be led gently into the car waiting to take him to his new home.

My guess now is that Mr. McCarthy continued to sit in that tiny, shadowed room and plied his trade until his hands no longer obeyed him. Ireland gradually changed, bringing therapies and medications that could treat a young life like that of Brendan. But in my childhood days, there had been no naming of such things. It had simply been seen that Brendan was not as a youth of his age should be, that the deep shadows in his mind would never lift, and that his parents were growing older and were poor. No clinics or social programs existed to respond to Brendan's needs, but, in quite another way, resources did, indeed, exist.

In Mount Melleray, and other large monastic communities across the country, there existed a separate world into which Brendan could enter. In that world, there was a community large enough to assimilate and accept him. There he could take his place in the community's life; there his limited skills could be put to use. Somewhere in the sprawling buildings of Mount Melleray, Brendan was given another bench and another set of tools, so that once again he could bend and shape the leather for the sandals and work boots of the community.

At Mount Melleray, he would have had security and identity as a lay brother in the life of the monastery. His parents would never again have to worry about his welfare. They could be assured that they would forever receive the gift of his prayers, and would enjoy among their neighbors the distinction and benediction of having a son numbered among a community of the church where he would live a secure life of daily labor, contemplation, and holiness.

Perhaps, on very rare occasions in their simple lives, they would make the long journey through East Cork, passing through villages and small towns they may very well never have seen before, crossing into Waterford, winding their way through the green countryside, climbing down from the bus, pulling the bell that rings echoing down the long halls beyond the gates. From such a journey, Mr. McCarthy would return to his bench, picking up again his apron and tools. He and his wife would remember with pride the robed and cowled figure whose silence, once sad and frightening, was now transformed for them into a holy silence, and thus given dignity and meaning. For the rest of their lives, Sunday Mass would always be an occasion of profound thanksgiving.

## 4. THE CHOIRMASTER
### St. Luke's Church, Cork, 1935

We Church of Ireland folk always knew that our institution was a much more modest affair than the Church of England. We saw this in no uncertain terms whenever the *Irish Times* displayed photographs of great events involving the Church in England: a royal wedding at Westminster Abbey, a royal funeral in Windsor Chapel, and most of all a Coronation. We were very aware that we could not offer anything nearly as splendid.

Not, of course, that we were resentful. After all, when we in Ireland might from time to time feel overwhelmed by the vast Roman Catholic majority all around us, we had the Church of England to look to as a kind of big brother, especially since in those days, Big Brother possessed an empire that was still quite impressive.

Mind you, we had ways of maintaining our pride. From an early age, we were taught in school that while the Church of England referred to the ecclesiastical provinces that had spread across the British Empire as "daughters" of the Church of England, we should understand that the Church of Ireland was nothing as inferior as a daughter church. Instead, since we could trace our lineage back to Saint Patrick himself in the mid-fifth century, we were a "sister" church to the Church of England.

All of which, in a meandering way, brings me to Mr. Garrett. Had we been English, he would have been referred to as the master of the choristers. But again, being Irish, his role was defined more modestly. Mr. Garrett was our choirmaster. I think you might wish to meet him.

Mr. Garrett was a small man. We choir boys would delight in making the biblical reference to the tax collector Zacchaeus, said by Luke the Evangelist to be a small man. You may recall his having to climb a tree to see Jesus pass by in his hometown of Jericho. Mr. Garrett had to find other ways of lifting himself to an imposing height. The grand piano in the center of our rehearsal room was a challenge to him if he wanted to see us choir boys at weekly practice. To achieve a heightened state, he would assemble four thick service books, place them on his bench, and sit on them. He was then ready for choir practice.

While we did not dislike Mr. Garrett, we nevertheless feared him. In that long-ago world, authority figures were much more acknowledged than today. We might make jokes about Mr. Garrett behind his back, but we would never dream of challenging his authority. He smoked incessantly, rolling his own cigarettes, getting out the strands of tobacco, licking the small piece of paper, wrapping these things together, and lighting up. Later, when the cigarette was well alight, it would cling to his upper lip as he sang a setting of the *Te Deum* or the *Magnificat* or some hymn. Although we always watched expectantly, we never saw a lit cigarette fall from that precarious position.

As choir boys, we were paid a small honorarium. To us, however, it was anything but small. It was exciting and anticipated beyond words. Once a month, Mr. Garrett would arrive with a small cloth bag of sixpences, shillings, florins, and half crowns. At the end of that week's practice, he would climb down from his small tower of service books and spill the change on to a cloth carefully spread on the piano. Next, he would produce a sheet of paper on which was listed all our names, our respective seniority in the choir, and the amount we were owed. This small liturgy produced an effect of absolute silence and stillness in the choir room. One by one, our names would be called. If we had missed any practices or Sundays, Mr. Garrett had calculated this precisely. Depending on absences, the unfortunate recipient would be docked some pay. No excuses were accepted, even sickness.

At the end of the day, what gifts did we receive in that long-ago choir room? Rich gifts, indeed. All unknowingly, I received a working knowledge of the church music of the Western world, one of the world's great musical traditions, and a gift for which I will forever be thankful.

My mother lived to the great age of ninety-seven. Through all those years, she never forgot that when her dutiful seven-year-old son received his first choir pay—the princely sum of one shilling and sixpence—he went straight to the local confectionary shop and spent exactly half of it on a small box of Black Magic chocolates, proudly bringing them home to her as a gift. Who knows? Perhaps on the basis of that childhood gift, she may appear at the great gates to champion my cause when Saint Peter rattles his keys impatiently to express his doubts about my worthiness to enter!

## 5. HEALER AND MENTOR
### Doctor's Office, Cork, 1935–1948

I was about three years old when I contracted my first ear infection. There were, I am told, great cries, tears, and distressed parents. Naturally, I have no memory of what was done for me. I suspect that it was a procedure of cleaning tiny ears as gently as possible.

George Barter was an ear, nose, and throat specialist in the early days of that profession in the Ireland of the 1930s. My relationship with Dr. Barter began when I was seven. I assume that our family doctor decided at some point that my continued infections required the attention of a specialist. Perhaps it was only then that such care became available in the Ireland of that time.

A particularly pleasant memory of those early appointments—
otherwise dreaded—was my discovery of the *Illustrated London News*.
Copies lay in the waiting room. Their photos took me to distant
places: not only to London itself, but also to the faraway reaches of
what was then still referred to as "the Empire."

Each visit followed the same sequence. The door of the vast,
high-ceilinged waiting room would open. The doctor's nurse would
appear and solemnly announce my name. It was not yet an age when
the vulnerabilities of childhood were catered to. I would rise and follow her into the cavernous hall of what I realize now was a rather magnificent Georgian mansion, one in a row of such houses that had once
been private dwellings but now were offices of various kinds.

I enter the surgery. Dr. Barter stands waiting for me, smiling,
warmly welcoming. Everything about his demeanor communicates
that he knows well my fears, and that he will be as caring as it is possible
to be. Later, as treatment begins, he takes the syringe and places it gently in my ear. Then he invites me to hold the metal tray beneath my ear.
I begin to cry from the pain. There is no impatience from the doctor.
He waits for me to gather myself. At the same time his voice conveys a
gentle sternness that tells me that this simply must be done, that it is for
my benefit, and that somehow we would get through it together.

Looking back, I can't remember exactly when the books began.
My guess is that I would have been about ten. One day, when we had
finished the procedure that by now had become a regular part of my
school holidays, he put away the instruments, pushed back the round
mirror that was strapped to his forehead, and pronounced my eardrums clear once again. The fact that both eardrums were punctured
meant that our meeting again was inevitable. However, this time,
before sending me on my way, he reached his hand to a small side table
and handed me a large hardcover book. "Herbert," he said—he was
a quiet-spoken, formal man—"I have a wonderful story for you. It's
called *The Coral Island*."

I was, of course, thrilled. Books were already beginning to claim
their permanent, central place in my life. That particular visit was
during the Christmas vacation. Every year, at subsequent Christmas

appointments with him, he produced another book: always a hard-cover, always new. He gave me two volumes of Robert Louis Stevenson: *Treasure Island* and *Kidnapped*.

The Christmas after I turned thirteen, he handed me what was in those days a boy's holy grail: a copy of *Chums Annual*, subtitled "A Book for the Boys of the Empire." After that, there would be copies of P. C. Wren's *Beau Geste*, Edgar Rice Burroughs's *Tarzan of the Apes*, Jules Verne's *Twenty Thousand Leagues Under the Sea*. On it went, until I left for university in Dublin. I have no memory of visits to him after that. It may have been that he retired. Toward the end of the war, antibiotics came on the scene. I recall a general improvement, never a complete recovery.

Many years later, sitting in the surgery of a Vancouver specialist and hearing of a new surgical procedure (which I accepted with good results), my doctor informed me that I owed a great deal to the regular treatments received in my childhood. They had prevented my developing a mastoid infection. I was about to tell him of George Barter's remembered kindness to a frightened boy when I realized that his nurse receptionist was discreetly indicating that his next patient was ready. However, he and I met several times over the next few years and I eventually found myself talking to him about books and recommending some good reading here and there. You might call it returning the favor.

## 6. JOURNEY WITH MY FATHER
### May 1937

One day in the spring of my ninth year, my father tells me that he has a free Saturday, and we will take the train to Cobh to see the harbor. It's a journey of about fifteen miles. Many years experiencing the vastness of Canada make me realize how short a journey that is in comparison to how magically huge it seemed then.

When the big day comes, we go to the small window in the station ticket booth to purchase our return tickets to what my father still calls Queenstown. Only recently has it been changed to Cobh (pronounced Cove), since the new republic has come into being.

The harbor, my father tells me, is so large that it could at one time contain the whole British fleet. He tells me of the occasion when he and a friend, both of them then sixteen, made this same train journey in January 1901, on the occasion of the death of Queen Victoria. A flotilla of vessels from the British fleet were in the harbor, their flags flying at half-mast, all solemnly draped in black bunting.

Much of that wonderful day is forgotten, save for isolated moments that remain like old sepia-toned prints. My father is pointing to the mouth of the harbor, where two great forts guard the entrance. He explains that just beyond the entrance is the open ocean, and only a few miles along the coast is the sunken wreck of the *Lusitania*, torpedoed by a German submarine with great loss of life. The awe and mystery of such an event reverberate in my young mind. I am far away in the heaving ocean, the outline of the great wreck looming in the depths.

Sitting on a bench, still looking out across the harbor, we share the lunch packed for us by my mother. My father jumps up, points out to sea, and cries "Look! Out there! As far as you can see!" On the very edge of our vision, we could just make out a grey shape moving westward above the ocean. "It's the Hindenburg!" my father cries. "The big new German airship. It's sailing to America!" We stand together, transfixed with excitement. My father acquires a new aura of high achievement in my eyes, as if he has personally arranged this amazing conjunction of the great airship and our train journey. All at once, we are in touch with the great world usually experienced only through our evening paper and the crackling voices of our home radio. Little did I realize that in a few days' time we would be sitting by that radio, listening to the terror of the same proud airship exploding and crashing, sending its crew and passengers to their deaths.

There were, of course, many other memorable times with my father, like the first movies I saw with him. The very first, I've already mentioned, was *The Texas Rangers*. I recall both my parents taking me to see *Sanders of the River*, the now politically so incorrect film starring

Paul Robeson as the Nigerian leader Bosambo. A third—they are coming to mind thick and fast—was the utterly thrilling *King Solomon's Mines*, Rider Haggard's wonderful story. We went to an early Tarzan movie, from which I came home attempting to imitate the great Ape Man's hunting call. My efforts were not met with appreciation! I realize now that my parents were very much into the then new world of movies or, as they were called, "the pictures." They certainly ensured that I would become a film buff and remain so for the rest of my life.

I recollect most vividly those moments when my father pointed me far beyond my immediate world. Three times a week, the big blue and white ferry, the *Inisfallen,* would come from Fishguard in Wales. My father knew the captain, so we would sometimes go aboard. I learned of the train that met the ferry in Wales, waiting to take people further on to a shining, infinitely distant London.

Nowadays we speak of someone being a "techie," able to do endlessly clever things on their iPhone and iPad. In those days, being a techie meant being adept in the still new world of radio. At times, I would share my father's forays into the exciting world of short-wave broadcasting. Voices came to us from some infinitely far-off part of the world, sounding tantalizingly near for a fleeting moment or two, only to be swept away in the whistling and shrieking of what we vaguely referred to as the ether, notwithstanding our frantic searches on the twisting dial.

Suddenly memory brings back the sight of something that was almost always on the wide kitchen windowsill. There, close to the radio and Dad's pipe and tobacco pouch (filled with Murray's Mellow Mixture) and his chair, was the current copy of a magazine of that time, *The Wide World*. As that title suggests, it specialized in articles from exotic places combined with the adventures of explorers, mountain climbers, dare devil pilots, and the like.

I realize now that my father was expressing a longing to escape from the prison that his job had become. He lived with unrelenting stress, robbing him of his health and the energy to participate fully in the lives of his three boys. He loved his family deeply, which added to his sense of defeat and futility. I suspect that his great fear was that his sons would also become prisoners of a society that at that time held little opportunity for a new generation. I have always regretted that he did not live long enough to know that life became very fulfilling for all three of us.

# 7. CORPUS CHRISTI
## Patrick Street, Cork, 1937

It was my best friend Jim who suggested we go downtown to watch the Corpus Christi procession. As Church of Ireland boys, we were not sure what it was, but it sounded interesting. We were both nine. We told nobody where we were going. As we got near the city center, we could hear church bells ringing. Soon we were moving within a great crowd. My memory is that it was a happy, boisterous crowd and this puzzled me. I was used to church occasions being quiet and serious.

Eventually we found ourselves in the main street of the city, surrounded by a solid mass of people. We knew we could see very little unless we got to the front, so we wormed our way through. We heard the distant sound of an army band, its music slow and solemn. Sunlight glinted on the brass instruments, the leader marched resplendent in white gloves carrying a staff that rose and fell to beat time for the band. Behind the musicians in their green uniforms marched a body of soldiers with rifles. There were other bands too: pipers with swinging saffron kilts led by a major who hurled his gleaming staff into the air and caught it without missing a step.

Then came the children. Whenever I read of the Children's Crusade in the Middle Ages, I think of this occasion. All the schools were closed, even our Church of Ireland schools, since Corpus Christi was a public holiday. The ruddy Irish faces of Wolf Cubs, Boy Scouts, and Girl Guides were beaming with excitement and self-importance. No effort was made to get them to walk in step. They flowed along in a solid mass, dressed in their uniforms, acknowledging the greetings from the crowd.

Then came the Catholic organizations: the Legion of Mary, the Confraternity of the Blessed Sacrament, the Solidarity of the Blessed Oliver Plunkett, and most dramatically the Knights of Columbus with their drawn swords and black capes.

The next and climactic part of the procession rounds the curve of the wide street, and it eclipses everything else on this day: the bands, the uniforms, the crowds, the closed shops, and schools. First comes the great white and gold canopy waving up and down, carried by priests. Under it, preceded and followed by more clergy, comes the bishop, magnificent in his vestments, blessing everyone to right and left. The thought occurs to me that he might have some way of knowing that two Protestant boys are in the crowd. He looks as if he knows everything. I am relieved when he passes by, leaving us undetected.

Every eye is fixed on what is being borne before the bishop under the white canopy. A disc of gold on a long pole is carried by a tall, robed figure. In the center of the golden frame is a small, pale circle: the Corpus Christi, the Body of Christ. The silence of the crowd changes to a strange sound, a kind of whispering wave of awe, as everyone kneels for the passing of the monstrance containing the Sacred Host. As Jim and I kneel, I feel a sense of guilt about my parents not knowing where I am and what I am doing.

My memory fades after that most solemn of moments. Many other groups marched: policemen, nurses, civic organizations, professional guilds. As I think back, I realize I could not have grasped then that I was given a vision of a world made whole: an entire society unified by the primacy of the sacred, giving it absolute precedence over everything else: commerce, schooling, sports. I had a glimpse of Christendom even as it was already beginning to disappear in the greater world beyond the small, newly independent island I called home.

The memory of that day also serves as a future hope for the fragmented culture I now live in. I realize that such a day cannot come again in the same way. However, that image of social unity inspires me to search for signs of wholeness about me, however faint and tenuous. The church that I watched passing by me on that Feast of Corpus Christi was at the time still glorious, confident, even imperial in its capacity to rule, to discipline, even to punish. Many faults are now ascribed to it in a very different age and society, and there is no doubt that they were, indeed, real and grievous faults. But for one glorious hour in those crowded streets, it challenged the so-called real world to dare to believe in a world much more real. Such were the gifts of Corpus Christi to a wide-eyed Protestant boy caught up in the surge of a vast, never to be forgotten, Roman Catholic tide.

# 8. A GIFT OF WORLDS
## Cork, Christmas 1938

As a small boy, one of my earliest memories is of a brightly colored tin box that contained my books. I say "*my* books" because I am told that these books—probably, in reality, very slim booklets—were very much mine, jealously guarded and grudgingly shared.

When I was seven, the nearby parish church claimed me as a chorister. In those days the newest young choristers had yet to learn how to sing psalms and anthems, so we participated only in the hymns. This meant there were long stretches in the service—the sermon was one such opportunity—when we could look through the books that filled the racks in the choir stalls. Most, of course, were prayer books and psalters and bibles.

However, boredom and desperation are powerful motivators. One day, I discovered the page in the prayer book that gives the yearly dates for the great celebrations of Christian faith such as Easter. I realized with a thrill that the page giving me the dates carried me far into the future—to the year 2000, no less. Considering that it was then 1935, you can perhaps understand how exciting it was to a small boy to think of that unimaginably distant future. I had enough early math in my parish school to be able to calculate how old I would be in 2000. I would be seventy-two!

Wonder might be the best word to describe that moment, or perhaps awe. At seven years of age, the very impossibility of imagining what it would be like to be seventy-two was overwhelming. After all, at seven you occupy a shining *now* that will simply always be. I still credit that page in the Book of Common Prayer, and its ability to waft me on a magic carpet into the far future, with giving me a lifelong passion for science fiction, especially stories of time travel.

There came a day in October of 1938 when my brother and I were excited because we had been told that we were about to welcome a baby brother. Small boys are not known for their expressions of delighted anticipation about the advent of small siblings. Excited does not necessarily mean delighted. Delight would come in a very different form, most certainly to me.

Our brother duly arrived. Over some weeks, we became used to his cries and shouts, his insatiable hunger, his napkins ("diapers" was a word yet to be used), and his constant demands on our mother's time and attention.

Christmas Day 1938 proved to be a day to remember. I had returned home from Morning Service when my father called me into the parlor. In Irish homes of that period, the parlor was a place of significance. Parlors were for special occasions, for important visitors, for reading or listening to the radio on Sunday afternoons, for great occasions such as Christmas. I knew that an invitation to the parlor meant something very important.

My mother was seated in the room. In front of the fire was a large box, wrapped in heavy brown paper. My father said, "Here is something you have wanted for a long time." Tantalized with curiosity, I opened the box. My delight knew no bounds. There before me were the ten magnificent volumes of *The Children's Encyclopedia*, edited by Arthur Mee. My father's reference to my longing for it referred to the fact that my uncle and aunt, whose nearby house I frequently visited, already owned a set. I had spent countless hours exploring their volumes. As my two brothers became old enough, they too explored these wonderful pages.

Arthur Mee's encyclopedia was the equivalent today of giving your child access to the Internet. Running though all ten volumes were streams of every conceivable area of knowledge, at least as conceived in those days: History, Philosophy, The Arts, Stories from all over the

World, Poetry, Science, Biology, Great Cities, Inventions in Technology, Famous Men and Women. On and on it went, and in the ensuing months and years, on and on *I* went, exploring, delighting, discovering, wondering.

Many years would pass before I would find myself leading parents of newly baptized children in a prayer naming the gifts they would wish God to give their child. The ultimate gift in that list is "the gift of joy and wonder in all [God's] works." As I have said those words, I have often recalled the magnificent gift I was given by my parents so long ago, a gift to be shared with my brothers, one that I now realize our parents could ill afford.

## 9. A WORLD FULL OF WEEPING

### Glanmire Railway Station, Cork, September 1939

"For the world's more full of weeping than you can understand."

—William Butler Yeats, *The Stolen Child*

**We lived about ten minutes' walk** from the Glanmire Station, and like most small boys, I was interested in trains. A large railway station of those days was the equivalent of today's airport: a place where one's mind was expanded, even if one was not intending to travel anywhere. We imagined great journeys. In reality, none of them were in any sense great—after all, we lived on an island only three hundred miles long—but imagination sufficed to make them great. We imagined travelling all the way to Limerick Junction in County Tipperary, there to change trains for that faraway city at the estuary of the great Shannon River, the longest river in Ireland. The greatest journey was to go all the way to Dublin. Most of us had never been.

A unique feature of Glanmire Station was the tunnel. What made this tunnel unique was that its great dark opening stood only about a hundred yards from the end of the station platform. Hardly had the pistons of the huge green engine turned half a dozen times, sending their pillar of steam high into the air, when the train plunged into the darkness of the tunnel, piercing the base of a mountain on which part of the city was built, not allowing its travelers to see daylight for many long thrilling minutes, during which time the pale electric lighting would come on in the compartment and the black walls of the tunnel could be seen rushing by.

I share these details because of the things that began to take place within weeks of the beginning of the war.

In 1939, it became obvious to the British government that Hitler was not going to be appeased. War appeared inevitable and the engines of war had to be made available. Factories old and new began to be refurbished or built all over England. Most of these were located in the north and west, in order to be as far as possible from the bombing that would surely begin soon. One thing more was necessary: with hundreds of thousands of English men and women about to be conscripted for service, a labor force was required to staff the factories.

For that labor force, the British government looked west across the Irish Sea to the as-yet young Irish Republic, which had stubbornly declared its neutrality in the coming conflict. Its depressed economy meant a high level of unemployment. Within weeks of the war's outbreak, the vast emigrations began. For tens of thousands, their first point of embarkation was Glanmire Station.

I remember the evening that we listened as a family, first at the tea table and then standing outside our front door, as a great wave of human cries filled the air. It seemed to come from the direction of the station. For months, those cries were a part of the city's life. Soon after they began, I asked if I could go to the station to watch. My best friend at the time said he would go with me. His family owned the pub opposite one of the side gates of the station. Grudging permission was granted, probably because my parents knew we would find our way to the station with or without it.

I picked up Maurice and we walked toward the station. The gates, which in our experience always stood open, were now closed and guarded by police. All around them was a vast crowd of milling humanity, the relatives and friends of those leaving for England. People were shouting, crying, beseeching, swearing. The police were trying to limit entry to those who were actually travelling, but their efforts were failing. People were breaking away from the crowd to seek other ways into the station. Maurice and I found a vantage point that allowed us to see the station platform. A dense crowd surrounded the waiting Dublin train. Since most of those leaving were young men (many to join the British forces as a job), most of the milling crowd was made up of their womenfolk, young and old. In time this pattern would change, as more and more young women sought employment in the munitions factories.

What has always remained in my memory from that first evening watching those wartime emigrations is what happened as the time for departure drew near. The station staff and the police tried to persuade people to step back so the train could move off. In an effort to help, the engine crew deliberately blew the steam whistle two or three times. Its shriek caused further pandemonium. As their efforts at persuasion failed, the police tried force, which only enraged the crowd. As it surged forward, the police found themselves pinned against the compartments of the train. Somewhere another whistle blew repeatedly. More uniformed militia began to move in, eventually succeeding in pushing back the crowd.

Very slowly, the engine began to move, pouring out steam that enveloped and distressed those nearby. Shouted farewells rang out, mingled with the cries of those who were weeping and far beyond speech. As the train gathered speed, many people began to run along the platform and down the slope at its end. Then came the most heart-rending moment. The last of the cars had just disappeared into the tunnel, leaving only smoke swirling and billowing out from the darkness, when scores of women, many screaming as if demented, ran into the tunnel, some tripping on the rails and falling, others crying uncontrollably, their cries echoing from the soot-grimed walls until they faded from sheer exhaustion.

In succeeding days and weeks, the authorities became more experienced in handling the crowds. This last desperate expression of despair was forestalled by assigning military personnel to block the tunnel immediately after the last car had disappeared.

Perhaps because I was young when I witnessed this expression of intense sorrow, it remains with me as a vivid memory. I realize now that what was being expressed on that wartime platform was all the accumulated sorrow of centuries of enforced emigration from Ireland: the Flight of the Earls in 1607, when the leading Gaelic land-owning families were forced into exile; the dispersal, after the Boyne victory of the Williamite forces in 1691, of the Irish Jacobite troops (popular memory called them the Wild Geese); the suffering in the 1840s when nearly a decade of famine forced the overcrowded "coffin ships" to set sail for North America.

The memory of what I had seen as a boy would return with special poignancy when I, in my turn, emigrated to Canada in 1954. I took my trunk to that same station, boarded the train, waved to my family, closed the window of the compartment, and waited to be engulfed in the long darkness of the tunnel before emerging into the daylight for the journey to Dublin, where I would catch the ferry for Liverpool and the waiting Atlantic liner.

Many years after that, when I returned to Ireland for one of numerous visits, the agent at the immigration booth opened my passport, saw the name O'Driscoll, and said with a smile, "Ah, the Wild Geese are coming home." I said, "It's good to come home." We both knew what we meant.

"Was it for this the wild geese spread the grey wing upon every tide . . . ?"

—William Butler Yeats, *September 1913*

In front of the farm house at Donaguile.

# CHAPTER TWO

# The Farm

*An old Japanese saying goes that a child lives with the gods until the age of seven. I am grateful that I was given that privilege for twice that length of time.*

*To live with the gods, you must discover their dwelling place, their magic kingdom. The truth, of course, is that magic kingdoms lie very close to this world, if only we can see them. My magic kingdom had small winding roads, a humpbacked bridge over a river, meadows of hay, fields of golden corn, horses, a donkey, cows, a wonderful black and white sheepdog named Billie, and a cock that crowed every morning. At the heart of this magic kingdom was Donaguile, my mother's childhood home, my grandfather's (now my uncle's) farm, and my enchanted place.*

## 1. THE MAGIC KINGDOM
### Donaguile, 1932–1942

My earliest memories of the farm tell me that in those years my father took my mother and me during the winter months, probably on some of his business circuits. He drove a Morris Cowley, complete with a rumble seat. I think I might have been four.

It is early morning, not long after sunrise. I am standing with my mother and grandfather at the door of the horses' stable that leads into the barnyard. The fields are white with snow, something not frequently seen in the south of Ireland. My grandfather has mixed a large bucket of feed for the calves. He opens the door, bangs on the bucket, and gives a loud call. Immediately, the calves turn toward us and then, with that skipping gait of the very young, they run toward the doorway, all jostling for a place, all trying to get their heads near or into the bucket, almost wrenching it from my grandfather's firm grip. He watches carefully to see that each one gets a fair share. He lets my mother place my small hand on the head of one of the calves. I feel the matted hair and the hard crown that is already showing the signs of what will one day become horns. My grandfather scrapes the last of the feed from the bucket and hurls it out into the snow, causing the calves to turn away and chase after whatever they can get. My grandfather closes the door on the cold white vision of the fields and a moment of vivid childhood memory is blotted out.

For me, the magic of Donaguile did not involve any magnificence or grandeur. The yard area in front of the house led for about a hundred yards to the gate that opened onto the unpaved road that rambled up the side of the valley. As you left the farmhouse and walked toward the gate, there were outbuildings to your right: first the stable for the two horses, then the shelter for the horse-drawn vehicles, then the barn for general storage, then the hen house, and finally the piggery.

As you reached the gate, to the right was a pleasant area of low bushes and small trees known as The Plantation. Here three brothers, later with younger cousins, found various worlds for adventure and exploration. Two of my abiding memories are of my brother Terry as the leader in mischief-making, and his ability even at eight years of age to eat the greenest and sourest apples in the orchard without once getting a stomach ache.

Attached to the farmhouse was the dairy. Here, when I had attained sufficient height and muscle, I took my turn with the heavy wooden plunger and the large steel churn in which my aunt made her country butter.

In the stable stood the large brown horse named Dan and the graceful black mare named Polly, held in separate stalls. The day came when I was lifted for the first time onto Dan's great haunches. I would cling to my uncle as we rode through the fields above the farmhouse, the horse's leather and silver harness jingling, until we arrived at the field where work needed to be done that day. We would dismount and my uncle would gently back Dan between the shafts of whatever piece of equipment had been left there overnight: the plough, or the hay bogey, or the mowing machine.

Beyond the horses' stable and behind the farmhouse was the Haggart. Here was the barn where the cows were gathered in each evening for milking, and the big hay barn where the precious crop was gathered to dry as winter feed for the cattle.

Eventually I was old enough to come in from the fields of haymaking to bring the meal prepared by my aunt for the men: meat sandwiches with butter from her dairy, and a deep pie made with apples from the orchard. Finally, she would hand me a large blackened kettle of strong tea, milk and sugar already added; all of it in two cloth bags to balance the weight. I would set off, taking short rests from time to time, but not delaying. On my arrival the men would gather in the shadow of a large haycock and enjoy the meal. Then, before returning to work, they would enjoy a single short smoke, my uncles reaching for their packets of Players Please cigarettes, my grandfather and the hired man reaching for their beloved short clay pipes.

By the time I approached my thirteenth birthday, early boyhood was coming to an end. Donaguile was about to be eclipsed by the new world of boarding school that was approaching. The oil lamps of my childhood and the candlelight beside my bed were about to be replaced by the new electricity sweeping across the countryside.

Again and again in later life, the sweet smell of new mown hay would return to me in places far from this remembered and beloved farmhouse. It returned on the farms of my first parish of Huntley in the Ottawa Valley. It came on the breeze not far from Cavendish Beach in Prince Edward Island, later in the foothills of Alberta and the rolling countryside of the Shuswap in British Columbia. Always the sweet windborne scent knits together an Irish boyhood and a Canadian adulthood, weaving them together into a seamless journey.

## 2. THE GREAT JOURNEY
### A Summer Ritual

Every July, we prepare to go to the farm. We will stay there about a month, sometimes longer. Our father will join us later for his two-week holiday from the office. Castlecomer is a hundred miles from Cork, an unimaginable distance to a child in those days on that small island.

Each year, the preparations follow a familiar pattern. For some days before we set out, Mother washes and irons, hoping for the sun to warm the small backyard and dry the lines of garments. Each day she reaches into the fire with a pair of tongs and takes out the red-hot stones that heat the iron. Piles of sweet-smelling clean clothes mount up. The evening before we depart, Dad comes home early from work. His role is to pack the bags. It is soon time for us to have our baths before going to bed early.

The morning of our departure, we savor the rare experience of taking a taxi to the bus station. The large American car has seen better days, but to sink back in its huge interior is thrilling. At the bus station, the bags are pulled out of the cavernous trunk and placed on the sidewalk. My father goes along the line of buses, seeking the one for Clonmel. Eventually, we are all on board. The engine starts, the bus—itself old and worn in a new and still impoverished republic—pulls away. Waving to our father, faces pressed against the vibrating window, we are off.

Through the city streets we go, riding above the great hidden marsh on which our ancient Norse city was first built. Eastward by the river we go, passing Blackrock Castle and turning north through villages that sing in the remembering: Tivoli, Dunkettle, Glanmire, Watergrasshill. Faster and faster the hedges fly by as the bus picks up speed. Horses and carts, donkeys and smaller carts, cyclists, all pull aside into the long grass at the roadside to let us pass. From time to time we slow down, not quite stopping outside some local shop or pub. The bus door crashes open, the conductor seizes a heavy roll of newspapers, throws them with unerring aim toward the small news agency doorway, and off we speed again.

Climbing now, we move out of Fermoy, passing the once British and now Irish army shooting range at Kilworth. On a hilltop in the far distance stands a white cross, stark against the sky. To me in my early years it was somehow "The" Cross. Later I learned that it was a memorial to more recent political and military agonies vaguely spoken of by our parents, remembering the flying columns, the ambushes and killings all over north Cork less than twenty years earlier, when the Republic was bloodily being born.

On we go through Mitchelstown before turning east, the tires singing their high-pitched song, the voice of the conductor calling out the names of towns and villages: Kilcoran, Ballyporeen, Clogheen, Ardfinnan. Away to the south rises the blue world of the Knockmealdown Mountains, to the north the rolling hills of Tipperary. Turning under the dark bulk of Cahir Castle, the fifteenth-century fortress of the Butler family, we finally drive along the north bank of the river Suir to Clonmel, where lunch waits, to be followed by the thrill of another bus.

All through the long afternoon we climb the low range of hills that brings us out of Tipperary into Kilkenny. Somewhere on the road down out of the hills there is a house with mysterious dark blue panels in its windows and a glittering fish pond in its garden. Year after year, I wonder what lies behind the windows.

As the day wears on, my brother, somewhere between sleeping and waking, leans against my shoulder. Our youngest brother, still a baby, rests in our mother's arms. As we enter Kilkenny, the Cathedral of St. Canice sends its spire and Round Tower into the sky to welcome us. We swing into the square under the shadow of the great Norman castle of William the Marshall, the seat of the Dukes of Ormond in medieval times, and there across the square is the small country bus that will take us the last twelve miles to Castlecomer.

My mother meets familiar faces, some of whom she has grown up with. They are returning to Castlecomer on the bus after a day's shopping, or perhaps a necessary appointment, in Kilkenny. They say the things of long friendship about herself and the boys, remarking how we have grown.

As the bus moves out of the city, the sun is lowering across the fields. We gaze from the front seat past the burly shoulders of the driver, watching for well-known landmarks, until we turn the last corner and come into Castlecomer, its row of shops now closed for the day.

At the corner of Barrack Street stands the light graceful carriage known as The Trap, the black mare between its shafts, our uncle at her head. There are hugs, greetings, laughter, a flurry of cases and parcels. Adult conversation is impossible with children's endless questions. We ask about the farm, the animals, the machines, the stream through the fields. On and on we chatter until the high wheels of the trap turn into the farmyard, and we have arrived.

Quick greetings are given to grandparents before a mad dash for the stables. The other horse stands in his stall, turning his great eyes that glitter in the shadows as we gingerly but affectionately stroke his haunches. From there to the cow barn, then to the hay barn, the pig house, the apple orchard, on to see the wooden gate our uncle has made since last year. We swing it wide, standing on the flagstone outside it that bridges the small stream where we will sail ocean liners made of six-inch slivers of wood.

Sloping away from us through the fields, an endless green land stretches to the dark wood that crowns the valley and stands as guardian and boundary of our boyhood world. At last, exhausted, we enter the house as the oil lamps are being lit and evening falls.

## 3. JOHN BRENNAN
### Teacher and Friend

John Brennan was a hired man on the farm. He has been spoken of already in this narrative, though not until now by name, and since he looms so large in it, I think you ought to meet him.

John wore a red scarf or kerchief around his neck, a cloth cap, trousers precariously held up by knotted binder twine, and boots with holes in the soles. He smoked a clay pipe with a metal cap on the bowl. He had a heavy mustache that dropped hot brown tea as his face emerged from a great steaming mug during breaks in the summer haymaking. I like to linger with the memory of him. I loved him, using the word as a child uses it.

There was one whole day when I became John Brennan. I announced this fact on rising, refusing all day to answer to my own name. Pushing a small hand truck, I went about the farmyard, the hay barn, and the orchard, doing the kind of things I imagined were John's duties. I recall that a wise grandmother took me seriously in my imagined role.

Between the horses' stable and the barn there was a flat stone about four feet long and a foot high, wide enough to provide a seat when needed. Very often, after the evening milking of the cows, John would sit there, fill his short clay pipe and have a smoke. Sometimes I would sit with him and he would chat away about all sorts of things. There were times he would tell me of his travels in earlier years. To this day I do not know if he had ever been further than Dublin, if indeed that far—all of seventy miles. But together we travelled, certainly in my imagination and I suspect also in John's, to Afghanistan and Baluchistan and what he called "the great falls of Nia-gara." This he would pronounce with an emphasis on the penultimate syllable. These were his favorite locales for adventures, probably because they were the most distant lands imaginable in those days in Ireland.

I learned things from John that I have never forgotten. He told me that crossroads—there was one very near the farm—were mysterious places. Crossroads, John would say, are places where you have to make a choice. You must choose the direction you will go. Each of those choices, even though they seem small and unimportant, changes the pattern of one's life. Very often, John said, both God and the Devil wait at the crossroads. Each of them tries to get the traveler to make the choice that will one day bring him or her to heaven or to hell. Therefore, John warned, one had to be most careful at crossroads. They were good places to make the sign of the Cross before deciding which direction to take.

One long summer's evening, long enough for the moon to come out even before the sun had set, John told me something that changed forever the way I would think about Christian faith. Looking up at the evening sky, pointing to the sun and the moon and the first faint stars of the coming night, John asked if I knew that they all moved. Sun, moon, stars, galaxies, all, he said, move all the time. I did not know this. I was filled with wonder. John then paused—for he was a consummate storyteller—and asked if I realized that once upon a time—only once since all of time began, he emphasized—they had all stopped moving. Sun, moon, stars, galaxies, all stopped moving. John remained silent for my wonder to grow.

Eventually, he resumed what has remained for my whole life a wonderful story. "When the angel Gabriel came to the Blessed Virgin Mary," he said, "he asked her if she would give birth to the Holy Child. The Blessed Virgin was puzzled and frightened. She didn't know what to say. She remained silent. The angel Gabriel waited. In that period of silence all the heavenly bodies ceased to move. The sun, the moon, the stars, the galaxies, all ceased to move. They waited for the Virgin's reply, and when she spoke, when she told Gabriel that she would give birth to God's child, they all began to move again."

I was stunned into silence. I had never heard anything so wonderful. I now realize that this simple man had shared with me a profound insight. Hitherto, I had seen the story of the holy birth playing out on a small stage: a baby in a manger in a stable in a village in a tiny country. Having heard John's story, I would henceforth set Christian faith in a vast cosmic arena of both time and space, which is where it remains in my consciousness to this day.

## 4. MY FRIEND NEDDY
### Donaguile, 1934

A photo turned up recently in a box in the basement: one of those small black and white photos that have become slightly yellowed, their corners curled up. In it, I am five years old. Looking quite secure and at ease, I am seated astride the farm donkey.

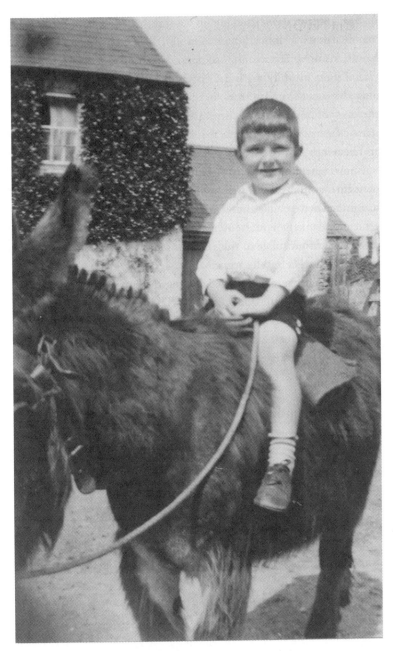

The author astride Neddy at Donaguile.

The person who lifted me up was John Brennan. And I remember clearly what John did as soon as I held the rope reins in my hands. Pointing to two lines of darker fur on the donkey's back, he traced them carefully with his finger, one across the donkey's shoulders, the other from his mane back along the spine. He then told me the story of how these two lines are found on every donkey. Before I share that story with you, let's think for a few moments about Neddy and his kind.

Somewhere on every Irish farm, there was a donkey who would perform many necessary lowly tasks. However, on our farm, the donkey had one role we could almost call genteel. Two graceful carriage-like vehicles were kept under cover in one of the farm barns: the traps. They were comfortable to ride in, their seats well cushioned and their rubber-tired wheels well sprung.

The smaller trap was for the donkey, the larger for a horse. Somehow you knew that the donkey liked his trap. Far more frequently than when he was pulling the plain old farm cart, he could be persuaded to break into a canter. I suspect he appreciated the lightness of the trap and the much greater ease of pulling it.

There were, of course, many adventures with the donkey. I recall the day my brothers and I decided that he could cheerfully accept all three of us on his back and take us for a short ride. I was fourteen, my brother Terry was ten, and Percy, the youngest, was about to be five. We put Percy up first as a kind of trial balloon. Neddy stood quite still. Terry then climbed up, hung on to Neddy's mane, and kept Percy in his arms. This time the donkey stirred sufficiently to communicate a quiet protest. It was when I got up on his rear haunches that the long-suffering animal decided he'd had enough of these summer visitors. Suddenly, he began to move off. Terry held onto his mane for dear life while at the same time holding Percy. I held on to Terry. Neddy's canter became a trot.

I could see that we were heading for a large clump of nettles whose sting I knew to be quite painful. In vain I yelled at Terry to steer Neddy away from what, I think in retrospect, was his plan to teach us a lesson. Just as we reached the spot, with devilish cleverness and intent, Neddy came to a sudden stop, whereupon we slid sideways from his back and ended up in the midst of the nettles, to be stung wherever our skin was bared: hands and arms and lower legs. Our weeping was loud and bitter and came to the ears of our mother, who spent the next half hour preparing a bowl of chamomile lotion, an old remedy for assuaging nettle stings. Its reputation was considerably better than its efficacy, as I recall.

I remember much of this small, humble creature who shared our lives for those sunlit summer days. I recall his graceful attributes, the way he walked with his small hooves pointed forward and placed almost delicately on the ground, his large soulful eyes, and the way he would allow his head to be cradled for a moment under one's arm.

Most of all, I call to mind the story that John Brennan told me when he first lifted me on to Neddy's back as a very small boy. He carefully traced with his finger the lines on Neddy's fur. "Every donkey has those lines," he said. "Do you see how they form a cross?" I was all attention. The lines of darker fur were very clear.

Then, very simply, in terms that a small boy could understand—and indeed would never forget—John told me the wonderful story of the day when Jesus chose to ride on a donkey as he entered Jerusalem, and how from that day Neddy and all his creaturely kind received those lines on their fur to remind us that it was a humble donkey, gracefully stepping on a vast carpet of soft green olive branches, who carried our Savior through the shouting crowd that filled Jerusalem.

## 5. MY GRAND UNCLE WILLIAM
### Donaguile, 1936

It was my Grand Uncle William who first showed me the sacred pages. They lay carefully preserved in the drawer of the huge sideboard in the parlor.

The year was 1936, the year, Uncle Willie announced to me solemnly, when England had three kings: George the Fifth, who died nobly; Edward the Eighth, who abdicated shamefully; and George the Sixth, who ruled faithfully. Such was Uncle Willie's succinct assessment of royal succession, as he proceeded to pass on to another generation his undying loyalty to the English crown.

Uncle Willie was tall. You might well think, who is not tall to a small boy? However, I have good reason for my assertion. He was a retired Royal Irish Constabulary officer. The RIC was the police force of the British occupation before the Irish Free State came into being. I would be surprised if in those days there were not a minimum height for RIC officers.

I am not entirely sure how long Uncle Willie had been retired, but a little math may help. The RIC was disbanded the same year the Irish Free State was born: 1922. By the time he came into my life around 1936, Uncle Willie would have been on pension for well over a decade—and not by choice. It is likely that his pension was minuscule, adding to his general displeasure at the new state of affairs.

Uncle Willie was a grump. He disapproved of the political world in which he found himself. An example of this is how he responded when a small grandnephew whom he barely knew other than for this fleeting summer visit asked him for the time of day.

Let me set the scene. Uncle Willie is wearing his customary grey jacket, waistcoat, white wing-collar shirt, bow tie, black pants, and impeccably polished black shoes. He leans heavily on a walking stick with a silver head. Across the waistcoat lies a heavy gold chain that begins in one pocket, is fastened halfway on its journey by a button hole, then finds its journey's end in the opposite pocket.

"Grand Uncle William," I say, gazing upward for the coming morsel of enlightenment, because my grandmother had warned me that this was the way to address this august figure, "can you tell me what time it is?"

The question releases a kind of mini-liturgical drama, unchanging each time it plays out. First, Uncle Willie would shift his stick from his right hand to his left. Then, with his now available right hand, he would reach across his slightly convex midriff, insert his fingers into the small pocket of his waistcoat, find the watch, slowly withdraw it, click open the gold cover to reveal the face, and hold it at arm's length. Uncle Willie wished to convey that he was not merely looking at the watch; he was *consulting* it.

Having done so, he would utter what I now realize was a kind of formula or mantra, intended to convey much more than merely the time of day. "Government time, my boy," he would intone, "is four o'clock." Then, his voice taking on a disapproving tone, he would add, "The correct time"—emphasizing the word "correct" with studied sarcasm—"the *correct* time is *three* o'clock." Whereupon he would close the gold watch with a flourish and deposit it safely back in its pocket.

It was only when I was older that I dared to ask for an explanation of Uncle Willie's response. The reason was simple, and once again it was linked to his resentment over the passing of the British occupation. Soon after the creation of the Free State, a decision was made to introduce Daylight Saving Time to Ireland. For Uncle Willie, this was a Republican imposition, to be stubbornly resisted.

I was mightily impressed by the imposing character of my grand uncle. Alas, he made his exit from the stage of my life quite early. I have no idea why he was living on the farm with us that summer. One did not wonder about such things. Like Mallory's Everest, for a small boy, Uncle Willie was simply *there*: a towering reality to be respected.

Many years later, my father described an incident that took place toward the end of that same summer. One day, a woman appeared at the end of the farmyard driveway. My grandmother, who was crippled with rheumatoid arthritis, always sat in the front window of her room, where she could see everything and everybody that approached the house. She called out to draw attention to the advancing female figure.

According to my father, Uncle Willie moved quickly to the window, uttered the words "My God!" in an urgent voice, grabbed his stick and jacket, ran through the kitchen and out through the back door. He was last sighted moving swiftly through the apple orchard, and was never seen again.

How wonderfully vivid a figure he remains, after all these years, and for one of the oldest of reasons: a tantalizing whiff of family gossip, and perhaps that even more delicious ingredient in family life and lore, a hint of scandal.

## 6. MEETING FATHER MARTIN
### Castlecomer, 1936

In the Ireland of my childhood, the relationship between the clergy and their people was one of deepest trust and affection. Certainly this was true in the Church of Ireland, and I have no reason to think it was otherwise among our Catholic neighbors. I realize now that this grew out of the myriad ways in which our clergy were involved in our lives. Not only did they play a key role in the large events of human life such as the baptism of a child, the marriage of a couple, or the care given in times of loss and grief. In all such events the presence of clergy was taken utterly for granted. But also, beyond such milestone occasions, people would turn to the clergy for advice on many matters. They would seek clerical help in finding a job, applying for a scholarship to school or university, and in many other circumstances.

With our Roman Catholic neighbors, the same strong reciprocal links existed between priest and people, and I am quite certain that in many cases such links included genuine friendship and affection. However, this relationship was always characterized by the assumption of an essential difference between the lay and clerical states.

Perhaps the best way to describe this is to introduce you to Father Martin. Martin was one of the siblings in a large family that owned a farm close to my grandparents'. I cannot be sure, but it is quite likely he was the eldest son.

In the 1930s, it was expected that at least one son from every Irish family would be offered for the priesthood. So it was that Martin went to Maynooth, a large complex of buildings west of Dublin. For Irish laypeople, whether or not they were Roman Catholic, it was felt that behind the doors of Maynooth lay another world, another set of laws, another mode of being. To go there meant severance from one's former life. Even within one's family circle, one would never again be referred to merely by one's name. Martin Brophy thereafter was always Father Martin.

News came to the farms that Father Martin, now ordained, was bound for Australia. In those days, Australia was thought of as infinitely distant. To go there had a ring of finality. So, before his departure, Martin was given leave for a visit home. It coincided with our family's annual summer visit to the Copley farm. During that time, I witnessed an incident that, as I think of it now, taught me much about the relationship between the two religious worlds of that time and place: Roman Catholicism and the Church of Ireland.

It took place at a bend in the road where a small lane branched off into the fields. My uncle was speaking to an elderly neighbor whose front gate he had just fixed. Both were leaning on the gate; I was perched on the top bar, my uncle holding me to keep me from falling. Martin came around the bend in the road, dressed as always in black clericals. As he came into view I felt a slight tension, a deliberate preparing for the encounter.

In spite of the initial formality of Martin being addressed as "Father," the meeting was pleasant and jocular. After all, he was well-known to everyone in the neighborhood. Greetings were offered and acknowledged, but familiarity was somehow bounded by intangible, but very real, limits. Martin, who as a boy had driven the cows morning and evening through this very gate, whose swinging hurley stick had sent a ball high over these very trees, was in some mysterious way not the same person. His stocky peasant body was somehow changed, like the Blessed Sacrament he would handle at Mass: familiar in appearance, but altered in substance.

Of course, none of these thoughts entered my childish head that evening. However, the fact that I can recall that passing encounter so vividly tells me now that I had come to sense how friendship could find itself transformed where unspoken, but mutually understood, lines of separation had been drawn between clergy and laity.

Perhaps also that long-ago evening may have been a first learning for me that so much of life is communicated in ways beyond language, as it was on that occasion among the adults present, but also from all three of them to an eight-year-old boy perched precariously on a farmyard gate.

# 7. A CHILD'S TRUTH

## Brennans' Cottage, Donaguile, 1937

It is almost impossible today to imagine the degree to which the world of the Bible and that of everyday life were interwoven in my childhood. A remembered moment will illustrate.

About a quarter of a mile along the country road from my grandfather's farm stood a thatched cottage. Three people lived there, two sisters and a brother: Mary, Lizzie, and Jim. They were all, if memory serves, in their late fifties, though this would have been further along in the cycle of life then than it is today, and of course for a small boy all adults are—well—adults.

One day, I was sent over the cottage to buy some eggs. Jim brought them out to me, and I duly handed over the money. For the first time I noticed something about him. I could see how hesitantly he walked, how weak and light his voice was, and how hollow-chested he had become. I was too young to realize that I was looking at the ravages of tuberculosis, a scourge that affected something like 35 percent of rural Ireland in those days.

But something happened as I stood in front of Jim. Having become aware of his fragility, the fact that he lived in this cottage with his two sisters, Mary and Lizzie, struck me with an utterly new significance that was both thrilling and frightening. Suddenly in a child's mind two households merged. One was this cottage in whose yard I was standing, while the other was a home in the pages of the New Testament.

On one of his early travels, Jesus came south to Jerusalem. The climb from Jericho up to the city was steep and tiring. First one approached the small village of Bethany, today a suburb of Jerusalem called El Azariah. Here Jesus met a woman named Martha who offered hospitality to him and his friends. The small house where Martha lived with her sister, Mary, and their brother, Lazarus, would come to be the one home where Jesus felt he was always welcome. This is where he spent what would be his last days of freedom. From here he would leave to enter the city riding on a donkey, thus acting out a prediction of one of the Hebrew prophets that a king of Israel would appear in Jerusalem in this way. The success of this challenge to power may well have sealed the fate of Jesus by its audacity.

Following this, each day of the last week of Jesus's life brought intense public confrontations between critics and supporters, as well as vicious verbal attacks on Jesus himself. Each evening, he would return exhausted to the Bethany home, the only place where he could find hospitality and respite. From here, he would eventually leave to share supper with his disciples, later to be arrested, tried, and executed.

Before all this happened, however, the Gospel writer John tells of a mysterious, even terrifying event: Jesus raises Lazarus from the dead. All of this I had absorbed in Sunday school classes. These were the vivid images that now flooded into my mind as I stood in front of Jim's tall, emaciated figure.

I said goodbye, thanking him for the eggs, turned, and began walking slowly homeward, dawdling as small boys are apt to do. As I went along, I thought about what had just taken place and the link my mind had made with Holy Scripture.

I remembered reading that Lazarus had died and that Jesus had called him back to life. I began to wonder about Jim and his sisters. After all, this household next door to our farm was very like that other home in Bethany, though far distant in space and time. In both houses, there lived a brother with two sisters. In both families, the brother had become ill. Could it be true then that Jim had died and been mysteriously called back to life? Who could have done that? Was there some corner of the cottage property where I might find a dark and hidden place with a stone guarding its entrance? The very thought was at the same time both fascinating and fearful. I have no memory of mentioning these thoughts when I reached home.

Looking back over at that small boy returning to the farm with the newly purchased eggs, I realize now that he had just experienced two elements of his life flowing together. One was the world of the Bible, and the other was the gift of imagination, both of which would remain with him throughout his adult life. Many times, in many churches, I have listened as the story of Jesus raising Lazarus from the tomb is read. As I listen, there is always a moment when I find myself standing again in the small yard in front of the Brennans' cottage.

# 8. DOOLEY'S LORRY
## Donaguile Farm, 1937

A child has a passionate determination to make the ordinary into the exotic and the romantic. In fact, one might say that for a child there is no such thing as the ordinary. Being now at the stage of life that looks back over many years to childhood, I find that the most unexpected things become doorways in time.

Downtown Vancouver is bustling and sunny in the springtime of 1972. The city is in the midst of an ongoing construction boom. Across from the cathedral where I work, there have been until recently two gas stations. Almost overnight, they have disappeared and in their place are two vast excavations from which two massive towers will assuredly rise, reaching for the sky, incidentally dwarfing the cathedral. Lunchtime crowds flow across intersections, defying increasingly impatient traffic. Change is throbbing and thundering in the air.

Suddenly I see it. It's coming down Robson Street surrounded by the traffic, but not giving an inch as it goes along. It is so magnificent the traffic seems to give it a wide berth as a sign of respect. Huge, high, open to the sky, its long, graceful bonnet reflects the sunlight. The coachwork is perfect, the headlights reminiscent of the design of the coach lights from which they are descended. The wheel spokes are thick and strong and solid. Its occupants are young. They sit high and proud, enjoying everyone's interest in their splendid vintage vehicle. But for me a doorway has opened to childhood and I am looking again at Dooley's Lorry.

I think I have delighted in describing this magnificent machine in downtown Vancouver in 1972 for the simple reason that it was so utterly different from the one I was reminded of from thirty-five years earlier. Yet for the small boy of 1937, that ancient motor car was not one whit less splendid than this glamorous creation.

Today it would be called a truck but in that long-ago Ireland it was a lorry. Every day Dooley—whom I was admonished sternly to address as Mr. Dooley—would arrive very early in the morning and park his lorry in a corner of the farmyard, between the pig house and the plantation. He would then gather up whatever he needed for the day and walk the mile and a half to the nearby town, where he worked. Since he could not afford the price of a license for the lorry, he had asked my grandfather's permission to park it in the farmyard.

Of course, to a small boy these mundane things mattered not a whit. When I came down to the kitchen for breakfast I would run to the half door, stand on my toes, just able to see out. Every morning, as if by magic, the lorry would be there. It would never just come, rather it would mysteriously *be there*.

It was a model of heaven knows what vintage. The tires were solid, the steering wheel formed of dark gleaming wood, the seat leather ancient and shiny and wrinkly and smelling of many things, among them Woodbine cigarettes, petrol, motor oil, Guinness Stout, and Irish whisky. This last aroma I would learn to recognize when I was somewhat older.

After breakfast I could not go to the lorry because I had to go to the creamery with my grandfather. In four heavy churns we would take the milk that had come from the cows the previous evening. I loved this journey to the town and the creamery, so it was no great deprivation to have to postpone my thrill, but when at last we returned from the creamery and the donkey, glad to be home, trotted slowly by the lorry, I would jump off the bench of the cart to the ground.

Stepping up on the running board, I would open the door to sit in the driver's seat, then reach out my hands to grasp the great steering wheel. For a moment I would look through the windscreen—peeking through the wheel, of course, because of my height, or rather lack thereof. I would plan my journey. Would it be to the town or up over the hills to Kilkenny? Then I would get down from the seat, walk around to the front of the engine and imitate Dooley using his crank to start it up. As soon as the engine coughed thunderously to life—in my imagination of course—the panels of the bonnet would shudder. I would run back to the driver's seat and, through the magic of childhood, travel across hills and fields and counties until an adult voice would call me for lunch and I would once again be in the world I grudgingly called real.

In the evening I would wait at the end of the driveway for Dooley to appear. I would watch him reach into the truck, take out the starter crank, plunge it into the front of the engine, and steady himself before fiercely turning the handle. Sometimes it would take two or three tries before the engine would catch. Then, as the whole truck shuddered and thundered, Dooley would run back to the driver's side, leap aboard, slam the door. The great wheels would move, Dooley would wave to me and I to him as he drove out of the driveway, turning right on the narrow road that ran up the side of the valley. I would stand and wave until the sound of the engine had died and the cloud of oily smoke had faded on the summer evening air.

## 9. MOLLY

### Donaguile, 1938

It seems only yesterday. I hear the sound of the latch lifting on the door by the stable. Molly is arriving for her day's work with my uncle and aunt's large family on the farm. She is a small young woman, but it is not the youthfulness of today. Molly wears a black shawl, an apron of black and white dots, black heavy stockings, and black laced boots. Her hair is lank and disheveled, pinned together here and there. She has lost almost all her teeth. Dental care of any kind is far in the future in these early years of the new Republic, as indeed is anything other than the most basic of medical resources. This has robbed Molly of the attractiveness that youth would otherwise have given to her, just as she has been deprived of stature by lifelong malnutrition.

Molly comes to help my aunt care for the children, my younger cousins. My aunt has to support the all-important harvesting of hay and corn in the elusive periods of fine weather. I myself am drawn into these chores each summer, as I become older.

Molly is the utterly dependable hub around which the household turns. She sweeps, washes, makes meals for the children, changes their clothes, all with unfailing kindness. She also feeds the hens, gathers their eggs, and drives away the odd calf or pig who wanders into the farmyard. Sometimes she complains of her lot, asking an invisible and seemingly uncaring deity why she is beset by myriad duties and troubles, but she never neglects her care.

In the evening, Molly takes up her shawl, wraps it around herself, sometimes taking some food set aside by my aunt, and once a week also wrapping her fingers around the precious coins of her wages and depositing them in the pocket of her apron. This done, she lifts the latch of the stable door, walks out into the barn field, crosses the small stream that runs through the farm, walks to the edge of the field, climbs the stone stile, stands for a moment on the earthen wall, and turns to wave goodbye to us children before stepping down the other side.

Between our farm and her home there are five fields to be crossed before she steps out onto what is known as the Old Road. About a hundred yards up the road is the cottage where the family lives: Molly and her parents, Jim and Ellen Clear.

However, we need to pause on that homeward journey. About halfway, there is a grove of trees. In the grove stands the ruin of a cottage, its low stone walls with their two tiny openings for windows and a larger one where a door once hung. All trace of a thatched roof has long vanished. Molly would pass this small, silent ruin every morning and evening.

Only recently, I found myself thinking about these two cottages: one with its ruined walls and gaping roof half-hidden in the trees, and the other on its small government grant of land, giving basic shelter and sustenance to Molly and her parents. These simple, two-room cottages had been built in the Irish countryside by the government of the new Republic. They were for people without anything more than the barest necessities of life. With the cottage went about half an acre of land where they could keep some hens, perhaps a cow, perhaps a pig.

From what I have since read of late nineteenth and early twentieth century Ireland, I believe I understand something of the background to this abject poverty. It's embodied in that other cottage, the ruined one. Around 1847, less than twenty years before I estimate that Molly's father Jim was born, I suspect a scene took place at that now-ruined cottage that was like similar scenes taking place all over the great foreign-owned estates of Ireland at that time.

Seven long years of dreadful famine were drawing to a close. In the previous six years, hundreds of thousands of people either died or emigrated on what became known as coffin ships. Countless poverty-stricken tenant farmers were unable to pay the rents on their pathetic holdings. The penalty was to lose their home. The bailiff would arrive, acting for a usually absentee landlord, and backed up by a detachment of the local constabulary. The family's pathetically few possessions would be dragged out to the roadside, and the thatched roof would be set on fire to ensure that no one could return after the enforcers had left. The use of the small tract of land would revert to the estate.

In the world of my childhood, none of this was spoken of—certainly not to children—but all over the country, the ruined walls of roofless cottages bore mute testimony to the horrors of famine and eviction and destitution. I think it very possible that either Jim or Ellen was born in the ruined cottage that Molly passed every day.

They would have grown up in the aftermath of the famine, both of them likely homeless and in abject poverty. Having met and married, they would have experienced the desperate struggle for land that began in the closing years of the nineteenth century and continued into the first years of the twentieth. In 1916, a short-lived revolt against British rule was followed by a savage and brutal civil war, which in turn brought into being a new but resource-poor Republic that would seek to redress the injustices of the past. One day, Jim and Ellen would receive a new home.

As she stood on that earthen wall each evening, turning to wave to us children, then walking through the fields past the ruined cottage, I wonder if Molly ever considered the irony that she was caring lovingly for a family who, by virtue of their Church of Ireland faith, were at least linked to the regime of occupation that had presided over the years of famine while daily exporting tons of corn that could have fed their starving tenants, Molly's family among them.

If she ever did think such thoughts, it did not lessen Molly's loving care for the children to whom she waved an evening farewell.

## 10. THE DARK WOOD
### Darby's Haggart, Donaguile, August 1939

It is late afternoon on a summer's day. I will soon be eleven, my brother seven. Our youngest brother is only a year old, so he is at the farmhouse. The rest of us—my grandfather, two uncles, the hired man John Brennan, my brother, and I—are in the field, making hay on this lovely afternoon. Such days are precious in the changeable weather patterns of Ireland.

The field, like all fields in those days in Ireland, has a name. This field is known as Darby's Haggart. It stretches along the side of a wide, gentle valley crowned by a dark stretch of woodland called Grant's Wood. From where we are, the wood is only about three fields away. My brother and I would like to go there, but we are afraid.

About three o'clock, my brother and I set off back to the farmhouse at our uncle's bidding, to fetch the ham sandwiches and apple
pie and strong tea our Aunt Bella has prepared for the men. Naturally, we boys are looking forward to a helping of pie as reward for
our labor. When we return, one of the uncles points to a haycock
and says, "Over there." Everyone stops work and gathers at the spot,
sinking gratefully into the sweet-smelling hay. Mugs are handed
round, tea is poured, sandwiches unwrapped, the cover taken off the
pie dish, and the meal begins. I recall the pie dish as vast—though,
if it really had been, we wouldn't have been able to carry it. Let's just
say that anticipation and boyhood appetite probably increased its
perceived size.

As we gather up the mugs and plates, John comes over to us. He
knows we want to go into the wood but are afraid. He laughs warmly
and says to us, "I'll take ye into the wood when we're finished the hay."

It is now early evening. Every hour of daylight has been taken
advantage of, in case the weather changes. John calls us over to him
and together we climb over the five-barred gates that separate the
fields. As we approach the trees, my brother takes John's hand. Because
I am eleven, I resist the urge to do the same.

In through the line of the trees we go. As we venture deeper, we
become aware of the lengthening shadows and the growing silence.
The further we go, the nearer we stay to John. There comes a point
when I, too, take John's hand.

The wood darkens around us. We reach a small clearing. John
comes to a halt, turns around, and quietly tells us to do likewise. We
are now looking back the way we have come, along the golden beams
of the evening sun. The woodland path, so dark and menacing when
seen from the distant field, is now bathed in light. For a few moments
John lets us stare in silence. Then he says, quietly, "You see, lads, the
wood isn't a dark place at all."

I never forgot that moment. Only in adulthood can we try to
express what such a moment means. In childhood, there is the all-
important thing itself, the actual experience, burning its way permanently into one's consciousness. Even now, so many years later, I grope

for words to name the gift I was given that day. So far as I can now understand it, my brother and I had been taught something about life that would serve us in many different future circumstances. We had been taught that light is stronger than darkness, and that companionship assuages fear. I have found these simple truths, given to two brothers through the kindness of a decent and sensitive man, a lifelong source of strength and courage.

In the vast and beautiful world of Orthodox or Eastern Christianity, the concept of Light is supremely important. It sounds in prayers and hymns. One of the most ancient of Christian hymns has as its Greek title "Phos Hilarion," or in English, "Hail Gladdening Light!" It continues:

. . . of His pure glory poured . . .

Holiest of Holies, Jesus Christ our Lord.

Now we are come to the sun's hour of rest,

The lights of evening round us shine . . .

I have sung that loveliest of hymns on many occasions. Whenever I do, I find myself once more standing in that woodland clearing, looking toward the setting sun, slipping my hand free of John Brennan's, because I am no longer afraid of the darkness.

## 11. THE VISITATION
### Donaguile, Summer 1939

The long summer holiday on my grandfather's farm is drawing to a close, the hay is being brought into the barn, the branches of the apple trees in the small orchard behind the farmhouse are heavy with fruit. From the front of the house I hear the voice of my grandmother. Immobilized by her chronic arthritis, she sits in her window looking down the driveway. "The canon is coming," she calls urgently.

I run into the kitchen. My aunt is already at the half door. Coming up the driveway on his bicycle is indeed the canon. St. Mary's parish has two clergy, the canon and the curate. To receive a visit from the curate is a pleasant diversion; to be visited by the canon is a serious occasion.

In swift succession, my aunt casts her apron in a corner, tidies her hair, puts a large kettle on the range, pauses to collect herself, and goes to meet the important visitor. The canon enters, tall and imposing. My grandmother gives him a warm and happy greeting. My hand is shaken from a great height.

Only now is the key taken down from the parlor door. This, in itself, is a measure of the importance of this occasion. The parlor is forbidden, particularly for small boys, attainable only on special occasions. It contains a large dining table, a long couch and two large easy chairs, a sideboard with a mirror, some silver pieces, and some photographs of various family members and occasions.

For me, the room's prize exhibit is a small table bearing specially bound issues of the *English Daily Sketch* for the year 1936—the year, as my elders have told me solemnly on more than one occasion, that England had three kings. In such moments, I am left in no doubt that in spite of being a citizen of a still relatively young Republic, I belong to a monarchist family. I am sometimes allowed to look at these pages.

The canon and my aunt go to the parlor. I push my grandmother's chair on its small wheels, finding a place where she can join them. Then I am sent to find my mother and my younger brother. This done, I am instructed to run as quickly as I can to the hayfield to inform my grandfather and uncles that the canon is in the house.

I am unaware that this is an age-old liturgy wherein every player knows their part. The canon, knowing that the men will be called in, has timed his coming near the end of the working afternoon so that they will not lose too many of the precious working hours. My grandfather and uncles know that they have a little leeway before leaving the hayfield, as my grandmother chats with the canon and my aunt prepares the tea. This is a world of tradition and predictability.

When I return, my mother and grandmother are with the canon in the parlor, my brother firmly held in my mother's lap. In the kitchen, tea is being prepared. Hot apple pie has already been put out, and fresh griddle bread with salty farm butter and homemade jam. As if all is being coordinated by an unseen director, the large tea tray is laid on the parlor table just as my grandfather and uncles arrive from the field. They have already thrown water on their faces from the rain barrel by the stable door. Greetings are exchanged, comments on the weather and the crops are made, heads are bowed as the canon says grace. He prays for the family, thoughtfully speaking loud enough for my grandfather to hear him. Startled, my baby brother cries for a moment but is firmly hushed. The hum of conversation goes on, its subjects above and beyond me. I am already enjoying my first slice of bread and jam, anticipating my helping of apple pie and cream. It remains for me as a long and fond remembrance: a gathered family, the layers of the generations, the richness of wholesome food, the church embodied in the tall figure of the canon.

Some years later in school I will learn a lullaby written by the poet Patrick Colum:

O men from the fields, come softly within,

Tread softly, softly, O men coming in.

Mavourneen is going from me and from you,

Where Mary will fold him with mantle of blue.

I realize now that such lines wove together one's own home and that of Mary and Joseph and their child in faraway Bethlehem, thus drawing together earth and heaven, making them one.

## 12. THE WELL

### Donaguile Farm, Summer 1940

In a corner of the farmhouse kitchen, covered by round wooden covers made by my uncle, there are two white metal buckets, always kept scrupulously clean. They are the source of drinking water for the family. Each morning, and often again at a later hour in the day, someone takes these two buckets to fill them at the well. In the summertime, now that I am twelve and old enough and strong enough, and because it is necessary that all available adult hands are put to work bringing in the precious hay, I am given this duty.

The well is about half a mile away, a distance easily covered with two empty buckets, but very different on the return journey! Down the farmyard I go, on to the narrow country road that serves the various farms along it, until I come to a lane that leads to the well. Because the trees arch thickly over the lane, it can be deeply shadowed, particularly on a dull day. This, coupled with the silence that falls once I leave the main road, makes me aware of my solitariness and brings a mild sense of fear.

At the end of the lane it splits, one path leading into the small yard where John Brennan's cottage stands, the other branching off as a narrow earthen track down a short slope. I am entering a long, grotto-like area. Down to my right flows a stream. It emerges from a large pool behind me, fed in its turn by a waterfall whose source is high up the valley. The grotto resounds to a mingled symphony of sounds: the splash of the small waterfall as it enters the pool, the chuckling of the stream as it gushes over the stones that litter the grotto's floor, the birdsong.

Then I come to the well. It is separate from the pool and the stream. Centuries or even millennia ago, it would have nestled naturally in the earth. By now, the local farmers have lined it with concrete and placed a sheltering cover over it, some feet above the surface. Because of this cover, the water is utterly still, clear and dark.

During the many times I came to this well, sometimes both morning and evening, I would find myself being spoken to in a way hard to explain but rich to recall. I would put the buckets aside and crouch down, searching the dark depths for—for what? As Thomas Hardy once wrote: "A boy's will is the wind's will and the thoughts of youth are long, long thoughts."

To the extent that I can now shape those thoughts in the hindsight of adulthood, I think I was searching for a world beyond the well—beneath it perhaps, yet at the same time beyond and in a different world. I would imagine beings emerging from the water, rising from the underworld into this doorway between the worlds. The interesting thing I now recall is that I did not feel fearful, rather filled with a kind of quiet wonder.

Then I would return to reality, dip the buckets one by one in the shimmering water, gently sweep aside the few leaves that had settled on the surface, pick up my now much heavier load, and begin the slow progress up the earthen path and homeward.

Many years later, in a world newly fascinated by ancient Celtic history, I would read of the mythic past of Ireland: how the people of the goddess Dana fled into the underworld before powerful invaders, asking only to emerge once in the cycle of the sun, at the time when autumn darkness was falling on the world. Their access points to our world were the wells, the orifices of the goddess. Eventually, the new religion of Christianity would name this season All Hallows' Eve or Hallowe'en, the time when the spirits of the dead are remembered.

Carl Jung tells us that eternal archetypes remain in the human mind, beyond and below our comfortable rational minds. I suspect that such may have been the source of a boy's wonderings as he crouched by a well in a grotto echoing with the voices of a once-divine nature.

## 13. A LOVE DISCERNED

### Summer 1937–Summer 1941

My grandfather's farm is the place from which I will draw my deepest memories for the rest of my life.

Night comes and I must go to bed. As I climb the narrow staircase with my candle, shadows leap on the walls. I am clutching a book that I have found in the small bookcase on the landing. It was given as a Sunday school prize in the late 1800s. Its cover proclaims *The Egyptian Wanderers: A Tale of the Fourth Century Persecutions*. The cover portrays a fleeing family leading their camels into the desert. One member of the family is a boy about my age.

I share a double bed with my grandfather. Sometimes I will be awake to feel the pressure on the bed as he kneels for his prayers. The memory of this quiet natural piety will come back to me as a dream of grace in the then-faraway 1960s in Canada, when clever books will sell a new Enlightenment announcing prayer as neurosis, sacrament as superstition, and God as only a memory.

Morning comes with the crowing of the cock and the banging of buckets in the nearby dairy. My Aunt Bella has breakfast ready for everyone before the day begins. The milk churns are loaded on the cart, my grandfather and I sit on the sack-covered bench, the reins are pulled, and we set off for the creamery about two miles away in the town square.

Our milk delivered, sometimes a few purchases made for the household, a copy of the morning paper bought, our return journey is up the side of the valley. To ease the donkey's burden, sometimes my grandfather and I dismount from the cart and walk. When the hilly stages of the journey are past and level ground is reached, we scramble back onto the cart until we reach the last bend in the road before the gate of the farm driveway. Knowing from long familiarity that home is near, the donkey breaks into a happy jog.

As we draw to a halt in front of the house, I can see my grandmother waiting in her chair behind the lace curtains. I know she will be reaching for her glasses in anticipation of slowly opening the pages of the newspaper with white and twisted fingers. She was nearly forty when the stiffness began, then the pain. The next thirty arthritic years would make walking a memory.

Every day, there were two periods when my grandparents would enjoy each other's company. Before lunch they would read the *Irish Times* together and discuss the news, she speaking loudly because of his deafness. Later, when the work in the fields was done, they would again sit together.

When she died in 1940, my grandmother's body was buried in Saint Mary's churchyard, just beyond the town. The following year, summer came again to Donaguile and once again we came to the farm. One day, my grandfather and my two uncles arranged to inspect some cattle in a farm some miles away. I was in the back seat of the car with my grandfather. As we passed the graveled driveway leading up through the tall summer grass to the churchyard, my grandfather, thinking he was unobserved, pressed his face against the window of the car and, with a small, half-hidden movement of his hand, he waved.

Somehow, even as a boy, I knew what he was doing. Our eyes did not meet, nothing was said, but for a child it was a moment of gentle yet immense growing. Like a traveler who comes to the edge of a great escarpment and sees beyond it a vast and mysterious country, I know now that I had come then to my first understanding of the majesty and vulnerability of human love.

All this was brought near again when our son Niall handed me a small packet for my seventy-fifth birthday. When I opened it, I discovered a rather weather-beaten copy of *The Egyptian Wanderers*. There once again were the camels, and the family fleeing into the desert, and the small boy. Once again, the candle flame flickered and threw its shadows on a small farmhouse bookcase, and time turned on itself to form an enchanted circle.

## 14. THE CHURCH ORGAN
### Summer 1940 and Summer 1991

As you leave the town of Castlecomer, at the end of the very fine town square, you cross a small stone humpbacked bridge across the River Barrow. Beyond this, you are setting out on what will become the Dublin road. About a quarter of a mile beyond the bridge, a gate and driveway lined by magnificent yew trees lead you up a gentle slope to the door of St. Mary's Church of Ireland parish church. The church is surrounded by its graveyard, still used today for burials and still carefully tended. In recent years, we have taken our adult children to St. Mary's to show them the graves of at least three generations of their Copley family.

The Church of Ireland has always had the ability to inculcate a deep loyalty in its people. This is true of my family even into the changing world of the twenty-first century. In my childhood, it was even more marked. The family in Donaguile, my uncle and his wife and their children, were in St. Mary's without fail every Sunday morning. Each week, a pattern was played out that could have been witnessed in every other rural Church of Ireland parish. Families would arrive as the bell tolled, some on bicycles, others in horse and trap, some walking up the driveway from the nearby town. The wives and children would alight and go in, while the men would tether the horses nearby before congregating around the church door, chatting about such things as the weather, local politics, the faraway war that was raging in Europe. While the men gossiped and joked outside the church door until the last toll of the church bell, the women and girls were practicing the music for the service. They would cluster around an object of pride and joy for the congregation: the church organ. Not every rural parish had one; some depended on a lowly harmonium, but not St. Mary's.

One summer Sunday evening, Evening Prayer was being celebrated in St. Mary's and my Auntie Bella asked me to go with her. Off we set on bicycles. When we arrived, the rector appeared, obviously very concerned. Nobody was available to pump the organ. He looked me up and down, and in a voice that did not brook argument, ventured the opinion that I was old enough and strong enough to perform this necessary task. I was naturally agog with eagerness at this suggestion. The rector steered me to my place. From the side of the organ casing, a large wooden lever projected. A chair was already there for the person who usually did the pumping. I was given brief instructions that lasted all of two minutes. The objective was to make sure that at all times there was sufficient air for the organ to sound. As I placed my hands on the pump handle, the rector pointed to two black lines painted on the wood. On no account—he almost hissed the words in his anxiety—on no account was I to allow the small lead weight to go above the top line nor below the bottom. Did I understand? There was no way I was going to say I did not. Just at this point, the organist sat on the bench, placed a piece of music on the rack, and indicated I should start pumping.

At first, there was indeed some anxiety. My eye never left the two black lines. Observing them would make the difference between abject failure or being the hero of the hour. Gradually I relaxed, and got into the rhythm of the work. Eventually the last notes of the last hymn sounded. Both organist and rector covered me in praise and appreciation. My aunt basked in the glow of family pride at the performance of her nephew. Who knows if it was not on that evening that the seed was sown of a clerical career?

There is an engaging sequel to this story. Fast-forward in time just over half a century. In St. Mary's, the organ of my childhood still stands, by now modernized and electrified. This time, the chief actor is my younger brother, who has by this time become bishop of the Anglican Diocese of Huron in far-off Canada. He is on a visit to Ireland, and has been invited to preach in St. Mary's because of his family connections with the parish.

As my brother tells the story, he was in the vestry with the rector of the day, both of them preparing for the service. My brother could not help noticing that the church wardens seemed to be paying a great deal of attention to the organ. Eventually one warden came and announced in great agitation that the organ would not work.

My brother could see the organ from where he stood in the vestry. He realized that no one was paying attention to a small metal box high up on the wall. Seeing the visiting bishop, clad in his episcopal robes, climbing onto a chair was sufficiently unusual to cause a stir among the gathering congregation. From his perch, my brother opened the metal box, which he had correctly assumed was a fuse box, flipped a breaker switch, closed the box, looked down to the wardens and said, "Try it now." The organist laid her hands on the keys. Lo, there was a most melodious and reassuring chord.

Relief was almost palpable. It was sealed by a wonderful moment that could only happen in the Irish countryside, a world where no situation can defy the ability of native eloquence to respond to it. One of the wardens looked up at my brother, still standing on the chair in full episcopal garb, and in a voice full of awe, exclaimed fervently, "By God, Bishop, 'tis you who have the Power!"

My brother hastily denied being anything remotely like the arm of the Lord in this crisis. He merely pointed out that he had worked at Ontario Hydro for ten years before being ordained, and knew a fuse box when he saw one. To this day, he has never been quite sure whether or not the effusively grateful rector, wardens, and organist of St. Mary's believed his disavowal of, if not divine power, at least divine inspiration.

## 15. HERBERT LORENZA COPLEY

### St. Mary's Churchyard, Castlecomer, County Kilkenny

The gravestone is mottled and stained by age. The inscription cut into it is becoming difficult to read, due to the deterioration of the surface of the stone. It reads: "Herbert Lorenza Copley. Born October 1899. Died April 16, 1905." There follow the names of his parents, my maternal grandparents: Abraham Copley and Elizabeth Copley (*née* Daly).

I know almost nothing about him other than the manner of his dying. I have a faint memory of once being shown a photograph of him by my grandmother. The picture is of a small boy not much younger than I would have been when looking at his face: perhaps five to my seven or eight. I seem to remember feeling the great mystery of how he could be dead and I alive. I can realize now the sadness my grandmother must have felt as she allowed me to hold the photograph for a moment. In her mind's eye, she must have been seeing her child, had he lived, as a fine young man in his early thirties. I recall my mother speaking of him, too, but she had only the vaguest memories of her brother since she, born in 1901, was only four years old when Herbert died.

Herbert's death was accidental, the kind of death that must have happened from time to time on Irish farms in those days. In the farmyard at the front of the house there was a line of buildings for storing equipment and supplies, and keeping animals. Beyond this, there was a deep ditch into which the refuse of the hens and pigs was thrown, eventually to be used as manure. That was true in that other Herbert's childhood, as it was in mine.

One day Herbert slipped and fell into the ditch. Hearing his crying, someone ran and brought him into the house. While in those days the knowledge of the nature of infections and germs would have been still in the future, there would have been a realization of the absolute necessity to cleanse the child, especially trying to prevent his swallowing what would have been fecal material. According to my grandmother, relayed to me by my mother, all seemed well for a few days. Then fever set in and Herbert died.

Just beyond that fatal ditch, a gate led into the adjacent field. I would go there often, standing on one of the rungs of the gate and gazing out across the fields toward the dark line of Grant's Wood that crowned the ridge of the valley. I remember one day stepping up onto the gate and thinking how that other Herbert must have stood here, probably on this very rung, his hands grasping the top rung just as I was doing, looking at what I was seeing. I began to wonder what it would have been like to play with him, so I began to talk to him, just to tell him what I was seeing: the barn field, the cows in the far corner sheltering from the summer heat, the fields beyond, the distant wood. To a child, death is a vast mystery, impossible to grasp yet at the same time communicating a sense not so much of fear as of great sadness.

Herbert has always remained in my memory, if only for my being named after him. I have often thought of my life as being in some sense a living of his life for him. There was an occasion when this sense, dormant for most of the time in my conscious life, was suddenly wakened. I was back in Castlecomer in my adult years, visiting my uncle who had been bereaved by my aunt's death. One of his old friends who happened to be with us remembered me as a boy on the farm. Confusing the generations, he referred to me as "Herbie Copley." I didn't correct the error. It was not a disturbing thought to be so addressed.

During all my growing years, I remained unaware of that second or middle name: Lorenza. When I did become aware of it, standing at Herbert's grave with my own children and grandchildren, it was too late to ask its source in the family. Only recently have I discovered that there was a Lorenza in an earlier generation.

Herbert Lorenza Copley. May he rest in peace and rise with Christ in glory.

# 16. THE BIG HOUSE
## St. Mary's Church, Castlecomer, 1952

The title of this reminiscence refers to a long chapter of Ireland's history when almost all land was in the hands of English owners. On these large estates, Irish Catholic peasants worked pathetically small holdings as tenants. Heavily taxed, they lived lives of ill health, poverty, and malnutrition. Human nature being what it is, life on some estates was better than on others. This depended on the care and compassion—or lack thereof—shown by the occupants of what was known as the Big House.

When our family in Donaguile cycled to morning service each Sunday during those summers of my childhood, we entered a scene that was to some extent mirrored all over Ireland. Ahead of us was St. Mary's Church of Ireland. To our left were the estate offices from which the lands and, in this case, their coal mines, were administered. To our right began the woods that hid from view the Big House.

Because this is not a history of the Anglo-Irish Ascendancy but rather a boy's remembrance of the Ireland of the 1930s, it may serve best if I relate what I came to understand about the family in the Big House, and their role in the life of the society at that time. While there was an acknowledged difference between us socially, families such as theirs and families such as ours were united by common bonds: religious, cultural, and political. When my grandfather picked up his copy of the *Irish Times* each morning, he knew that the Captain and his family in the Big House were reading the same pages. The engraved portraits of the reigning monarchs on the walls of our farmhouse parlor would also be hanging somewhere in the Big House.

And on Sunday mornings, our lives crossed in public worship. Near the church, on both sides of the road, were two small pedestrian gates: one set in the graveyard wall and one in the wall of the estate. At a suitable time, the estate family would appear at their gate. Crossing the road, they would enter through the graveyard gate, walk to the church door, and climb a wooden staircase to a small gallery. As they passed, greetings would be exchanged.

During worship, the two lessons were invariably read by the Captain. Once a month, Holy Communion was celebrated. When the time came for Communion to be received, the estate family would rise, descend the stairs, and walk slowly up the main aisle to kneel at the rail. They, and whatever visitors they might happen to have, received the sacrament, rose, turned, and walked back down the aisle to resume their places in the family gallery. Only then did the rest of the congregation begin to stand and move forward to receive Communion.

The last year I spent the summer on the farm before heading off to boarding school and university was 1942. A decade later, in 1952, I was preparing for ordination at Trinity College Dublin. Word came that the rector of Castlecomer was ill and a senior ordinand was needed to conduct Morning Prayer in St. Mary's. Because of my connection with the parish, I found myself robing in the small vestry as the bell called the congregation to assemble.

All went well until we reached what is known as the petitions and responses. I came to the line "O Lord, guide and defend our rulers," expecting the congregation to respond, "and mercifully hear us when we call upon thee." To my consternation, there was not a sound. Not a single voice spoke. I knew I had to think clearly and quickly.

Mercifully, I recalled that this particular petition was familiar only to my own generation.

At the previous Synod of the Church of Ireland, the Irish government had asked the Irish House of Bishops to consider that some three decades had now passed since the founding of the new Irish Republic. With admirable diplomacy and delicacy, they had enquired if the Church of Ireland might consider it reasonable to cease offering a petition for a monarch who was no longer reigning over the population of Ireland.

The said House of Bishops had duly responded by acceding to the request to change the traditional petition, "O Lord, save the King." But the words they substituted were Jesuitical in their subtlety. The new petition, "O Lord, guide and defend our rulers," was one about which the worshipper could have many unsaid reservations.

To my new generation of theological students and clergy, this change had presented no difficulty. Looking back from another century, it is easy to see that the ties of Empire, even of Commonwealth, were already loosening in those postwar years. However, to an older generation, and most certainly to the last Ascendancy generation seated in the gallery of St. Mary's on that Sunday in 1952, such a change was utterly unacceptable.

I would later learn that the Captain had given strict instructions that the old petition was to be used in the worship of St. Mary's. If by some misfortune or impertinence the new petition were to be uttered within its walls, there was to be absolute silence. No one had thought to tell me. But now, in the echoing stillness of the church, realization dawned. I broke the silence by resolutely declaiming, "O Lord, save the King." A loud and firm response filled the church: "And mercifully hear us when we call upon thee."

At the end of the service, I prepared to encounter the Captain when he descended from the gallery. I need not have been concerned. He was immensely gracious, as was the rest of the family. He said quietly, "I understand you are a Copley," naming my mother's people. He and I both knew that when the Captain's predecessors had come from England in the early 1800s, they had brought with them from Yorkshire an ancestor named Copley to be the steward on their estate.

It occurred to me that the other reason for the Captain's graciousness was that he knew that there was no reason to be other than gracious. After all, he had already very effectively made his point.

Confirmation Day, 1943: the author at St. Fin Barre's Cathedral, Cork, where worship has been offered since 606 CE.

CHAPTER THREE

# Student Days

*I* *n my formative years in Ireland, one entered the past to be prepared for the future. From 1941 to 1945, I was a boarding student at Midleton College, a school founded in 1673 on the estates of the Earl of Midleton. From 1948 to 1952, I attended Trinity College Dublin, a foundation of Elizabeth the First in 1592.*

*In July 1952, I was ordained in Dublin's Christ Church Cathedral, having entered by walking past its Norman remains. Pointing from the pulpit that day, directing our eyes to the stone step on which we were about to kneel to be ordained, the homilist said: "Never forget that men have been ordained on this step for 950 years."*

*The sense of possessing this long story would prove invaluable in the changing world already bearing down on our generation.*

## 1. THE DONKEY
### Midleton College, 1941 and 1943

September 9, 1941, saw me boarding the early morning train for Midleton College, all of fifteen miles distant, saying farewell to my parents, and being welcomed by the housemaster at the entrance to the platform, my name ticked off on his list. Many years later, I relived this wrenching experience as I sat with grandchildren and watched Harry Potter and Ron and Hermione catching the train for Hogwarts Academy of Magic.

What images does one choose from those years? Faces and voices come easily; rugby, hockey, tennis, and cricket matches won and lost; the anticipation and pleasure of receiving parcels of "tuck" from home; the fun of preparing for the Christmas concert followed by the journey home for the holidays. There is the immense pleasure of being selected as editor of the college magazine for a year or two. The growing appreciation of good teachers—masters as we called them—especially in English Literature and History and Latin. I owe them a lifelong fascination with these subjects.

One abiding memory: summer term, 1943. I am in the fourth form. Our classroom is near one of the entrances to the school. For some unknown reason the school donkey, used by the grounds staff to haul a cart hither and yon, decides to enter the hallway through an outside door, then amble along the corridor to the partly open door of our classroom. We are busy with our Latin master, Mr. Cox, probably wrestling with some chapter of Julius Caesar's self-obsessed books about his Gallic Wars. Slowly the door creaks open and the donkey sticks his head in. There is instant and delighted pandemonium. This is a heaven-sent excuse to interrupt Julius Caesar and celebrate a moment's freedom from study.

Amid great commotion the donkey is led outside. Class settles down again, all eyes on Mr. Cox. But he does not immediately return to the first century BCE. Instead, he looks at all of us reflectively and then, with great satisfaction, quietly quotes a verse of scripture that earns him a line in the history of the school. Indicating the door by which the donkey entered, Mr. Cox presents his chosen citation with just a hint of sarcasm. "You boys will, of course, be aware of the text in Saint John's Gospel, Chapter 1, Verse 6." With exaggerated patience he waits for one of us to identify the passage. None does or can. Deliberately, he continues, "Chapter 1, Verse 6 of Saint John's Gospel states that our Lord 'came unto his own and his own received him not.' I cannot help thinking that these words could be applied to the visitation we have just received." For a moment there was silence, then Mr. Cox gave a wide grin and the class exploded with applause.

There is a sequel to this wonderful moment, a tribute to the fine mind of Richard Cox. A few days later in Latin class, before calling us to open once again our copies of Caesar's Gallic Wars, he said he wanted us to listen to something he had remembered after the visit by the school donkey. He reached for his copy of the New Testament.

We listened as he read to us the short passage about Jesus choosing a donkey, the humblest of beasts, to ride into Jerusalem. When he had finished, Mr. Cox paused and said, "I want you now to take out your English Poetry books and look in the index for a poem by G. K. Chesterton. The title of the poem is 'The Donkey.'" Mr. Cox waited for silence and then began to speak:

When fishes flew and forests walked
And figs grew upon thorn,
Some moment when the moon was blood
Then surely I was born.

With monstrous head and sickening cry,
And ears like errant wings:
The devil's walking parody
On all four-footed things.

The tattered outlaw of the earth,
Of ancient crooked will;
Starve, scourge, deride me, I am dumb,
I keep my secret still.

Fools! For I also had my hour,
One far fierce hour and sweet.
There was a shout about my ears,
And palms before my feet.

I remember Richard Cox very clearly, perhaps because I liked him and I found Latin interesting. In appearance he was a slight figure, physically stooped and slightly lame. Sometimes he could be the butt of cruel and hurtful schoolboy jokes, but when he read aloud, he did so with a quiet and memorable authority. I also remember noticing that as he read, he did not have to look at the page. He looked at us as he delivered Chesterton's lines from memory.

There was silence when the reading ended. Mr. Cox made no further comment. He then closed the book and said, "Now, I think we were beginning chapter 3 of Caesar's *Gallic Wars.*" At least some of us saw that Caesar and his wars were not the real lesson of that day.

Good days and indeed good years on the whole, punctuated with the usual anxieties, personality clashes, fears and friendships lived out under a sometimes harsh authority: the general nature of boarding school life at that time. Around our small island revolved the turmoil of Europe in its agony of war. From time to time at morning prayers, the names of Old Boys who had died on active service were read aloud solemnly and prayed for.

Years later the headmaster, by then long retired, told me of at least two occasions when the school was alerted to the possibility of invasion by German forces. He had been warned of the potential necessity to arrange for the return of students to their homes. This did not happen and life went on. The coming of peace coincided with our graduation from boarding school. For most of us, university awaited; and after it, the choice of a career.

## 2. THE GRAMOPHONE CONCERT
### Midleton College, 1941–1945

The first person a new boarder bound for Midleton College met was Mr. McBride. He greeted students at the entrance to the railway platform from which the Youghal train left at 6:15. One of the stations along the line was Midleton.

Mr. McBride was the housemaster. As such, he was responsible for our welfare. When term began, he would travel from his home in Belfast to the college in Midleton, where he would spend a few days with the headmaster and the matron discussing the coming term, any changes there had been over the summer, the list of new boys, and much more. Then, on the day we were to return for the Christmas term—usually the first or second Tuesday in September—he would catch the train to Cork to take up his position at the platform entrance. With pen and writing pad, he welcomed boys and parents as they appeared.

Mr. McBride was experienced with new boys and their parents. He knew that a boy's first time leaving home was something of a trauma for both parents and son. Sensitive to this, he was well practiced in communicating warmth and understanding, while at the same time making it clear that the moment of parting should pass without any overt emotional displays. He was also understanding with boys who had been attending the school for some years and were now seniors. Those boys took great care to say goodbye to their parents before arriving at the spot where Mr. McBride awaited them. To be seen giving your parents a farewell hug would result in merciless ribbing from your peers.

Andrew McBride was a good and kind man. Living in the college throughout the term meant that he was thoroughly aware of its daily life, of problems that might occur, of issues such as bullying, of difficulties one of us might have fitting into a new kind of life. He was also immensely generous in giving us his time far beyond the call of duty. An example of this was the weekly Gramophone Concert.

Every Saturday morning, Mr. McBride would come into the fourth form classroom and pin two sheets to the notice board. In his neat copperplate writing would be the list of music that he had selected for us that weekend. Then on Sunday evening, precisely at 8 p.m., we would assemble. There were a few rules. As we listened to the program, we were allowed to read a book, write a letter home, or simply sit and listen. Doing "prep"—schoolwork for the coming week—was strictly forbidden. Mr. McBride prepared meticulous notes on each musical item that told something about the composer, or the piece itself, or the society of the time when it was written. Each Sunday evening, two readers were chosen to deliver these notes. Once a term, we were allowed to request our own favorites.

There are musical works I first heard at those evenings which I remember very clearly, partly because I have heard them throughout my life ever since. A partial list comes to mind: Handel's "Hallelujah Chorus" and *Water Music*, the Overtures to *William Tell* and *Tannhäuser*, the Chorus of the Slaves from *Aïda*, Bach's "Jesu Joy of Man's Desiring," Ravel's *Bolero* (the last a particular favorite requested on every possible occasion). Piano pieces like Beethoven's "Für Elise" or a

Chopin nocturne. And so many others. To hear them now is to return to those attentive Sunday evening sessions so many years ago.

A classmate named Hector Johnston was, like me, interested in English literature and drama. We decided that we would try an experiment. Both of us would listen to the music of the evening and write whatever thoughts it brought to mind, then allow the other to read what we had written. Sometimes those responses to the same musical work would be so different; sometimes there would be intriguing common nuances. We did that a number of times in our final year. Hector would eventually put his fine writing style and brilliant brain to good use in the nuclear physics papers he would write in Oxford. I went on to be a compulsive scribbler of books.

Such was Andrew McBride's gift to us. I assume, life being what it is, that some among us appreciated the gift he was offering more than others. For me, his generous spirit enriched my life beyond measure.

# 3. A COUNTRY DISCOVERED

## School Holidays, Cork, 1941 and Christmas Term, Trinity College, Dublin, 1949

As with most families during the years of the Second World War, the radio was at the center of our lives. Source of news, commentary, music, drama, it was in fact the wellspring of everything that informed, entertained, educated, and fascinated us. And because almost all of it came from the BBC and Radio Eireann, our national broadcaster, it was generally of a high order.

Kept handy beside the radio receiver was an indispensable weekly publication, the *Radio Times*, providing schedules and other details about the many programs on offer during the coming seven days. One week, while home for the holidays from my first year of boarding school, I noticed a name I recognized. C. S. Lewis was giving a series of short talks on Wednesday evenings.

The reason I knew the speaker's name was that he was the author of a paperback I had just read and had found fascinating entitled *Out of the Silent Planet.* What had drawn my attention to it was that it was a new kind of science fiction. I didn't quite understand it, but somehow it gripped me. The fact is that a naïve teenager tuned into the BBC that Wednesday evening in the hope of getting more science fiction. What I got instead was a brief presentation about Christian faith that absolutely fascinated me because it was so simple, logical, and crystal clear. It made sense. I did not realize then that it was all those things because I was listening to one of the finest Christian minds of that era. There were a few more Wednesdays before we headed back to boarding school. Each evening I was an avid listener. About two years later, still in boarding school, I read another tale of Lewis, *Perelandra*; it, too, whetted my appetite for more. It would be a few years more before I came across a small book by Lewis called *Broadcast Talks*, some of whose chapters were the same pieces that had first drawn me on those Wednesday evenings. They were eventually consolidated into *Mere Christianity*, a classic that is a best seller to this day.

Then came the great discovery. I have never been quite sure why it took so long. Perhaps my reading patterns changed in the way that they do at that stage of life. But one day early in the Christmas term of 1949 at Trinity College, I picked up a copy of *The Screwtape Letters* in a large Dublin bookshop. I was immediately enthralled by the device Lewis used to tell his tale: a young man is taken under the dark wing of a demon assigned to bring him to the nether regions. I realize now that in this brilliant collection of letters from a senior demon to a junior nephew Lewis was once again appealing to my lifelong fascination with fantasy and science fiction. But of course it was far more than that. These letters are one of the great works of moral reflection in Christian history. They have been an endless resource for a lifetime's ministry. I have given away at least a dozen copies of the book over the years. I simply cannot imagine it becoming irrelevant in any recognizably Christian future.

There remained still more for me to discover. It had to wait until children came along in our marriage. Thanks to C. S. Lewis, our whole family, along with countless others, were taken in our imaginations to a magical country called Narnia where two boys and two girls, aided by a mighty lion named Aslan, would find themselves the heroes and heroines of a great struggle between good and evil.

It was only in later years that I became aware that the Narnia adventures were conceived against the backdrop of the Second World War and its titanic conflict against the very real and present evil of Nazism. Another reason these tales were, and are, so significant for me is that they are imagined as taking place in the rolling hill country of County Down where Lewis grew up, very near to my wife Paula's family home. When he came to write *The Voyage of the Dawn Treader* and *The Last Battle*, he envisaged them being played out on Carlingford Lough, the long fjord-like inlet of the sea that separates County Down from County Louth.

I realize these reminiscences are really a way of expressing gratitude to an Oxford and Cambridge don named Clyde Staples Lewis, a writer who conveyed the essence of Christian faith to me and millions of my and subsequent generations with unmatched eloquence and effectiveness.

## 4. THE HILLS OF DONEGAL
### Rockwell College, Tipperary, 1943

This is not the place to attempt a social history of Ireland, but a remembered moment in boarding school needs some context if it is to have any meaning.

From the last decade of the seventeenth century to the last quarter of the nineteenth, a system of repressive statutes called Penal Laws severely limited Catholic education, preventing the development of a Catholic professional middle class in Ireland. One consequence was that almost up to the Second World War, virtually all aspects of professional life in what had become the Republic were dominated by Protestants. In the late 1800s, the orders of the church—among them Dominicans, Christian Brothers, and Benedictines—decided they would bring into being schools to create such a class. This ambitious project was still building a new Ireland in the 1940s, when I was at boarding school.

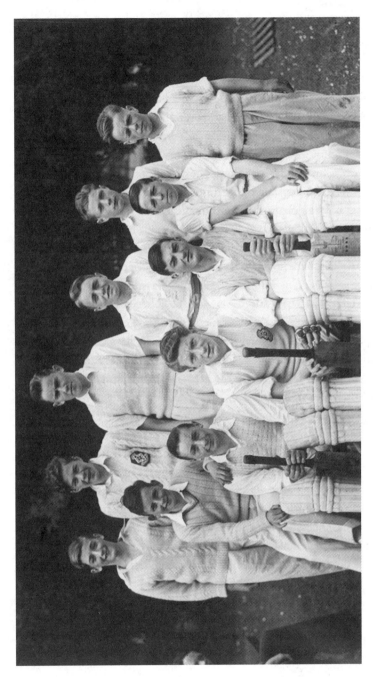

Midleton College senior cricket team, 1943–44. The author holds a bat in the centre of the front row.

The summer term of 1943 saw us fifth and sixth form boys excited about the coming cricket season. As usual, we played matches with other Protestant schools, but that particular summer brought the exciting news that we would also be playing Rockwell College. We had all heard of Rockwell, though none of us had been there. We knew of their proficiency in rugby, but we had never played them in cricket. Indeed, the mere fact of their playing such "foreign games" at all went very much against the strictures of the powerful Gaelic Athletic Association that only "traditional Irish games" be played at Catholic schools.

The great day came, for those of us lucky enough to have made the team. In 1943, travel of any kind in Ireland was at a minimum; any journey was an adventure. The trains were running on turf fuel and thereby slowly destroying their boilers. Petrol was strictly rationed; only certain people, like doctors, nurses, and clergy, were allowed to have cars.

The headmaster had the use of the college car; the rector of the parish had one; a local doctor had a son in the college, so his car was roped in. That made three vehicles; there must have been one more to carry us all, but its provenance is lost in forgetfulness. Anyway, off we went: out of Midleton, onto the Fermoy Road, through Fermoy, north to Mitchelstown, eastwards with the Knockmealdown Mountains on our right in the distance, past Kilcoran, into Cahir, under the walls of the castle and north toward Cashel, until eventually we turned into the gates of Rockwell.

Everything we had heard about it turned out to be true: beautiful grounds, magnificent buildings, a school population far more numerous than our small Protestant college. We were impressed. This quickly turned to concern about their prowess at cricket. We reassured ourselves that we Protestants had been playing cricket for more than a century, while these Catholics had only just discovered it. In such simple mental devices the teenage mind seeks solace—perhaps even the adult one.

Time has taken away the details of the game itself. I do recall that we won, but not overwhelmingly. But time has not taken the vivid memory of the hospitality we received after the game, and of how I found myself responding to that hospitality in a surprising way.

The hall in which we gathered after showering and changing was a most beautiful setting: surrounded by walls of dark wood paneling, a high vaulted ceiling, stained glass, huge windows looking out on a distant vista of the green rolling countryside of Tipperary, the lingering late-afternoon sun lowering in the sky.

After the meal, one of the Rockwell staff suggested a short impromptu concert. Perhaps there was a song that was especially liked in each school, that someone would be willing to perform. After a slight hesitation, one of their senior boys stood and began to sing. He possessed the makings of what would become a classic Irish tenor voice. He chose a well-known Irish song, "The Hills of Donegal," that speaks of love of Ireland and the longing of an exile to see again those "Irish hills, the hills of Donegal so dear to me."

I was deeply moved. Certainly, it was the song, both its words and music. I had heard my mother sing it many times. But this time I heard it differently. As I think back, I recognize that my response was made up of many things: the graciousness of my surroundings, the warmth of the hospitality, the beauty of the grounds, the camaraderie of the day. But it was even more. I felt myself part of a community that exuded strength and energy and confidence. Beyond the windows, I could see a green land that was my land. All this stirred in me an intense longing to identify in a total way with the country of my birth, instead of feeling at times like some hybrid creature of conflicting and ambivalent loyalties.

I realize now there were reasons for this welling up of deep feelings. My family on my father's side had only become Church of Ireland in the very late 1800s, and then only one branch of it. Many generations of Catholic faith lay behind that recent change. Also, unusually among Church of Ireland children, I found school classes in the Irish language interesting and enjoyable. In the precociousness of youth, I even tried translating English poetry into Irish Gaelic, with predictably mixed results.

Strangely, I cannot be sure that any of us from Midleton offered a song. If we did, it was probably a popular song of the day. The gathering drew to a close. We had a return journey ahead of us.

Goodbyes were said, plans for future matches exchanged, and we piled back into the cars. Like most adolescent waves of emotion, the tide of my feelings waned quickly amidst the chat and laughter. I had glimpsed a road that I would never take, but now I was on the road home.

## 5. THE SONG OF CREATION
### The Rectory, Midleton, 1943

**Decades after my four years** as a boarding student at Midleton College, when my wife, Paula, and I took our family to see the school, one of our children remarked that it didn't look as if it had changed much since its founding three centuries earlier. As I've said, my memories of it are not unhappy ones. There were periods of homesickness, especially in the early months but, as with most things in life, they passed and one entered into the life of the school with one's peers.

Nevertheless, life was, you might say, spartan. Actually, the motto of the school incorporated that very term. On our caps and blazers was emblazoned the Latin motto "*Spartam nactus es, hanc exorna,*" reminding us that we were indeed Spartans and we were expected to live up to that title. Spartan also might be applied to such things as the food in the dining room—plain—the desks in the classrooms—hard—and the beds in the dormitories—old.

Sometimes we longed for the comforts of home. There came a time when for a few short months something of home was provided from an unexpected source: the local Anglican rectory, which was within walking distance of the school. I recall the rector as a quiet, cultured man. To be in his company was, at least for me, a great pleasure.

In those days, confirmation classes were mandatory and usually happened in your fifteenth year. Previously they had taken place in the school library, a bare and dull room cluttered with desks that had been retired from the classrooms. But this year, the rector suggested to the headmaster that candidates for confirmation come to his study in the rectory. And so it was that on a certain Thursday we were sitting on the floor of the rectory study, its warm rug beneath us, a cheerful fire burning. The rector perched on the edge of his desk, his legs dangling. His wife brought the juice and biscuits. We had had a month of these classes and we looked forward to them eagerly as an oasis from the Spartan ambiance of the school.

On this particular Thursday I am to be given an enduring gift. Each of us has a Book of Common Prayer and a Bible. The rector directs us to open the prayer book at a certain page. He asks one of us to read. A boyish voice proclaims:

Therefore with Angels and Archangels,

and with all the company of heaven,

we laud and magnify thy glorious Name;

evermore praising thee and saying:

Holy, Holy, Holy, Lord God of hosts;

Heaven and Earth are full of thy glory.

Glory be to thee, O Lord Most High.

The reader's voice falls silent. Then, very quietly and deliberately, the rector speaks to us. "Those are very powerful words. When they are said in church something rather wonderful happens. If you listen carefully to the words, and if at the same time you keep looking at the window over the communion table, you find your imagination being drawn through and beyond the window itself. Sometimes when I lead you all on Sunday morning as you say these words, I find myself looking out at the whole of creation: every conceivable kind of being God has created, from great shining archangels to the tiniest and most humble creatures you can think of. Then, beyond the creatures, I see millions and millions of people of every kind, color, and race.

"Who are those people? I think we're looking at everyone who has worshipped God before us, and everyone who will do so after us, right back to the beginning of time and on to the very end of time: countless people, countless generations. And who is in the middle of them all? We are, we who are alive today. When we say these words in church, we join in the great song they are all singing, and for that moment time and space are opened up, and we and every part of creation sings the Song of Creation."

The rector paused. The room was silent. Then he said, "That song of creation has a name. We call it *Sanctus*. It means holy."

Those awe-inspiring images have remained with me, and the passage we call *Sanctus* has remained a song in my heart.

## 6. LEARNING BY HEART
### School Days—Lasting Memories

When education experts wish to demean the value of memorization, they use the slighting term "learning by rote." It conveys dismissal of what they consider to be a hopelessly outmoded and discredited method of imparting information. I would plead for another view, represented by a similar phrase, but with a very different connotation.

I grew up in the twilight years of what was then called "learning by heart." While I admit that we did indeed learn our multiplication tables by rote, learning by heart went far beyond imparting the fact that eight times eight is sixty-four while nine times eight is seventy-two.

We could sing off the names of the three main towns in every county in Ireland: "Cavan, Cootehill, Belturbet." We knew the medieval words that were still the titles of our Church of Ireland dioceses: "Ossory, Ferns and Leighlin, Killaloe, Kilfenora, Kilmacduagh." We could sound the roll call of the great battles of the Napoleonic Wars in Europe: "Blenheim, Ramilles, Oudenard, Malplaquet." Learning by heart was a kind of magical doorway to a vast country of cultural knowledge, beauty, and wisdom.

We did, of course, have literary resources: books of English poetry and prose. We had the plays of Shakespeare, the Psalms of David, the Book of Common Prayer, and the Bible. I realize now that our relationship with the Bible was far more about literature than it was about religion. I have no memory, even in senior years in boarding school, of any teacher being the least bit concerned whether such and such a piece of scripture was literally true or not, but I have a very clear memory of passage after passage being chosen for the beauty of their language. Some such selections might also contain deep truths about life that went far beyond our understanding as children, but, because we were assigned the task of learning them by heart, they stood a much better chance of serving us in adult years.

From Shakespeare would come Antony's plea to his audience at Caesar's funeral: "Friends, Romans, countrymen, lend me your ears." Or Portia's impassioned assurance that "the quality of mercy is not strained." Or Hamlet's soliloquy on the battlements of Elsinore: "To be or not to be, that is the question." Or Henry's words to his army before Agincourt: "We few, we happy few, we band of brothers."

From the library of the Hebrew Bible (known to us in the Authorized Version) would come the story of creation: "In the beginning God created the heaven and the earth." The contents of the two great tablets brought down from the mountain by Moses: "Hear, O Israel: The Lord our God is one Lord." David's heartrending lament for Saul and Jonathan: "How are the mighty fallen, and the weapons of war perished."

In the New Testament, we would learn (again in the language of the King James Bible) much of the second chapter of Gospel of Luke and its telling of the birth of our Lord, also the song of his mother Mary when the angel asks her to bear the sacred child: "My soul doth magnify the Lord." From the letters of Paul, his great tribute to the nature of love or charity: "Though I speak with the tongues of men and of angels . . ."

Collects and Psalms from the Book of Common Prayer were learned by heart: "Blessed Lord, who hast caused all holy Scriptures to be written for our learning . . . the sun shall not burn thee by day, neither the moon by night . . . they that go down to the sea in ships and occupy their business on the great waters . . ." And so much more.

I think some of us began to realize toward the end of schooling and the beginning of university that we had feasted on language, and for some of us the very richness of that language carried the faith into our lives.

Flash-forward three decades to Vancouver in 1972, about eight o'clock on a lovely summer evening. I am leaving a private ward in Vancouver General Hospital. Along the corridor, a few of the more mobile patients are getting a little exercise before sleep. I stop for a moment to greet a nurse on duty, who happens to be one of my parishioners. At that moment, another nurse emerges from a doorway, supporting a patient who is small, walks very slowly, and with great effort. Her grey hair is disheveled. There is about her a kind of bird-like fragility. She is helped into a wheelchair. A strap is fastened to make sure she does not fall forward. The nurse turns the wheelchair and begins to move away from where we are standing.

Then a most unexpected thing happens. A low but strong and perfectly audible voice begins to recite without pause or hesitation:

I wandered lonely as a cloud
That floats on high o'er vales and hills,
When all at once I saw a crowd,
A host of golden daffodils.

It is more than the groping recollection of a long-forgotten memory. Rather, it is the celebration of something treasured for a lifetime, and now reached for as a resource to nurture a weary spirit. It is not learning by rote. It is learning by heart.

# 7. ENCOUNTERING JUNG
## Patrick Street, Cork, 1945

The store was in what we would today call the city center. It sold a wide variety of musical instruments and sheet music. I had gone in for nothing more ambitious than a humble harmonica. I knew the manager because he was also the organist in one of the city churches. I had been a boy chorister in his choir for a year or so when as a family we moved temporarily to that part of the city. That afternoon, Mr. Marchant showed me various models of harmonicas. My choice was severely constrained because I had very little disposable income. It was my last year in boarding school. Just as Mr. Marchant handed me my purchase, he beckoned me to a bookcase. Taking out a book, he said, "I think that you will like this," then added, "maybe not now but some day." Without showing me the book, he wrapped it and handed it to me. As he saw me hesitate, he shook his head. "No, don't worry about payment. It's a present."

As the venerable double-decker bus labored up Summer Hill toward home, I opened the parcel to find a copy of Carl Jung's *Modern Man in Search of a Soul*. What I could not know then was that this book would enrich my future life and thinking in ways I could not have begun to understand.

The Ireland of the 1940s was very different from that of today. There was almost no awareness of the world of psychology. On the part of the churches, it was held in deep suspicion, if not downright antagonism. Many years later, I learned that at that time there were precisely three practicing psychologists in the entire country. You can perhaps understand why I looked at my gift with some mystification. I tried hard to read it. I did not understand what I was reading, but as I struggled to puzzle my way through passages here and there, I felt I was being introduced to a world of whose existence I had not previously known. At the same time, I also sensed that this new planet was hauntingly familiar, and that somehow I had been there before.

I know now why I had that feeling. When I was nine, I had discovered another book on my own at the top of the stairs in my grandfather's farmhouse as, holding my candle, I turned onto the small landing toward my bedroom. It had the most wonderful drawings by someone I had never heard of named William Blake. About the same time, too, my school textbooks were not only replete with the Christian tradition that came to Ireland in the fifth century CE, but also rich in the millennia-long Druidic tradition that came to the island a thousand years before Christianity. The plays of O'Casey, Yeats, and Synge were being performed in the Abbey Theatre in Dublin as I was fingering the pages of Jung's book. This was a culture where a youthful mind and personality could be richly formed in the humanities, in imagination, in story, in saga, in legend, in poetry, in long memory. All these things served to enrich immeasurably one's unconscious. That, of course, was the first big thing I was to learn from Jung: my conscious mind existed within a mysterious and much greater mind, or level of mind, called the unconscious.

All these gifts given in youth were, unbeknownst to me, preparation for the gift of Jung's book. It wasn't that I was taught as a child in a way that would allow me to understand what it said intellectually. Instead, the world I grew up in nurtured my unconscious and helped me in many ways to encounter Jung's mind *experientially*, even as I turned the pages of his book feeling at times totally confused and bewildered.

As years passed, Jung would give me the concepts now intimately associated with his work. I learned of conscious and unconscious, of anima and animus, of persona and shadow, of archetype. With his help, I came to understand my life as a single day: the glory and energy of morning, the pride and achievement of high noon, the gathering quietness of afternoon, the gratitude, regret, and sometimes peacefulness of evening, the fears of night and the dark. All of these are Carl Jung's gifts to me, for which I offer this inadequate expression of gratitude—not only to the great man himself but also to Cecil Marchant, who gifted me with a book that began a life's journey.

## 8. TRINITY COLLEGE DUBLIN

### Dublin, 1948

The wonderful thing about the place is that when one returns, it looks as if it has remained precisely as it was all those years ago when one walked in through Front Gate with all the excited anticipation that only the nineteen-year-old mind and heart are capable of.

Leaving behind the noise and bustle of College Green, one moves through the dark interior of the small rotunda to step into the brightness of Front Square. There is the Chapel, there is the Exam Hall, the Campanile, the Dining Hall, the Graduates Memorial Building, the Long Room, and Reading Room. In the twinkling of an eye—were it not that ancient knees tired from walking the surrounding city remind one otherwise—it is 1949 again. But then one has only to look at the humanity all around one to know it is very much 2015: the year of this particular visit. The consistently casual but calculated dress of both young men and young women announces a world different from ours, a world at once more overtly sexual and at the same time more mutually wary and sharp edged. Not to mention, of course, the ubiquitous smartphones in every hand.

Many thoughts come as we wander the squares, mostly of people. A glance at Number 7 block brings back H. R. F. Keating, who would give the world brilliant whodunits. Also striding Front Square was J. P. Donleavy, his brilliant novel *The Ginger Man* gestating in his fertile brain. The Rubrics remind me of a friendship with Douglas Hyde Sealy, the critic and translator who bore the names of his grandfather, Ireland's first president. Norman Rodway comes to mind. Active in the Trinity Players in my time, he carved out a respectable acting career on the English stage, and in film and television. I would see him decades later playing opposite Judi Dench in *As Time Goes By*. Wandering into the Graduates Memorial Building recalls the weekly debates of the "Phil," the Philosophical Society. How pretentious the topics argued over each week sound today: "Moved that this House believes that Christopher Columbus went too far." Predictably, perhaps, the distinguished visitor on that particular evening was the American ambassador.

In those days one could still sit in the cheap (one and sixpence) gallery seats of the Abbey Theatre and watch the later years of the first great generation of its company of players: Sara Allgood, Arthur Shields, Barry Fitzgerald. Lennox Robinson, one of the Abbey's founding fathers, would occasionally appear in the tiny foyer. He too would grace the Phil debates as our distinguished visitor. A few years later, I would get to know him as a member of the congregation in my first parish.

Exciting as all this sounds in retrospect, the fact is that that first year of university was not the happiest of times for me. My father was increasingly ill. As you've read, I had almost no money. I could not afford to live in residence, which made friendships more elusive. It also meant, under the university regulations of the time, that I could pursue only a "pass" degree, not the "honors" degree I coveted. I recall feeling despair as my tutor took me to task for living in unapproved lodgings. When I tried to explain my situation, he dismissed it with disdain. Indeed, my first year ended with the news that family finances made it impossible for me to remain in university at all. There followed a year of school teaching on minimal salary, with board and lodging, which at least meant I could set aside some modest savings.

Near the end of this "gap" year came the offer that would make all the difference. The rector of one of the large suburban parishes in Cork had been given one hundred pounds to use as he wished. In those days, that was a substantial sum. He offered it to me if I would return to Trinity and enter the Divinity School. So, in the fall of 1950, I found myself back at university, living in the Divinity Hostel on Mountjoy Square. This time, rich community and companionship lasted until ordination. Resuming my membership in the Phil, I participated in its public debates. I also joined the Theological Society.

Nonetheless, anxieties about money remained. A few weeks after my return to Trinity, a prominent Dublin heart surgeon phoned the hostel seeking a tutor for his young son, who has been born with a large hole in his heart and needed to be homeschooled. I applied and got the job—five days a week, 2:00 p.m. to 5:00 p.m., three guineas a week. The fact that my charge was a brilliant student made the work a pleasure. Later he went into the sciences, eventually joining the faculty of Canada's National Research Council. That tutoring job provided the wherewithal to bridge the chasm between penury and survival. It paid my expenses in the Divinity Hostel. Life was good. I knew I had chosen the right path.

Trinity gave me something else: a love that time has not diminished. I had been ordained about two years when I found myself back in Front Square one particularly auspicious day. I was walking toward the Dining Room when I became aware of Paula Lucy approaching me across the cobblestones from the door of Number 6, her coat open, her hair auburn, her eyes smiling. It was not our first encounter. I knew her as a member of the choir in the parish where I was curate, but for some reason that moment in Front Square changed everything. We walked out of Front Gate, turned toward Grafton Street, and went for coffee at Bewley's. To this day, whenever we return to Ireland, we go for coffee at Bewley's, sometimes accompanied by our adult children and their children. They all agree the coffee is magnificent. It has remained so for over six decades.

# 9. A GREATER MUSIC
## Divinity Hostel, Mountjoy Square, Dublin, 1950

To be Church of Ireland in the 1930s and 40s was to be conscious of always hearing a greater music, that of the life of the overwhelming Roman Catholic majority. Brought up in a Church of Ireland family, I was a spectator to the world of Roman Catholicism that surrounded me. However, I realize now that the presence of that world affected in many important ways my understanding of Christian faith.

The Angelus bell rang every evening at six o'clock for every ear to hear. Unlike our churches, Catholic churches were open every day, people coming and going to and from confessions, weekday masses, funerals, and so on. This made me aware of a church that was obviously woven through every aspect of personal life. In addition, every year there was that huge Corpus Christi procession, with representation from every aspect of public life. To witness this was to see church and society utterly interwoven.

There was also the effect of language constantly overheard. In his book of essays *Finders Keepers*, the poet Seamus Heaney speaks of what he calls "the enforced poetry of our household," by which he means the many names for the Blessed Virgin used in popular family devotions. As I read his recollection later in life, I realized that I too had grown up aware of such language merely by a kind of constant overhearing, either from childhood companions at play, or through references in the daily papers, or by public devotions on the radio. "Ark of the Covenant," "Gate of Heaven," "Morning Star," "Star of the Sea," "Health of the Sick," "Comforter of the Afflicted," "Queen of Heaven"—I knew them all. Heaney's comment resonated with me:

> None of these were consciously savoured at the time, but I think that the fact that I still recall them with ease, and can delight in them as verbal music, means that they were bedding the ear with a kind of linguistic hardcore that could be built on some day.

So much for the way in which one heard and absorbed the "greater music" of Irish Roman Catholicism, all powerful and all pervasive as it was. But there was a later overhearing of that same music that was heard quite consciously.

It was a November evening in 1950. I was living in the Divinity Hostel of the Church of Ireland. The house stood in what George Bernard Shaw once called "the most noble slums in Europe." Street after street was bounded by magnificent Georgian houses that had long since decomposed into cavernous open doorways, smashed windowpanes, and an all-pervading odor. That sea of poverty had within it islands of what might be considered institutional opulence but in reality, as in the case of our hostel, were much more scrubbed austerity. The north side of the square contained the buildings where James Joyce had sat at school, not that many years before, a student absorbing the images he would soon deploy to paint a devastating verbal portrait of that world.

On this particular evening, a fog coming in from the Irish Sea mingles with the smoke of coal fires, railway engines, and double-decker buses. The sky is overcast with the last of a watery sunset etched along the line of the western suburbs. I am standing at an open window to hear a sound coming from the center of the city. Everyone knows the reason for the sound. There has been brought to Ireland a most sacred relic: the right arm of Saint Francis Xavier. Tonight, it is to be placed on public display as the focus of evening devotions in one of the city's huge churches.

The response is overwhelming. Traffic is almost at a standstill. A friend who happened to be making his way back to the hostel from the university told me afterward that men and women were kneeling in the wet streets, the church long since packed beyond capacity. The sound of the chanting within is picked up by those outside. It lifts on the evening air and moves across the city, overwhelming the usual noises of urban life. Rising and falling, it gives voice to a great tide of emotion that is neither joy nor sorrow but an ecstasy beyond both, a passion beyond explanation, a mystery beyond any theological expression.

I recall thinking that evening that while I may have lived within a Protestantism that sometimes saw itself as a kind of ghetto, albeit a comfortable and influential one, I was also a willing listener to this greater music, which filled the world of that time and place and irresistibly drew me in to itself.

## 10. AN EVENING IN WALES

### Aberystwyth, 1951

After the Second World War, many things—activities, associations, institutions—began to spring to life again. One of them was the tradition among the universities of the British Isles and Ireland of holding what were called inter-varsity debates.

The format was quite simple, but the tradition was quite old. A motion was chosen on some theme. It usually began with the words "Moved that this House . . ." and a statement followed. The motion for the debate in which I had the good fortune to be involved was "that this House maintains that the Celtic Twilight was one of the wonders of the world." If that sounds to you rather out of this world, you are quite correct. It was intended to be so.

The host university selected the motion to be debated, and a speaker from its own ranks. Then it invited seven other universities to name speakers. Four spoke for the motion and four against. The audience assigned victory or defeat by acclamation. The group of institutions usually included Oxford, Cambridge, London, Edinburgh, Queens in Belfast, Trinity in Dublin, one of the colleges of the National University of Ireland, a Welsh university, and so on.

Sometime in the winter of 1951, an invitation came from the University of Wales in Aberystwyth to the University Philosophical Society at Trinity College Dublin. It happened that I was chosen to carry the Trinity banner that year. I was delighted. In those war and immediate post-war years there was very little travel and very little money, so I had never been outside of Ireland.

I had to take the ferry from Dublin to Holyhead in Wales, then catch a train down to Aberystwyth. The trip itself was exciting enough to compensate for the seasickness felt while crossing the Irish Sea. Seeing north Wales from the train window provided the novelty of discovering a country other than my own, though, truth to tell, the lack of sleep from the night's voyage caused me to doze intermittently in my compartment.

Arrival at the station in Aberystwyth forced me to wakefulness. There was a big banner to welcome us delegates to the university. The group assigned to host me could not have been warmer in their welcome. I was swept away to some restaurant or tea room, taken on a tour of the town, out onto the great sweep of the strand to see the bay, then around the university. I learned something very moving about its history. It is sometimes referred to as having been built by the pennies of Welsh miners. Two or three generations of miners all over the country had each given a penny from their pay packet week by week for many years in order to give a new generation access to scholarships which could help them escape the mines and aspire to professional careers.

Evening came: time for the debate in the large assembly hall. A dinner beforehand gave the speakers a chance to meet one another. The Cambridge delegate regarded the whole thing as a bit of fun. He confessed to not have the remotest idea what the Celtic Twilight was, surmising (correctly, as it happened) that it might have something to do with, as he put it, "dear old Willie Yeats and that sort of thing." Give him his due, when he did speak he was brilliant and amusing, so we earnest Celts, who had all debated the motion seriously, forgave him.

Perhaps a word of explanation may be in order about this Celtic Twilight. In the last two decades of the nineteenth century in Ireland, Scotland, and Wales (and, incidentally, also in Brittany), there began a revival of consciousness about Celtic history and culture. Theatre, art, music, dance, literature, as well as a great deal of historical research, all sprang to life, earning the overall title "the Celtic Twilight."

There is something about a large and appreciative audience that energizes a speaker. Suffice it to say that an enjoyable evening was immensely appreciated by the large gathering of about eight hundred students. To no one's surprise, wild acclamation made it obvious that this almost wholly Celtic gathering did indeed most fervently maintain that the Celtic Twilight, which more than one speaker declared to be more of a sunrise than a twilight, had indeed been one of the wonders of the world. And indeed, as I write this memoir almost seventy years later, there continues an unabated interest in those Celtic centuries in the British Isles.

No sooner had the clapping died down than a student leapt from his front row seat on to the large heavy table from which the addresses had been given, and in a heavily Welsh accented voice full of excitement and passion, exhorted the gathering, "Let us now show our visitors how we can sing!" The result was immediate and electrifying. The crowd divided, seemingly spontaneously, into soprano, tenor, alto, and bass sections, forming a vast four-part choir. On and on they sang, in both Welsh and English, finally building to a massive climax in "Men of Harlech." It was extraordinary and unforgettable.

Long after the party that ended the evening and continued into the morning hours, long after the few hours of sleep snatched before being escorted to the railway station, long after the train journey north to Holyhead and the evening ferry for Dublin (a smoother crossing this time, from what little I remember of it), I was still reverberating to the enthusiasm and intensity of it all. To this day, I have only to hear the name Aberystwyth to hear the thunder of those young voices. Not, of course, that I thought of them then as young voices. After all, I too was young. Perhaps Wordsworth's lines about the French Revolution apply equally well to my experience:

> Bliss was it in that dawn to be alive,
> But to be young was very heaven.

## 11. A LONG STORY
### Christ Church Cathedral, Dublin, July 1952

Sunday morning in Dublin, still early, the city quiet after its Saturday night revels, I am walking up Dame Street from Trinity College to Christ Church Cathedral. For the first time I am wearing clerical clothing, every stitch new. Grey suit, clerical collar, black vest. I am walking to the cathedral for the service in which I and three others will be made deacons in the ordained ministries of the Church of Ireland.

As I look across the decades at that twenty-three-year-old, while I have no idea what exactly was going through his mind, I can recreate a general impression of how he was feeling. As so often at such turning points, emotions were mixed. There was joy and anticipation, of course. There was relief that university years were over, not because they had been in any way unhappy, but mainly because it had been a difficult financial slog. My father had died the previous year. Being the eldest of three brothers, the loss gave me a new sense of identity and responsibility.

One thing I do recall vividly from that morning walk. I had been instructed to dress in clericals in preparation for ordination. Other parts of my wardrobe—black cassock, white surplice, black stole— were waiting for me at the cathedral. I was aware that I was about to become part of something much greater than myself.

Since earliest years in school, I had been taught that as an Irish child, I possessed a long story. Later, in boarding school, I had been introduced to John Henry Newman's essay on *The Isles of the North*, in which he tells the story of the contribution made by the Irish Church in the centuries between the fall of the Western Roman Empire and

Ordination Day, 1952: the author (second from right) with two fellow ordinands and Arthur Barton, Archbishop of Dublin (second from left).

the emergence of the early Middle Ages. That morning in 1952, I could have no way of knowing that interest in this chapter of Christian history would emerge again in the last decades of my own century, a recalling of the past that will be called Celtic Christianity.

A corollary to possessing a long past was the parallel assumption that I was about to become part of the ordained ministry of a church whose life would extend far into the future. Again, I could not predict then that within a scant decade of my ordination the tsunami of cultural change that would sweep over the world of the 1960s would challenge the church to find its role in a radically changed world.

The first foundation of the cathedral in which I am about to be ordained stands on what would have been in the eleventh century a low hill above the south bank of the River Liffey. Outside the doors of the present building are traces of the walls of the Viking cathedral laid down in 1030. In a side chapel is a preserved human heart, relic of the life of Laurence O'Toole, archbishop of Dublin at that time. As I walk up the side aisle toward the clergy vestry, I pass the tomb of Richard le Clare, Earl of Pembroke, also known as Strongbow, the powerful Norman who led his knights on to the quayside at Wexford in the invasion of Ireland in 1170. In succeeding centuries, the cathedral would experience many periods of devastation and of restoration.

Entering the building, I am conscious of being enveloped, even welcomed, into this long history. Something said to me in the liturgy this morning will make it possible for me to move through the decades of change ahead without feeling that the continuity of that faith is fundamentally threatened. I quoted them in the introduction to this chapter, and now I can put them in their proper context.

The homilist is the dean of the Cathedral, Tom Salmon. I have come to know and like him as a professor in my college years. At one point, he turns in the pulpit, points to the worn, smooth, stone front step of the chancel, looks at the four of us who are to be made deacons, and speaks slowly and deliberately. "Never forget," he says, "that on that step where you will kneel, men have been ordained for 950 years."

I remember little of the rest of that day, but that moment I never have forgotten. Over the seven decades since then, being reminded of the long tradition of the church that formed me has been a wonderful help in weathering the tides of change that have come and gone over a lifetime of ministry. *Deo Gratia.*

## 12. THE QUARE FELLOW
### Dublin, 1950 and 1954

To be in Dublin—indeed to be anywhere in Ireland—in the early 1950s was to have heard of Brendan Behan. He was a well-known, one could say notorious, public figure in the life of the country. He lived a lifestyle (a term unknown then) that challenged all those gentle and fragile things we call the proprieties. Most of what he said and did was done with a sublime (some would say diabolical) disregard for that vague and amorphous thing we call public opinion. Brendan was a revolutionary in every sense, even to the point of violent acts. He used language in public that most people used only in private, or not at all. He had a hearty contempt for authority, in all its forms. All of this was acted out and volubly expressed in a miasma of alcohol: an affliction that would bring Brendan's life and gifts to a tragically premature end.

My first meeting with Brendan was in the rooms of the University Philosophical Society in Trinity College. Putting it mildly, it was an unlikely setting in which to find him. He had been invited to act as what tradition called the "distinguished visitor" at one of our weekly debates. The convention was that the debate would take place on whatever topic happened to be scheduled, and then the floor would be turned over to the distinguished visitor.

Inviting Brendan was a typical student decision. We thought it daring and controversial. Here was this wild man who would proffer the ribald sallies we could not dare to utter. His presence in our august halls would surely guarantee the attention of the press—and a full house. He might even challenge the university authorities. Brendan, perfectly aware why he had been invited, certainly delivered. His dress was suitably bohemian, his language colorful, and the influence of alcohol obvious. But as his remarks continued, some of us gradually realized that there was far more to him than met the eye. In his earthy yet eloquent way, he was letting us know that in our cossetted middle and upper middle class lives, we had little idea of the reality of the streets of Dublin and the lives lived therein.

After the evening was over and the crowd milling about Brendan had thinned out, I was deputized, as a member of the Phil committee, to escort him to Front Gate. We had just left the Graduates Memorial Building when Brendan turned to me and demanded, "What's a good Catholic like you doing in Trinity?" I replied that I wasn't Catholic. That stopped Brendan in his tracks. "For the love of God," he expostulated, "what do you mean you're not Catholic! Your name is O'Driscoll. You *have* to be Catholic!" I explained that in the 1860s one part of the family had changed from Roman Catholic to Church of Ireland. When I finished, Brendan emitted a two-word invocation of the second person of the Holy Trinity, followed by, "I never thought I'd meet a [expletive deleted] Protestant O'Driscoll!" He was still shaking his head in disbelief as we parted on College Green.

Brendan and I would meet again. A few years went by. I graduated, was ordained in the Church of Ireland, served my first curacy in the Dublin suburb of Monkstown. In 1954, I was invited to come to Canada as a member of the staff of Christ Church Cathedral in Ottawa. There came the September day I was to leave Ireland. That very morning, I was running a last-minute errand in Dawson Street when I encountered him. I was ready to say who I was, but it wasn't necessary. He remembered me from the evening at Trinity. I suspect it was because of the shock of meeting what was for him a very strange life-form, a Protestant O'Driscoll. He greeted me warmly. However, the language was more muted. He seemed in better physical shape. There were no signs of alcohol.

Brendan was thoughtful, even kindly. I told him I was leaving for Canada, and he asked if I knew anyone there. When I said I had family who had emigrated back in the twenties, he said he was glad for me, that family was important. He hoped that I would return some day, that we might meet again. Then emerged what I think was the reason for his apparent well-being. He told me that he might be crossing the Atlantic himself one of these days. He had been writing a play about his prison experiences. The title was *The Quare Fellow*. It was going to be staged in Dublin and maybe London. Depending on how it went, he might even be off to New York. He had a few friends there who wanted him to come. They were trying to get backing for a production.

It was moving to see Brendan in that brief, happy time of his troubled life. The happiness would not last. The old ways would return. A lifestyle of excess would cost him dearly. I'm glad that for twenty minutes or so I met what I would like to think was the real Brendan, the Brendan he longed to be. Looking back, I wonder if the reason our conversation that September day on Dawson Street remains so vivid in my memory is that, without realizing it, it was my first real learning about life and character, appearance and reality, or to put it in language that Carl Jung gave us, about persona and shadow in all of us.

# PART TWO

# New World

The author crossing the Atlantic aboard the RMS *Franconia*, October 1954.

# CHAPTER FOUR

# Canada

*I*t was a crisp, brilliant, early fall morning. The Atlantic crossing had been rough. At dinner the previous evening, someone had been heard to say that during the night hours we would enter the Strait of Belle Isle, which separates the mainland peninsula of Labrador from the island of Newfoundland and marks the northern entrance to Canadian waters.

Early in the morning, I got up and went out on deck. The sea was calmer than it had been for days. Stretching out from northeast to southwest as far as the eye could see lay the north shore of the Gulf of St. Lawrence. Love affairs often begin with an unforgettable moment when a face is glimpsed. That morning, it was not a face, but rather a vast heaving seascape and a rocky wooded shoreline viewed from the slowly rolling deck of a venerable Cunard liner that captured my heart.

## 1. CROSSING THE UNKNOWN SEA
### October 1954

Strangely enough, I cannot recall the actual moment when I made one of the most significant decisions in my life, to relocate to Canada. Perhaps much of our decision-making is like that. We think we take a particular step at a certain time on a certain day, but the fact may be that our subconscious has been working away at it for a long time and what we imagine to be a decisive turning point is really just the last stage in a process.

I had heard all through childhood about members of the family who had emigrated to Canada. Images of what the country might be like had always been in my mind at some level. Link this with the adventure stories I read as a boy, some of them set there, and you can begin to understand why Canada called.

Looking back, it's almost as if something or someone pushed me. One very obvious incentive was a letter of invitation from John Anderson, then rector of St. Aidan's in Winnipeg. It so happened that his church warden, Victor Copley, was a first cousin of my mother, whose family had emigrated in the 1920s. He had heard of my ordination in 1952 and told his rector, who was looking for a curate, so off went a letter to me in Ireland. I had to decline that first offer. The Church of Ireland had helped me with the cost of my training. I could not leave its ministry for at least two years. However, a year later John Anderson, now dean of Christ Church Cathedral in Ottawa, invited me again.

Canada was still very far away then, and rather romantic in the mind's eye, so to receive that second letter was very exciting. However, life became more complicated. I had met the person who would one day become my wife. I was torn between wanting to go to Canada and not wanting to leave Paula. In the end we agreed on a plan. We would become engaged. I would go to Canada and return the following summer for the wedding.

I set off on my solitary journey: first across Dublin to the docks, then by ferry to Liverpool for the transatlantic trip. My large wooden trunk had to be deposited at the Liverpool docks some hours before the ship left, duly stamped "Not Wanted on the Voyage," after which I was free to spend the rest of the day around the city.

I had heard how magnificent Liverpool Cathedral was, so I went there. I sat in a pew and let the cathedral surround my rather miserable, small, lonely self. At least, that's how I felt at the time. All the usual questions came to mind, chief among them, "Am I doing the wrong thing?" I stayed there about an hour or so. By the time I left, things were somehow alright. I had a sense of doubts being eased, a stiffening of resolve. I knew I simply had to go forward. I have always been very glad I climbed the hill to Liverpool Cathedral.

It's hard to explain today how deep and powerful the hold of the church was on my imagination. All my life it had provided context and community and meaning. I had accepted ordination into something I thought of as universal and timeless. I wasn't losing that world; I was simply moving to another part of it. Paula, my fiancée, was part of that world here; I would be part of it there. In less than a year, we would be part of that world together.

Back at the docks, the RMS *Franconia* was preparing for departure. I mounted the gangway onto the liner and a crew member showed me to my cabin. There were four of us sharing the small space, all roughly the same age. Two of the others hailed from Belfast and one from Manchester, all three heading for jobs in Toronto. In those days, Canada was growing quickly, and work was plentiful. One of the Belfast lads, named Harry, had grown up as an Evangelical Christian. From time to time, he would lie on his narrow bunk and quietly, with a twinge of sadness, sing a chorus:

> Further along, we'll know all about it;
> Further along, we'll understand why.
> Cheer up, my brother, live in the sunshine.
> We'll understand it all by and by.

The four of us got along well in our cramped quarters. I remember the lounge of the ship thick with cigarette smoke. Somewhere in my photographs, three of us stand together on the deck. I notice we are braced against the wind and the movement of the vessel, as if readying ourselves to meet the unknown Canada each of us has chosen. When we disembarked at Montreal, we caught different trains— theirs for Toronto, mine for Ottawa. As it turned out, the paths of our lives never crossed again.

## 2. A REMEMBERED MORNING
### October 1954

The morning was glorious, the air crisp and clear, the sun still low on the eastern horizon, lighting the vast expanse of the Gulf of St. Lawrence. As I have said, I promptly fell in love at first sight with Canada.

Even now, more than sixty-five years later, the name of this great river holds romance for me. As a child in Ireland, I had heard of its endless journey from vast lakes large enough to be inland seas, through endless dark forests, by towns and cities, then forming this immense gulf that finally flows out into the wild, open Atlantic.

Before her postwar sailings back and forth across that ocean, bringing countless immigrants like me to Canada, the RMS *Franconia* (second of three vessels to bear that name) had served valiantly as a troopship during the Second World War. She and her sister ships had been requisitioned for the war effort because their power and speed allowed them to go faster than the Atlantic convoys, leaving U-boats in their wake. The *Franconia* also served as a floating headquarters for Churchill's English delegation at the Yalta Conference.

As I stared out across the wide expanse of water that morning, perhaps it was my ship's wartime associations which triggered a memory of my own from the still recent war years. In my hometown of Cork, our next-door neighbor's eldest son, about ten years older than me, had joined the Royal Air Force. I remembered Eddie Senior as an older boy in school. Along with many other recruits, he had been sent to Canada for flying instruction. One very sad morning, word came to his widowed mother that he had drowned when his plane crashed in this very same gulf on which I was now looking.

All that day, the shoreline came nearer as the old Cunarder beat her way west and south toward Quebec City, where I would get the train for Ottawa and my first Canadian home. As the hours passed, I returned again and again to the rail to drink in my first glimpses of my newly adopted country. As the gulf narrowed, I realized that its north and south coasts were like vast arms reaching out to welcome me to this magnificent land that was both unknown, yet somehow known in my imagination since childhood. All was about to become reality.

I carried the questions of countless immigrants before me, though without many of the burdens and anxieties many immigrants face. How would this decision to come to Canada work out? Could I go back if it turned out to be wrong? What lay ahead? There was much to give me confidence: a warm invitation to join the cathedral staff in Ottawa; an equally warm invitation from an aunt, an older sister of my mother who had emigrated to Canada in the 1920s, to live with her for at least some months; the realization that I would be returning in less than a year to marry someone I loved very much and to bring her to Canada if all went as we hoped. All of these thoughts blended with the throb of the ship's engines to induce a last restful night of sleep on board.

Morning came again. I got up early, because I knew the shore would now be much nearer. I went out on deck and as far as the eye could see was an endless line of richly varied color: pale yellow, deep gold, fiery scarlet. I was experiencing the glory of my first Canadian fall. Then I saw a silver spire and the small houses of a village. I would enjoy the beauty of autumn in my adopted country many times in the years that followed, but the thrill of that first morning encounter—the flaming beauty of those trees and the sun glinting on that spire—has always remained.

A couple of days later, it's 9:00 a.m. and I am in the chapel of the Cathedral in Ottawa. I feel as if only my body has arrived. The rest of me is homesick and disoriented. This moment, like the one in Liverpool Cathedral not long before, speaks of the way the church helped me through a challenging transition.

There are only about three or four other people in the small chapel. John Anderson and I are about to say Morning Prayer. We kneel, and the dean begins with the old words, "O Lord, open thou our lips." With the ease of total familiarity, I reply, "And our mouth shall show forth thy praise." This versicle and response mark the start of both Morning and Evening Prayer in the Anglican liturgy. I had made that response since I was a seven-year-old choirboy in St. Luke's Parish Church. To hear and say those same words this particular morning, thousands of miles away from everything familiar to me, had an immensely reassuring effect. The old world I had left behind and the new world I had come to were instantly bridged, seamlessly knit together within the shared world of the Book of Common Prayer. I had left home and at the same time, in a wonderful sense, I had come home.

# 3. THE GIFT OF MYTH

## The Bishop's Office, Ottawa, 1954

Much has been said and written about J. R. R. Tolkien and I make no claim to add anything significant to that mountain of erudition and eloquence. I mention him because these short reflections are about those riches in my life that I have come upon as discoveries or disclosures, and high among these gifts is the vast and wonderful world of Tolkien given to me within days of my arrival at Ottawa's Christ Church Cathedral.

I had come to the office of Bishop Ernest Reed to be formally inducted as a priest in the Diocese of Ottawa. I had taken the Oath of Allegiance to the Queen and then the Promise of Obedience to my bishop. I was just about to leave when the bishop handed me a large hardcover book from his desk and smiled, "I think you will like this."

It was *The Lord of the Rings*. I was not aware of it. It looked interesting. I was to discover that it was far more than interesting. I devoured it, thrilled at the knowledge that there were two more volumes to come. Later, I learned of a fourth book, *The Hobbit*, that had been written earlier than the trilogy. I now realize that in this wonderful mythic creation I had been given the key to a theme that would demand pursuit and expression for the rest of my life: the Christian faith as a quest—a wondrous and mysterious narrative always calling us to journey further and deeper.

Tolkien created a world. I suspect he would have demurred at that verb "created," and might have preferred the term "imagined." He gave that world heroes and villains, battles, victories and defeats, landscapes, geographies and histories. Above all, he gave us a vision of the human journey with a power that some consider not equaled since the great epics of Homer.

When I set out to pursue my own journey of imagination from the Shire to the Mountains of Mordor, I was still early in my ministry. I know now that I received at least three gifts from Tolkien. The first gift was realizing the power of narrative as a means of communicating insights about life. The second was learning that one of the richest and most revealing lenses through which to look at the human story is to see it in terms of a journey. The third was the gradual understanding that both of these other gifts could be further enriched for preaching purposes by linking them with a rediscovery that was happening in those middle years of the twentieth century. Something that was both very old yet also very new was beginning to affect the use of Holy Scripture in Christian preaching.

Many were realizing that the Enlightenment had allowed the narrative power of the Bible to be neglected, almost forgotten. Even as late as the decade of my own ordination, the very term "Bible stories" had been relegated to being little more than material for ministry to children. Forgotten too was the fact that by far the greater part of Holy Scripture is story and image rather than explanation and concept. For many years, I would use these insights about the recovery of "story" to enrich my own preaching and, later, the homiletic skills of many clergy in seminars and conferences. Time and time again it was rewarding to see men and women applying these lessons in their own ministries.

Within the Tolkien trilogy itself there were, of course, countless insights into human experience. To encounter the four Hobbit friends, chief among them Frodo, was to realize the mysterious power of such things as mutual loyalty and common purpose. In the faithfulness of Sam, often shown when he struggles desperately to understand, I learned that greatness can be found in simplicity, and that without such simplicity and even innocence, intellect and sophistication can be vulnerable and even helpless. Again and again, I was reminded of the necessity of resolution and resilience in the face of what life can sometimes bring.

A last thought about the loss and subsequent rediscovery of narrative in Christian teaching and preaching: in my years conducting seminars with clergy I was always aware of the great irony that never at any time was this loss suffered by either Jewish or Black preachers. However, considering that the purpose of this reflection has been to thank J. R. R. Tolkien for opening a world to me, that must remain another story.

## 4. SEEKING A BETTER COUNTRY
### Ottawa, 1957 / 1965 / 1967

To enlist as a chaplain in the Royal Canadian Navy, you must be a Canadian citizen. When I accepted the invitation to join the chaplaincy in 1957, I had been in the country three years and had not yet acquired citizenship, so one day in February I left the cathedral and set off to begin the process.

I recall standing at the counter of an office in downtown Ottawa and being given an application form. The task completed, I was asked to hand over five dollars: a token amount these days, but in those days a substantial subtraction from my curate's income of ninety dollars every two weeks.

I emerged not yet a citizen. Some checks had to be conducted and I would be duly notified. I was told some time later that an RCMP officer from the Canadian Embassy in Dublin came to the parish I had left two years before to come to Canada. He must have been satisfied that I was not trailing any legal baggage behind me and that I really was the person I claimed to be, because some weeks later, I was asked to return to the citizenship office to swear allegiance to Her Majesty as Queen of Canada and to receive my citizenship certificate, a valued piece of paper that has been carefully preserved over the years. Two further things happened over the succeeding decade that would deepen my sense of belonging to my adopted country.

Friday, February 15, 1965, was a bright, cold winter's day in Ottawa. It was almost noon as I drove west along Laurier Avenue toward Elgin Street and the Church of St. John the Evangelist where I was by now the rector. As I drove onto Laurier Bridge, I could see the National War Memorial in Confederation Square to my right, and beyond it the East Block on Parliament Hill. All of this had become familiar from our years in the city, but that noonday something else registered on the edge of my vision. I saw a flag being lifted to the top of the Peace Tower—a new flag, one that I had heard a great deal about but not seen until then: a maple leaf, red on a white background, with red side panels, against the blue of the February sky. I recall being deeply moved. For me at that moment it was far more than a flag. It was the new symbol of a land to which Paula and I were still comparative newcomers. While we had already lived in the Maritimes, and explored the beauty of Cape Breton, the St. John River valley, and the Gaspé, we had yet to come to know the vast reaches of Western Canada.

Another memory that I treasure happened two years later, in 1967. In those days, the Canadian Council of Churches arranged an annual breakfast at which senior government officials and senior church representatives would meet. That year, I happened to be the invited speaker. At some stage in my remarks, I quoted from that list of great people of faith given by the unknown writer of the Epistle to the Hebrews. At the end of the catalogue, the writer identifies what all of these people had in common: they all "desired a better country."

Following the breakfast, the Honorable John Matheson approached me and asked if he and I could sit together for a few minutes. Matheson was then Liberal MP for Leeds County and parliamentary secretary to Prime Minister Lester Pearson. Coincidentally, he had played a key role in the design of the Canadian flag, and would later become a judge. That morning, he told me confidentially of plans that would soon be completed to create a Canadian honors system called the Order of Canada. It appeared that the process was being delayed by the inability to agree on a suitable motto for the Order. Matheson told me that he was almost certain that the quote I had used in my address could be the answer to their quest. Together, quickly pooling our memories of boarding school Latin classes, we decided that the Latin words would be "*desiderantes meliorem patriam*." Later checking confirmed that we were right. And so it was, as the best stories say, that the Order of Canada acquired its motto.

Why do I share this? Because I would like the church I love to know that its sacred text contributed to the creation of the Order of those honored by our country. Speaking personally, as an

immigrant, I am proud and glad to have made that modest contribution to the country that welcomed my wife and me: a country in
which we would discover dear and lasting friendships, and in which
our children would learn and live the story called Canada that is
theirs by birth.

## 5. A LONG-AGO LOYALTY
### Parish of Huntley, Ottawa Valley, 1960

To become the rector and incumbent of the Parish of Huntley
in the fall of 1960 was to inherit a long tradition of rural Anglican
life in the Ottawa Valley. Loyalties ran deep and strong. Respect
for tradition and authority was paramount. A bishop who was a
long-time good friend used to say of such places that their commitment to the church was so steady, so unwavering, so instinc-
tive, that if they had the best parish priest in the country, there
would be at most three people more in the pew on Sunday, and
if they had the worst priest going, there would be at most three
people less.

Huntley was what is known as a three-point charge: within the
one parish there were—and indeed still are—three churches: Christ
Church, out on the Carp Road, east of town (dedicated in 1838);
Saint John's, in the agricultural lands to the south (1885); and Saint
James the Apostle, right in Carp Village (1892). This meant that the
parish had three of everything—three choirs, three graveyards, three
parish councils, three annual vestry meetings. Everything except
three rectors.

Because it was the oldest building, Christ Church was the official parish church. But because St. James was built of stone, stood at
the heart of the village of Carp, and had the rectory beside it, it sub-
tly assumed that *it* was the "real" parish church. St. John's, the smallest congregation, had no such pretensions to importance. However,
the congregation was justly proud of their handsome brick building, with its steeply pitched roof and beautiful large stained-glass

windows. They kept a close eye out to ensure they participated equitably in any privileges or improvements accorded to St. James or Christ Church.

By the time I arrived as rector, a number of voices were suggesting that the parish as a whole needed a parish hall. Up to this point, any large parish-wide events had used either the Orange Hall or the Women's Institute. The very complex, challenging, and fraught question, given the rival interests of three congregations, was where the hall might be built. After much deliberation the decision was made to build in the center of the village, beside St. James. The next major question was financial. How much, if anything, would each congregation commit to the project? Each congregation naturally held its own special vestry meeting, where all the duly enrolled members of that congregation were entitled to attend and to vote.

Not surprisingly, St. James said yes to the project. Next came the meeting at Christ Church. Again, there was a positive response—not quite unanimous, but a healthy favorable majority. St. John's was a different matter. Of its fifteen farming families, the female head of one was known to be adamantly opposed to the proposal. Since the vestry meeting was to take place in the parlor of this same worthy matriarch, the chances of a majority "yes" vote seemed slim indeed.

When all was ready, a resolution duly moved and seconded, voting papers distributed around the large family table, the official list of those attending having been read and checked off—the names including the rector and his wife, the church wardens, the vestry clerk, the two lay delegates to the diocesan synod, and the two parish delegates, one of whom was also our formidable hostess—the last solemnity was a request that the rector offer a formal prayer for such an important official occasion. Voting by secret ballot proceeded in silence. After a suitable interval, papers were folded and gathered, the vestry clerk and a warden took them into the adjoining room. We sat and waited.

When the result came, there was a gasp of disbelief. It was a unanimous "yes" to the project. All eyes turned to our hostess. Voices asked how it could possibly be that she had changed her mind. For a few moments she was silent, as if unable or unwilling to say anything. Then, almost as if she could not believe what she was hearing herself telling that small circle, she said, "I wanted to vote 'no,' but how could I when I was sitting beside the rector's wife!"

Salt of the earth, those people were. The parish hall they built still stands, and still hosts a wide variety of dinners, social events, service organizations, community meetings, and a co-op nursery.

## 6. THE DOUGH BOX
### The Rectory, Carp, Ontario, Christmas 1960

To this day, in the living room of our home, an old pine dough box fits snugly into the bay window. Now, a dough box—in case you've never encountered one—is a very plain piece of furniture that, in its simplicity, could easily be mistaken for a Shaker piece. It has that clean-lined, timeless look. It was likely made on a farm at the request of the woman of the house. Each evening she would have removed the flat pine lid, put inside the dough she had just made, replaced the cover, and left the dough to rise overnight, ready for baking in the morning.

Many decades after bread was no longer regularly prepared in this way, we discovered our dough box, roughly painted and slightly damaged, in the loft above the old stable that adjoined the rectory of our first parish in the Ottawa Valley. We brought it in, stripped and polished it, and gave it a home. In our house, it had no particular use other than being a lovely, eventually beloved, piece of traditional furniture. Pine polishes beautifully.

In the case of this particular dough box, something almost magical happened every year to make it mysterious and even sacred. It became a crib for the baby Jesus in the annual Sunday school pageant. Before it was taken out to the church, it was polished until the old pine shone. Then, because it was going to become a resting place for the Christ Child and therefore needed to be open, the cover was taken off. Hay or straw was placed inside to transform the dough box into a manger.

When we were in city parishes, the question would arise of where to find the hay or straw. However, there would always be somebody in the congregation who knew someone else who had acreage, and all would be well.

Before we left the house for the church, some other things went into the dough box that would eventually be carried solemnly by various children. A brass box, shining and ornate, served as the gift of gold to the Holy Child, and two pottery vases, one blue and one green, represented the gifts of frankincense and myrrh. Thus equipped, we would drive to the church for the first rehearsal of the pageant.

Invariably, those families who were new to the congregation would express admiration for the dough box. Some would tell how their grandparents or elderly friends of their parents had once possessed such an object, but somehow it had been lost. You could see that some now regretted that loss as they ran their fingers along the gleaming pine of the box standing in the chancel.

As the day of the annual pageant approached, something rather mysterious invariably began to happen. You couldn't help noticing the way in which people would begin to relate to the old dough box. They appeared no longer to regard it as merely a piece of farmhouse furniture. Somehow, perhaps because it had been brought into the sanctuary of the church, it seemed as if it had now been elevated, prepared and ready to serve its purpose, a purpose that was both far away in the infinitely distant village of Bethlehem, but at the same time also among us in our parish church. Most mysteriously of all, both in Bethlehem and in our church, the dough box became a humble manger, then, leaving behind every vestige of that humility, it was again transformed to become the sleeping place of the new-born Son of God.

Many years have passed since the old box carried its royal burden. Since then, it has travelled with us over many miles and stood in various rectories. In its travels and in its various homes it has been used in various ways, mostly for humble purposes. It has stored school books, supported potted plants and vases of flowers. At one time it became a bookshelf in someone's room; at another it shone with candles placed for a party. The thought came to me one day how readily this simple but lovely piece had laid aside its sacred role of bearing the Holy Child of Christmas, and accepted a humble and even mundane existence in our home. But then I remembered how Saint Paul tells us that our Lord Jesus "emptied himself, taking the form of a slave, being born in human likeness," and I understood.

## 7. THE COMMUNION RAIL

### St. John's Huntley, Winter 1960–1961

In the wonderful world of Harry Potter, there is a frequently repeated scene. Every time the three friends return to Hogwarts for a new term, they take their luggage to the station, put the cases in a luggage cart and push the cart faster and faster toward what seems to be a solid wall. Just as they reach the wall, it melts away and they find themselves on Platform Nine and Three Quarters where their train stands, its great engine steaming, ready to whirl them through the English countryside to where a new term awaits them.

Long before J. K. Rowling brought Harry and Ron and Hermione into being, I had what I might call a Platform Nine and Three Quarters experience. It was 1960 and I had just gone to be the very inexperienced rector of a small three-point parish in the Ottawa Valley of Ontario. One weekday in the depths of my first winter, I drove to the smallest of my three churches, St. John's. I can't recall why I went there on that particular day.

I was quite alone. A heavy overnight snowfall had blanketed the whole valley. Something about the stillness made me kneel for a moment at the altar rail. As I did, I received what I have always believed to be a vision. This seems to me to be the simplest, and at the same time the most mysterious, term for such a moment. I remember looking along the wooden altar rail to my left and then to my right, seeing the rail anchored into the wall. But then I found myself in imagination going through the wall and out into the silent fields of snow, still seeing the communion rail as it set out with me on what became a vast journey. On we went across the great river that gives this Ottawa Valley its name, across the incalculably ancient rocks of the Laurentian Shield, over the grey heaving wildness of the Atlantic, on and on across continents—first Europe, then Asia—and the endless vastness of the Pacific, above the Rockies and the Prairies, over the Great Lakes, across the white silent fields of my little parish and—wonder of wonders—back into my tiny St. John's through the other wall.

I have never forgotten that simple and wonderful vision. Each Sunday in St. John's there would be about thirty people, but I had brushed up against the mighty invisible reality that surrounded our smallness. In a moment, "in the twinkling of an eye," I had knelt with millions of people, stretched my hands forward with them, eaten bread with them, shared wine with them.

Much has changed in the world and in the church since I knelt at that rail. Nevertheless, the next time you kneel at a communion rail, you may wish to remember Harry Potter's and Ron's and Hermione's experience, and mine. You may protest: what have such magical, mystical, visionary experiences to do with the realities I must live in day by day? As you kneel in a world in which the 1960s are nothing more than a memory to older people and history to those who are young, you will be aware of a church very different from my little St. John's, a church that faces a very different world and that grapples with massive change. However, as you wait for the Sacrament to be placed in your outstretched hands, look left or right to where the rail seems to end at the wall of the sanctuary, then wait for the Spirit to take you through the wall and show you the Church, the worldwide Church, the Church as our Lord sees it. Through God's eyes you will come to see it differently, and when you rise from the rail and return to your pew you will see *yourself* differently too. You will come to know yourself as a living cell in the Body of Christ, and you will be changed.

# 8. MAKING HISTORY
## Parish of Huntley, 1962

To speak of the Book of Common Prayer is to tap into centuries of history. The very mention of this deceptively small volume takes one onto a stage where all is larger than life. One thinks of kings and queens, bishops and archbishops, cathedrals and palaces. My tale, however, is set on a much more modest stage: a small country parish in the rich farmlands of the Ottawa Valley. It was my very first parish responsibility. I was all of thirty-four, my wife, Paula, twenty-six, and our first two small girls aged four and two. We had been here for two years. We did not know it yet, but the bishop was about to call us to a church in the nearby city. But before that happened, we were excited by something historic that we knew was coming. The first Canadian Book of Common Prayer had been duly authorized by two successive General Synods of the National Church, had been published, and was being distributed in all Canadian parishes.

The day the big heavy boxes arrived in the rectory was an occasion of great excitement. Our first job was to install the new books in the pews of our three churches. Putting them in St. James was easy; it was just across the road from the rectory. I carried the box and our four-year-old eagerly ran among the pews, placing books at intervals, while our two-year-old tried valiantly to follow her sister. St. James completed, we returned to the rectory, loaded the other two boxes into our VW Beetle, fit the girls in beside them on the back seat, and set off *en famille* for Christ Church and after that St. John's.

For the children it was a thrilling day. Looking back, I realize that they sensed that their parents were also thrilled. Driving home along the country roads that late afternoon, we had a sense of making a modest contribution to a magnificent history. We were present at the birth of the next generation in a tradition more than four hundred years old. Let me share seven tiny gems I treasure from the Book of Common Prayer.

An Offertory Sentence: "You know the grace of our Lord Jesus Christ, that, though he was rich, yet for your sakes he became poor, that you through his poverty might become rich."

From the Collect for the Fourth Sunday after Trinity: "O God . . . increase and multiply upon us thy mercy; that . . . we may so pass through things temporal, that we finally lose not the things eternal."

From a General Intercession: "Remember for good all those that love us, and those that hate us, and those that have desired us, unworthy as we are, to pray for them. And those whom we have forgotten, do thou, O Lord, remember."

From a Thanksgiving for Family Use: "For life and health and safety, for power to work and leisure to rest, for all that is beautiful in creation and in the lives of men, [women and children], we praise and magnify thy holy Name."

From a Prayer at Eventide: "O Lord, support us all the day long of this troublous life, until the shadows lengthen and the evening comes, the busy world is hushed, the fever of life is over, and our work is done."

From the Collect for the Fourth Sunday after Easter: "Grant . . . that [we] may . . . desire that which thou dost promise; that so, among the sundry and manifold changes of the world, our hearts may surely there be fixed, where true joys are to be found."

And finally, from the Prayer of Humble Access: "We do not presume to come to this thy Table, O merciful Lord, trusting in our own righteousness, but in thy manifold and great mercies. We are not worthy so much as to gather up the crumbs under thy Table."

Later, I will share a few memories and treasures from the other prayer book that came into the life of the Canadian church during my ministry as an Anglican priest.

# 9. DALI'S CANVAS

## Beaverbrook Art Gallery, Fredericton, New Brunswick, Summer 1962

In an age when even the word "doctrine" sounds more than a little threatening, the term "The Doctrine of the Most Holy and Undivided Trinity" can be depended upon to stop conversation in its tracks. Yet the fact is that these words express, albeit obscurely, a beautiful and even awe-inspiring truth about human existence. Most unexpectedly, I was once given a way to grasp that truth.

The summer of 1962 was wet and miserable, at least in Nova Scotia. We had gone there on holiday with two small children. Our lodging was modest: a single room in a B and B within walking distance of the beach. However, thanks to the inclement weather, there was hardly a day when the beach beckoned. We decided to cut our time short and head home.

We had driven to Nova Scotia through New York and Maine, so we decided to return via New Brunswick and Quebec. We had another reason. Just three years earlier, the generosity of Max Beaverbrook made it possible for the City of Fredericton to open a fine new art gallery. We had read that the gallery's collection boasted a huge and most impressive painting by Salvador Dali, entitled *Saint James the Great.* We decided to stop and see it.

When we pulled into the parking lot, both children were asleep. We decided not to wake them to see the painting. Looking back, I'm not sure—as with many parental decisions—that it was the wisest course of action. Nevertheless, Paula and I agreed to take turns going in to see the Dali painting, while the other stayed in the car with the children.

On entering, I discover that the painting has its own gallery—and no wonder. The gigantic canvas measures about thirteen feet by ten. In the middle of the gallery, a bench allows one to sit and engage this wonder. As I do, I am unaware that I am about to be taught something about my Christian faith, and indeed, about the way I experience the world around me.

My first impression is of the painting's power over me. The armed rider, the massive horse pawing the air, everything speaks of power. I feel myself confronting an act of creation utterly and literally above and beyond my own small human scale. As I continue to sit and stare, I realize that the painting is drawing me into dialogue. It is taking me through some history that I know, some traditions of the apostles. The details and iconography invite me to explore the work more closely. The painting and I are in a relationship. Eventually, I force myself to stand and leave so Paula can have her turn.

A few hours later, after a noisy family lunch, we resumed our homeward journey, driving along the lovely St. John River valley. But I could not stop thinking about the painting. At some point, it dawned on me why. What my encounter with this masterpiece had given me is a way of understanding why generations of Christians have been at such pains to conceive of the nature of the divine as a Trinity.

After we'd put the children to bed, I pieced together the sequence of my experience. I recollected it very clearly as a sequence. Dali's painting first humbled me as something above and beyond me. Then it engaged and conversed with me. Then it haunted me. It came to me that my relationship with everything and every person follows that same pattern: first separate and apart, then in relationship, then internalized within. So it is with the ultimate reality that is the divine. God is outside me in creation, relates to me as a Christian in Jesus, and dwells in me as Holy Spirit. How far is that from the conventional image of God as a bearded old man in the sky!

Some years later, as I studied the coming of the then-new Christian faith to northern Europe, I would learn that all through the millennia of pagan religion, the Druids had thought of the divine in terms of a Trinity; because of this, the old and new faiths shared some common ground.

The Beaverbrook Art Gallery has since been expanded considerably, and the Dali painting continues to attract visitors. If you're ever passing through Fredericton, stop in. You may find your Christian faith enriched in surprising ways.

## 10. EARTHQUAKE

### Anglican Congress, Toronto, 1963

Michael Ramsay, archbishop of Canterbury in the tumultuous decade of the last century we call "The Sixties," was speaking at a world gathering of Anglicans in Toronto in 1963. I was only a little more than a decade ordained. Our youngest at that time, Moira, was a few months old. Her two sisters remained at home with an obliging friend who acted as babysitter. We participated in the conference as a family of three, baby included. When I think of it now, I realize that bringing her into that session was itself an indication of the changes taking place so rapidly at that time.

The archbishop was commenting on chapter 12 of the Letter to the Hebrews. He explained that the unknown writer was reminding his Jewish readers of something that had happened far back in their history on their trek from Egypt to what they regarded as their promised land. In the Sinai wilderness, there had been a strong earth tremor and some had died. But then, Ramsay continued, the writer goes further. The earth, he writes, will again be shaken. The primate then came to the point he wished to make. Why, asks the writer, does God shake the earth from time to time? The answer comes in verse 27: "So that what cannot be shaken may remain."

As I listened that day, I could not know that the image of earthquake would remain a recurring theme in the rest of my ministry, so much so that, to this day, when anyone asks me what the overarching image of ordained ministry is for me, I tend to respond "earthquake," and then try to explain that cryptic response.

I was ordained in 1952 and retired from stipendiary ministry in 1993. That puts me in the generation of clergy whose working lives straddled changes that have utterly transformed ways of ministry, understandings of Christian faith, roles of clergy in society, and relationships between clergy and their congregations—just about everything. For my generation, it has been more than half a century of continual upheaval: theological, pastoral, cultural, professional, personal.

Out of that experience of unrelenting change, images of earth-quake come easily to mind as vivid metaphors for Christian ministry. In the mid-1970s, a strong quake shook an area of northern Italy. A television camera in the rear of a large crowd at an outdoor mass on a hillside captured the image of an elderly priest standing by a rough altar of assembled stones. He was just about to elevate the chalice when an aftershock struck. The tremor rippled through the crowd until it reached the priest. He staggered but succeeded in keeping the chalice aloft with one hand while steadying himself on the makeshift altar with the other.

When I saw that scene, I immediately identified with it. I realized that what was demanded of my generation of priesthood was to live out our ministry in a world whose foundations were being shaken, and our task was to decide what, if anything, remained solid and lasting.

Another decade later, a major earthquake hit Los Angeles. After the quake was over and time had been left for possible aftershocks, a TV crew gained permission to return to a damaged apartment block with an elderly Hispanic woman who had escaped from the building some days before. The camera showed the woman standing in the darkness at the back of what had been her living room. She told how the dishes in her cupboard suddenly began to rattle. She pointed to the cupboard itself that had fallen over, and to a giant crack in the wall. She told how she had run toward the door, only to find it torn off its hinges and hanging sideways. She showed where she had fallen while trying to run along the concrete path that was twisted and crumpled by the tremors. Then she stopped in front of a large opening in the ground. In a hushed voice she said in Spanish, "I knew then that the earth had moved."

I could not but hear that simple statement as a summing up of what had taken place in Western Christianity in the latter half of the twentieth century. The changes began in the sixties. They gathered strength and significance until, in my own late years of ministry, I too could say that "the earth has moved."

Hearing that preacher's insight in 1963 has been a golden thread through my years of ministry. It has become a metaphor of vocation I have offered to others many times. To serve in an age of cultural and theological earthquake is to be forced to decide what it is for each one of us that cannot be shaken.

## 11. THE COLORS OF FALL
### Gatineau Hills, Mid-1960s

In Canada, intimations of change were in the air. A dashing young intellectual named Pierre Trudeau would soon arrive on the political scene. A new Canadian flag would soon fly over the Peace Tower. I was a priest in my mid-thirties, newly arrived in downtown Ottawa as rector of the Church of St. John the Evangelist on Elgin Street, and feeling glad to be back at the center of things; then again, perhaps when one is in one's mid-thirties, one always feels at the center of things.

Gradually, I got to know some people in the large congregation. Twice a week, I went to the Civic Hospital, in those days on the western edge of the city. The diocese had a first-class hospital chaplain, who would leave a list of parishioners who were hospitalized for their respective clergy to consult. All you had to do was to go into the doctors' lounge, review the list, copy the names and room numbers of your parishioners, then head up to the sixth floor and work your way down.

I forget what floor I'd reached when I looked at my list and saw the name "Jackson." I knocked softly and entered. The blinds were drawn. In the shadows, I saw an elderly figure in the bed with two large strong hands, fingers touching on the bedspread. Farmer's hands, I guessed; hands that knew work that was manually demanding.

"Hello, Mr. Jackson," I said in a deliberately cheerful voice, and introduced myself. The information seemed to take a little time to register; he had been dozing. I probed a bit, asking about his illness, how things were going, when he hoped to go home. Nothing brilliant;

simply pastoral and positive, as I had been taught. He became a little more wakeful.

"Mr. Jackson," I ventured, "what do you do?"

"What do I do?" he responded, grinning.

"Yes," I said. "You know, what do you do for a living?"

He thought for a moment, wiggling the large strong fingers on the bedspread as if deciding what to say. Then he replied, "I guess I'm a painter."

I had an immediate vision of him in paint-spattered overalls and cap, a folding ladder on his shoulder, a large can of paint in one hand. Armed with these images I was just about to ask "Who do you work for?"

I would like to think that a merciful God sometimes intervenes in the human situation, particularly if someone is about to make an unimaginably appalling gaffe. At that moment the name Jackson began to sound in my mind. Then it suddenly dawned on me to whom I was speaking. I think I just stood there, struck dumb as I looked at Canada's most famous living artist, a person whose name, Alexander Young Jackson, will always be associated with the Group of Seven, an innovator who had the courage to lead Canadian painting out of the prison of English traditionalism. And I had been about to clothe him in overalls and equip him with a ladder, a gallon of paint, and a large brush.

Stuttering, stammering, I apologized. He was wonderful. Face creased in laughter, fully awake now, he said "Oh, that's fine. That's fine. Glad to see you." I stayed a few more minutes and left, promising to return.

Over the next few years, I saw him frequently. By then, he walked slowly to and from his apartment very near the church. When he did come to worship, he sat in a side pew near the back.

One fall day I had an idea. I knew that the Gatineau Hills would be alive with glorious autumn color. I knew also that "A. Y." did not get out very much. So I asked if he would like to arrange a day to go for a drive. He said he would love it. We set off down Wellington Street, the Peace Tower on our right; across the bridge, then the exquisite drive up the Gatineau Parkway. We paused here and there for vistas. Sometimes we stopped near a particularly beautiful grove of trees, their gold and scarlet vivid against a blue sky. It seemed to me that I was seeing these colors in a way I never had seen them before and perhaps never would again.

We drove home as dusk began to fall, the lights of the city starting to shimmer in the twilight air. When we parted, he expressed his thanks. I assured him that it was for me to thank him. He had given me a memory I would treasure for the rest of my life: a memory of a day amid the scarlet and gold of the Gatineau when, for a few hours, I saw Canada through the eyes of one who has given its beauty to all of us forever.

## 12. THE BICYCLE MAN
### Kerrisdale, Vancouver, 1970s

There is an old hymn, rather out of fashion now, that tells a great truth. It tells us that saints do not live only in stained-glass windows; you can meet a saint anywhere, at any time. You just need to have an eye for one when you run across them.

The first time I met him, he was stooped over a child's bicycle, expressing extreme frustration in a broad Scottish accent because whatever he was trying to fix simply refused to be fixed. Since we had just moved into the neighborhood and I didn't know him, I hastily concluded that he was cantankerous and impatient, and, judging by the look of his shop, also untidy and inefficient. Over the years we lived there—a time when our children were young and in frequent need of bicycle repairs—I would learn that my initial impression was utterly mistaken.

His hands were always oily and, no matter how assiduously he wiped them on an endless succession of grubby cloths, they appeared to stay so. Meanwhile, the rags themselves turned up on counters, on the floor, or hanging out of his pockets. He always looked as if he was far behind in his work. Bicycles of every size and vintage and condition seemed to accumulate endlessly. In time, I came to understand that this was mainly because he found it impossible to say no to small people who wanted their bicycles repaired and returned as soon as possible.

He had started the business almost thirty years earlier, after returning from war service overseas. He had seen bicycles, once the sole domain of only the very young in Canada, begin to be an adult enthusiasm. He was a blunt man, and he could indeed express impatience, but because he had become a kind of father figure in the community and was trusted as such, and because he was a genius at what he did, his impatience and grumbling were expected and understood and permitted. After all, by now, some of the young parents who brought their children to him had visited his shop themselves as children.

Time passed and there came a day when he and I stood in the shop, just the two of us. It was an empty shell. All the stock was gone, the tools boxed up, the benches pushed against the wall. The building was coming down the following week. The block was being redeveloped. Rather than try to start again elsewhere, he had decided to retire. There would be no more Saturdays with broken chains, flat tires, seized gear shifts. No more glittering new bicycles would come ticking and gliding out of the downstairs stockroom to thrill a child. We talked for a while about the past, every moment of which he had enjoyed, and the future that he hoped would allow him some good years, and then we said goodbye.

A few years later, I conducted his funeral. It turned out that he had, as they say, a "heart." I know that medical tomes give little credence to the phrase "a broken heart," but I believe there is such a thing. I recall that he used old-fashioned terms for boys and girls. He would call them "sonny" and "girlie." I am very glad our children and I knew him.

The last verse of that old hymn I mentioned says of saints:

They lived not only in ages past;
There are hundreds of thousands still.

The world is bright with the joyous saints
Who love to do Jesus' will.

You can meet them in school, on the street, in a store,
In church, by the sea, in the house next door.

They are saints of God, whether rich or poor,
And I mean to be one too.

I've been trying for a long time myself to be a bit saintly, without ever quite making it. But I'm glad I met one once in a store.


## 13. THE PALM
### St. John the Evangelist, Ottawa, 1971

In the 1960s, the Anglican Church of Canada, in company with many other provinces of the Anglican Communion, went through a period of much liturgical change. A consequence of this process was the introduction into church life of many alternate ways of worship. Naturally, there was reaction. Some were excited by all this, some were deeply distressed. Even now as I write, half a century later, these feelings are still present among some.

I spent a good part of that decade as rector of the Church of St. John the Evangelist in Ottawa. A few years after we had moved to the West Coast, I was invited by another Ottawa church to deliver the Holy Week addresses. Hearing that I would be back in town, my successor at St. John the Evangelist took the opportunity to ask me to give the homily on Palm Sunday. It was an immense pleasure to return to well-known haunts and renew acquaintance with old friends.

I asked one small favor: to be allowed to sit in the congregation with my wife, Paula, then to come up from the congregation to preach. That request was readily granted. I was free to be a worshipper in a pew that morning, which meant that I would do something I had seldom done: enter the church through the main door. As clergy, I had always gone to the vestry door.

Palm Sunday dawns, and we walk up the steps of St. John's to receive a warm welcome from familiar faces. Then I begin to receive other things. First a bulletin for that Sunday with its order of service, then a prayer book, then a sheet with a liturgy that is "experimental" and therefore not in the prayer book. Then I receive a hymn book, plus a separate hymn sheet containing the texts of two hymns not in the hymn book. Last of all, I receive a palm cross.

On my way to the pew, I am struggling to make sure I don't drop any of this veritable armload of worship resources. Reaching my pew, I am still wondering where I will keep the palm. Shall I slide it into my hymn book? How about my breast pocket? Maybe I should just keep it in my hand? My inner self-questioning is still going on when I hear a voice. It's the voice of the rector reading the passage that tells of Jesus entering into Jerusalem and being welcomed by people waving palms.

As I listen, I do not realize that I am about to experience something that will for the rest of my ministry play a part in forming my understanding of the Gospel. I have read this Palm Sunday scripture countless times, and I have heard countless others read it. Yet today, something is about to happen to make me hear it in a very different way.

To this day, I am grateful that I decided to keep the palm cross in my hand. As I listen, the palm becomes a kind of time machine to free me from categories such as past, present, and future. I realize that it is not just a long ago and far away crowd crying, "Hosanna!" We too as a congregation are calling out our hosannas. And like that other crowd, in less than a week we will be shouting, "Crucify him!"

More than that, I come to realize that those voices will continue to sound anew in every generation until the end of time. That is because what is always happening is nothing less than our Lord asking each and every human being, in his or her turn, to choose our allegiances in life.

At that moment, past, present, and future are briefly woven together in my mind into a divine present. The events of our Lord's Passion will never again be for me merely past events in history. They will become more than history. They will become mythic—in the best sense of that word—speaking a truth that exists outside of time. I experienced that truth one Palm Sunday morning in a pew in my former church in Ottawa. I continue to experience it to this day, at the deepest levels of my being.

## 14. THE HEART OF THE MATTER

### St. John's Cathedral, Hong Kong, 1972

It is 7:00 a.m. on an October morning; I am waiting for the doors of the cathedral in this teeming city to open. I am in Hong Kong with a CBC Television crew, filming a program on the life of a very active Anglican congregation, the Church of the Holy Carpenter. We have mostly finished our work and wish to take a few final shots of the cathedral before leaving. Before the doors open, I am about to see something that offers me a new lens on Christian worship.

I suddenly become aware of people all around me who are doing something puzzling. I watch an elderly man put his bicycle aside and begin to turn very gracefully in this direction and that, while stretching out his arms. He then faces forward and leans outward, again extending his arms. When I inquire, I am told that these are the movements of the ancient Chinese exercise regime called *tai chi*, something at that time still new in the West.

As I watch, I find myself for some reason interpreting his graceful movements as first a delving into the past, then a stepping forward into present experience, followed by a reaching for the future. Only at this point do I recognize that he is enacting physically something that I am beginning to express verbally in Christian worship back in Vancouver.

When Christian liturgies in the West began to change in the 1960s, we were given the gift of a sequence of three simple, but profound, statements. We say them whenever we use certain liturgies for our celebrations of the Holy Eucharist. The celebrant invites us to "proclaim the mystery of faith," and the people respond: "Christ has died. Christ is risen. Christ will come again."

I have often thought that these three statements are to Christian faith what the formula $E=mc^2$ is to physics. Both formulations express something deeply wonderful and supremely important.

The roots of Christian experience will always go back to those fleeting three years beside the lake and along the highways of Israel, on into the narrow streets of old Jerusalem, then to an upper room, then to a screaming judgment hall and a terrible hill of execution. These things must and will be passed on from generation to generation. All this we express when we say, "Christ has died."

But mere remembering cannot of itself constitute a faith. Christianity must also be a present living experience. This is what we mean when we say, "Christ is risen." That use of the present tense expresses a great truth at the heart of our belief. Our Lord's Resurrection, though it originally took place with massive and transforming power in the lives of those who had known him, continues to take place in the lives of men and women who choose to serve him in their own time.

We make one more statement in what I have called this $E=mc^2$ of Christian faith. We say, "Christ will come again." Christians believe that what we see in Jesus is a glimpse of our own humanity lifted to its ultimate quality. If that is true, then we also believe that the destiny of all creation—humanity, nature, the planet, even the universe—is to be filled with the perfection embodied in a life lived among us and, if we choose, living in us. This is the future toward which we aspire.

As I write of this beautifully succinct summation of Christian faith that we have recovered from the ancient liturgies, there comes to mind again that elderly figure in Hong Kong moving so gracefully and reflectively in a pattern that spoke to me of past, present, and future. I realize now that what I learned in that moment was the mysterious way in which what you and I think of as an acclamation of Christian belief expresses a universal truth about human experience that is beyond religion. Much more than a formula, it is a great poem, groping toward a vast truth.

A christening inside a crowded Christ Church Cathedral, Vancouver, 1979.

## 15. THE MAN WHO LOST SIX MONTHS
### Christ Church Cathedral, Vancouver, July 1973

In the 1960s, the bishop of New Westminster appointed one of his priests to serve the Dzawada'enuxw people of Kingcome Inlet. An American writer named Margaret Craven wove a story about this priest in that remote and beautiful part of the diocese. The title of her book is *I Heard the Owl Call My Name*, and it has since sold over a million copies. A few years later Daryl Duke, a Vancouver-born, internationally renowned television and film director, was commissioned to turn the book into a made-for-TV movie for a major US network.

There is a scene in the movie where the bishop and his priest discuss the appointment in the days before Christmas. One day during my time as dean, I received a phone call asking if I would be open to chatting with Duke about the use of the cathedral as a location. Over coffee across the street in the now long-gone Spanish Grill of the Hotel Vancouver, he made me an offer. He wanted to set the scene during a Christmas carol service. He would need as large a congregation as possible. As incentive, he would offer the cathedral fifty dollars for each person who attended. For a wild moment—perhaps it was the influence of the strong dark roast—I was tempted to ask for a hundred, but I demurred. In those days, fifty dollars was worth a great deal more in downtown Vancouver than it is today.

Our chat took place on a sunny day in late June. Daryl said he'd like to do the shoot about two weeks later. This, he assumed, would give me ample time to get in touch with our congregation. I recall wondering if this mogul, used to demanding instant obedience from a thousand extras with his megaphone, had the remotest idea of the glacial pace of church decision-making. However, all went well. The wardens gave their blessing and a letter duly went out, informing the congregation of the opportunity and requesting their attendance on a weekday evening in mid-July. They were instructed to dress as if the event were in mid-December. Fur coats, heavy wraps, voluminous scarves, and gloves would be ideal.

The day before the event, the cathedral was taken over by a work crew who decorated it for Christmas to a degree it had never before witnessed. A gigantic Christmas tree, heavy with decorations of every kind and blazing with colored lights, was placed beside the chancel steps. Lastly, a set of narrow-gauge tracks was laid up one side of the center aisle, so the director's camera could move up and down the nave.

The members of the choir were directed to occupy the choir stalls in their robes, and to be prepared to sing "The First Noël." They did so again and again at Daryl's direction, as he swept up and down the cathedral behind his all-seeing camera. At the prayer desks were seated the actors representing the bishop and the young priest. As always in filmmaking, everything was repeated a dozen times until the director was satisfied. The choir sang the carol over and over. The congregation began to swelter in their winter garments. However, in the interests of cathedral finances, they stoically bore the warmth of the July evening.

Now came the crowning moment. Since I was not needed for this contrived Christmas celebration, I was standing at the back of the cathedral in the narthex, where the large doors on either side allow for public entry. One of these doors opened and I watched as a figure— not one of our regulars—stumbled in. I realized from his gait and general demeanor that he was, to use a gentle term, under the influence. He moved further into the narthex until he was able to see up the center aisle. His befuddled brain was assaulted by the sight of a huge Christmas tree blazing with colored lights, pews filled with people in their winter attire, and the choir singing "The First Noël" at the top of their voices.

For what seemed a long time he stood there, weaving slightly, trying to make sense of what he saw. Eventually, he turned and made his way to the door. As he struggled to open it, he expressed all his bewilderment and incomprehension in a single loud, exasperated cry, "Holy God Almighty," and disappeared into the bustling world of downtown Vancouver.

I would like to think that the experience might have shocked our guest into a lifetime of sobriety. However, I recall reflecting at the time that his exclamation was a remarkably suitable comment.

## 16. HOLY WAR AND SCONES
### Christ Church Cathedral, Vancouver, 1973

One August morning in 1973, the front page of the Vancouver *Sun* informed its readers that a plan was afoot to demolish Christ Church Cathedral at the corner of Burrard and Georgia and build a high-rise office tower on the site with, deep in its foundations, a new underground cathedral. Newspapers want to attract readers and, if possible, to evoke emotions ranging from visceral rage to ecstatic approval. This story succeeded immediately in creating two armies of readers at each end of the paper's hoped-for spectrum of reaction.

Warfare always requires villains and heroes. For some, I was a cultural barbarian and philistine. For others, I was the harbinger of a newly invigorated Christianity. I received a mountain of letters from friends wishing to be supportive. I also got another mountain of anonymous mail that increased steadily in viciousness as time went by.

One of those anonymous writers, knowing I had emigrated from Ireland, urged me in no uncertain terms to go back where I came from. This request was accompanied by lurid pictures of Belfast streets complete with tanks and armed troops. Another anonymous correspondent pointed to Albert Speer, Hitler's architect, as my obvious role model. Amidst all this *Sturm und Drang*, I remember one person more clearly than anyone else, perhaps because it would never have occurred to her to send an anonymous letter or make an anonymous call. She never tried to hide the fact that she was implacably opposed to our plans. The result was that she and I were able to relate to each other as human beings while the drama unfolded.

Isabel was a born activist. Whatever cause she chose to espouse, she did so with all the resources at her disposal. Because she was a devoted royalist, anything that might in any way demean or diminish the role of the monarchy would find the Queen's champion on the steps of City Hall, vociferously protesting whatever change was being considered. And since the Queen was Head of the Church and Defender of the Faith, nothing was going to happen to the Queen's Cathedral if Isabel could prevent it.

Sunday by Sunday, there she was in her pew. From time to time during the service, she would take out a small camera and snap a photograph. She usually took a shot of any visiting preacher, sometimes much to their surprise. They would look down to see this woman focusing on them and clicking the shutter.

One week, a distinguished English bishop had just launched into his sermon when Isabel approached the pulpit, pointed her camera, and took her photograph. In his most impressive British accent, the bishop curtly said, "Madam, will you please sit down," whereupon Isabel, nothing daunted by this figure of authority looming above her, replied defiantly, "I can't, because somebody is sitting in my seat." The bishop, nonplussed, beat a hasty retreat, striving valiantly to recover both his dignity and his thoroughly derailed train of thought.

During the early stages of the cathedral issue, I tried to discuss things with Isabel, but she would have none of it. As far as she was concerned, the whole thing "would come to no good." After a while I noticed a pattern. If Isabel and I met outside the cathedral, she wouldn't mention the issue unless I brought it up. She would chat about this or that in the most pleasant way.

One morning, in the middle of Choral Eucharist, Isabel appeared holding a large placard on a pole whose text read, "The dean should resign." As a hymn was being sung, she bore her sign slowly up the center aisle, turned at the head of the aisle just in front of where I was presiding at the altar, showed her message silently to the congregation, and returned to her pew.

It was a strange kind of friendship. I never at any time felt that Isabel disliked me. I was grateful because I knew there were many who detested me. On more than one occasion, she made a most unexpected gesture. As I stood at the door greeting everyone at the end of the service, Isabel would come along with a small paper bag containing half a dozen delicious small Welsh cakes she had baked for our family. While I knew it did not mean that she had relented one inch in her resistance to our plans, I also knew that this good and generous woman was quite clear about distinguishing mutual disagreement from personal enmity.

There came a time when the ambitious plans for change had to be abandoned. New opportunities presented themselves. Some years later, after I had left for ministry elsewhere, other changes were conceived and brought to fruition, enhancing the traditional cathedral's life at the center of the city in ways that make it today a most vibrant and creative congregation. I am certain that had she lived to see that renewed cathedral, Isabel would have approved. I am quite certain that from time to time, on special occasions, she would have expressed her approval with a large plate of freshly buttered Welsh cakes.

## 17. THE MISSIONARY BOX

### Saskatoon Airport, 1975

In the war years of the 1940s, Canon John Adcock was the deputation secretary in Ireland for the Colonial and Commonwealth Church Missionary Society. His duty was to travel ceaselessly around the country, visiting parishes and schools and synods, drumming up support for missionary work, primarily in Western Canada.

John Adcock radiated boundless energy and enthusiasm for his work, which made him charismatically attractive to young people. I first heard him as a small boy at St. Mary's in Castlecomer, and later as a youth in boarding school. He brought with him a large and heavy machine that he called his magic lantern. He would tie a sheet to the wall of the school room or the church hall, insert large glass slides, and project scenes of church buildings on the Canadian prairies. We looked in awe, not realizing that we were looking back at the world of the twenties and thirties.

When the lights came back on, each of us received a small missionary box shaped as a log cabin with a tiny chimney. Over the next few months, using the small slit in the roof, we filled the boxes with our pennies or other coins. On his next visit, the canon collected whatever we had saved.

Firmly glued to the roof of the cabin was a drawing of a line signifying a distant horizon. At the left-hand side stood a grove of coniferous trees. Emerging from this forest was a dog sled, the driver's whip whirling in the air, the dogs straining at the leads. In the sky above flew a small single-engine plane. Etched on a boy's imagination, this scene drew more than my pennies for Canada; it eventually drew me!

A few years later, after graduating from school, I was casting about as to the direction my life might go. I was interested in teaching. I was also vaguely interested in, as the term was in those days, "going into the Church." In October of 1947, John Adcock came again to our parish. As always, he would issue a challenge to any youth present; if we would offer ourselves for God's service in Western Canada, we would be given free passage by ship to Montreal and on by rail to Saskatoon, where we would become residents of Emmanuel College and be prepared for ordination in the Canadian Church.

I thought about it for days. Eventually I wrote him a letter. I was about to take my letter down to the mail train that left for Dublin at 9:00 p.m. when my mother said gently, "You know, sometimes when we write a very important letter in the evening, it's a good idea to wait until morning to post it."

The letter was never mailed.

My life went in another direction because of that decision. Many things happened. My father became ill and died a few years later. I decided to be ordained, but I went to Trinity College Dublin to do so with the help of a scholarship and various grants. After ordination, I was carrying out my first curacy in Dublin. One day, I received an invitation to join the staff of Christ Church Cathedral in Ottawa. In 1954, I walked off a liner in Quebec City into a new life. A year later, I returned to Ireland to marry my wife, Paula, and bring her back with me to Ottawa. Children would come to us. We would move to various parishes until we arrived in Vancouver in 1968.

One day in 1975, a letter came from the Diocese of Saskatoon inviting me to conduct a retreat for its clergy. It took place as spring was just about to come to the prairies. At the end of the retreat the bishop, an old friend, drove me to the airport to catch the flight home. After he dropped me off, I learned my flight was delayed by an hour and a half. It was a glorious late afternoon, so I decided to go for a walk.

My walk had taken me half a mile or so east of the airport when I heard the sound of a single-engine plane. I turned and there, rising into the western sky, was none other than the plane on my missionary box roof all those years ago. I was deeply moved. It brought to mind the long-ago rainy night when I stood at the end of the dining room table and listened to a parent's advice. I had not mailed the letter, and I had not gone to an unimaginably distant Saskatoon. And yet here I was in that very place half a lifetime later. Shakespeare said it best when Hamlet observes to Horatio, "There is a divinity that shapes our ends, rough-hew them how we will."

## 18. THE REGULAR
### Christ Church Cathedral, Vancouver, Christmas 1975

**The early seventies in British Columbia** saw a policy change that affected those wrestling with mental health. Up to that time, if a person's condition demanded it, they could be placed in institutional care. However, by the early seventies the world of mental illness saw the development of therapeutic drugs. The current wisdom was that thanks to the new drugs, mental problems were best cared for within the community. Since no social policy can prevent people falling between the cracks, we began to see many more such individuals in and around the cathedral at the corner of Georgia and Burrard. As a result, not only did we clergy become more aware of the prevalence of mental illness but so did the congregation, who gradually became more comfortable and skilled in responding to those in need of understanding.

Downtown churches tend to have "regulars," people who become familiar to staff and with whom relationships form. Some regulars get to know the times that church organizations have coffee or tea or meals, gradually come to mingle with the members of whatever group is meeting, and in time become familiar faces and voices. Most will not come to worship, but they become part of the scene. If they don't appear for a while, someone will wonder if anything has happened, and will check. Sometimes another regular will know. If they have ended up in hospital, someone tries to find them.

As the new social policies of drug treatment unfolded, so did a sad pattern. Some regulars who were on a drug regimen changed for the better in appearance and deportment, but another personality emerged. Anxiety or depression was replaced by greater ease and even joy. This would continue for a short period, but then, precisely because the drug had brought about a sense of well-being, the person would decide they could stop taking it, whereupon the unfortunate effects of illness would return.

One of the things that make ministry in a large downtown church interesting is that you never know who is going to walk in off the street for one reason or another. The Sunday before Christmas 1975, about four hundred children are in the cathedral celebrating their membership in Brownies, Wolf Cubs, Girl Guides, and Boy Scouts. I am speaking to them about the season when I see a figure enter at the back. At first, I don't recognize him. His face is chalk white, his shoulder-length hair wet and stringy, a long black coat hangs down to his ankles. As he moves slowly up the aisle, I see his gaze is fixed on me. When he is about fifteen feet away, he suddenly shouts, "Kneel down before me!" Two things strike me at once. First, I realize he is one of our regulars but utterly changed.

Second, I notice he has one hand in his coat pocket and I have no way of telling what he may be holding.

The children, especially the very young in the front seats, are now frightened, the adults with them concerned. Realizing that the most important thing is to separate him from the children, I quickly suggest that the two of us should go further into the cathedral, where there is a large altar. I address him by his name. For now, let's say it's John. He silently agrees.

When we get to the altar area, I make another suggestion, again using his name. I point to a door and say, "John, there is a small room in there where I could kneel down." After a moment's hesitation, he agrees. I fervently hope that one or two of the adults on duty as ushers can see that we are approaching the vestry, and are coming to provide support. When I open the door, two people are indeed standing there, just beyond the sightline of the doorway. I turn to face John, kneel on the floor, and for the third time use his name: "John, why don't we both kneel down here together, just you and me?" I recall adding that so the two other people would take the cue and stay where they were.

To my immense relief, John kneels down. I don't recall the exact words I said, but their gist is that I thank God that John has found friends in the cathedral, and I express the hope that he will know the joy of Christmas. I thank God that John has the gift of his medication to give him peace, and assure him that we will see him again whenever he wants to come. Very short and simple, because I also know I have to get back to where the children and adults are waiting. I invite John to go downstairs with the two bystanders, who will give him a coffee and something to eat. I heard later that he asked them if he could return into the cathedral, but they wisely didn't allow that.

When I go out, I speak as reassuringly as possible to the children, telling them of the many people in our city who are lonely and troubled and sometimes very ill, and that we should help them when we can. Then we all sing "While shepherds watched their flocks by night," but not before I point out the lines where the angel stills the shepherds' fear:

"Fear not," said he, for mighty dread
Had seized their troubled mind.
"Glad tidings of great joy I bring
To you and all mankind."

## 19. A PLACE OF ONE'S OWN
### West End, Vancouver, 1970s

She does not need a name, although it is very familiar to me, as is her remembered face. At the time of this conversation, she was elderly and becoming increasingly feeble. As with many in their later years, she needed less and less sleep, and so she would frequently go for a walk at five o'clock in the morning through the streets of the West End. A friend who saw her on such a morning said that she looked as if a puff of wind might blow her away. There were signs of other changes. She was beginning to become a little confused. Not always, only now and then, as she would assure you. She would forget where a friend lived. She would drop off for naps in public places.

She had a small apartment a few floors up in her building, from which she had a view of the distant inlet. Friends had begun to say to her that perhaps it might be time to move to a place where there would be other people and she could enjoy pleasant companionship. Quietly, always with a smile of appreciation for friendly concern, her answer remained a definite "no." Many friends tried. Finally, as rector of the parish, it was suggested I might try, not with any thought of introducing some kind of authority figure, but rather because there might be sufficient trust in our relationship.

We arranged to have a morning cup of coffee in her apartment. When I arrived downstairs, she took a long time to answer the apartment phone. Eventually there was a quiet voice expressing welcome and the sound of the door buzzer inviting me to enter.

The room was spotless. A small table neatly laid for two stood by the window. The china was delicate and light to the touch. For some reason, I recall noticing that the small milk jug was Beleek. It possessed the same qualities of delicacy and almost transparency as the hand that lifted it to pour milk for a guest. We chatted about this and that: the weather, the cathedral which had been dear to her for many years, a friend who was ill. Slowly, I steered toward the subject I had come to broach. She listened. There was not the slightest sense that she in any way resented my voicing concern for her. Yes, she realized she was a little slower. Yes, sometimes she did indeed forget things, but, as she assured me with a chuckle, never things that were really important. She felt she could and would carry on as things were. She was pleasant but firm, and, she said, grateful for my visit. She looked forward to being in her usual pew on Sunday.

She did carry on for some months. Friends kept a close eye. Then came the news that she had fallen. This time, there was no choice about being taken to the nearby hospital where, as quietly and gently as she had lived, she did her dying, very much at peace, and in the company of a few friends who had come to care deeply for her.

I will always remember our morning together at that little table. I have already said that she does not need a name, but all this is many years ago and, as it happens, hers was a very beautiful name: Gertrude. I was conscious of an immense courage and dignity about her, vulnerable and fragile though she may have been.

Each of us lives out our life in our own way, hoping that we will be able to live it gracefully to the end of the story. I have always felt that Gertrude managed to do that. Thinking of her now across many years, seeing her again at that small, impeccably arranged table with its embroidered linen cloth, I recall some lovely lines by Joseph Campbell:

As a white candle
In a holy place,
So is the beauty
Of an agéd face.

## 20. THE WARDEN

### Lighthouse Park, West Vancouver, 1970s

He was my churchwarden many years ago. When we first met, he was at the height of his powers, physically and professionally. He had spent a distinguished career in the Royal Canadian Navy and then went into business. He had a most wonderful *joie de vivre*. The ethos of his Anglicanism was that of a tradition absorbed in boarding school and never subsequently doubted. I mention this because being a boarding school survivor myself, I know well that the regular application of school prayers and religion classes does one of two things. It either turns one off for good, or it captures one's allegiance for the rest of one's life.

One day he asked me to lunch. Much to my surprise, he appeared in the restaurant accompanied by a very attractive person whom I already knew because she was also one of my parishioners: a young widow with two children. They were intending marriage—a marriage that I would have the immense pleasure of conducting.

Three or four years went by; the children grew; their parents lived full, rich lives. Then one day, he phoned to tell me that she was ill; something had to be looked at, just to make sure it was nothing threatening. She would be in hospital for a few days. Within a month she died, ravaged by a deeply malignant and implacable cancer.

How can we describe the aftermath? Some of us already know the terrible journey that must be taken after ultimate loss. Some of us have walked, or tried to walk, that road with devastated friends.

Within the next year, he suffered a severe stroke. With the children in mind, he fought back. Endless hours of physio over many months yielded partial recovery. We remained friends. During all this time, he kept her ashes in their home: out of sight, but near him on a high shelf in what had been their bedroom. He said that he would tell me when he was ready to choose a permanent resting place for them.

The summons came in early fall. He wished to place the ashes on the waters of the gulf. He had decided on the following weekend. He

felt that around sunset would be the right time of day. On the evening chosen, I drove to the house and found him ready. He cradled her
ashes in the crook of his good arm and with the other hand he held a
small wreath.

We drove out of the city, over a bridge, along the marine road. We
parked the car and began walking down to the shoreline. It was not
the easiest of approaches, because between us and the water there was
an area of dense growth, mainly thorn bushes. A narrow winding path
gave difficult and grudging access. I offered to carry one or other of
the ashes or the wreath, but he was adamant. Along the path we went,
making for a high rock that jutted out over the water.

For him, the walk was a supreme challenge. Three times he lost
his balance and fell into the bushes, but managed to keep a firm hold
on his precious burden. The third time, he surrendered the wreath
to me as we continued our slow and laborious progress toward the
rock. He had calculated carefully that the time of our arrival would
coincide with an ebb tide. Below and beyond the high rock there was
a protruding rock shelf where I was able to stand. Giving him the
wreath and accepting the ashes from him, I stepped to the edge of
the shelf, said some ancient and loving words which we had agreed
on, then placed the ashes as far out into the water as possible. I then
climbed back up beside him, because I knew he was determined to
deal with the wreath himself.

Steadying himself on the rock and reaching for my hand with
his weakened arm, he bent his once athletic body as low as he could,
swept his good arm in a powerful arc, and hurled the wreath out to
where the pale ashes were already moving seaward along the golden
line of the setting sun. For a while we stood together in silence. Eventually, he turned and once again made his way slowly back along the
path to the car.

I consider that evening to be one of the great privileges given to
me in a long ministry. The word that has always come to mind when
I recall his friendship and his fellowship in the faith is a word seldom
used today. That word is nobility.

The Dean greets the Dalai Lama on the steps of the cathedral, October 1980.

# 21. THE DALAI LAMA

## Christ Church Cathedral, Vancouver, October 1980

In my childhood, Tibet might as well have been beyond the Rings of Saturn. I knew where it was, up above the Himalayas on the globe that sat on the teacher's table. Geography was well taught in Irish schools, even at primary level. However, there was something mysterious, even ethereal about Tibet that made it unlike other countries.

Teenage years began to alter that infinite distance, but not to diminish it. I began to relate to Tibet through two wonderful stories. One was James Hilton's *Lost Horizon*, published in 1933. I was too young to read it at that time, but when I was nine my mother took me to see the 1937 movie. Recalling this makes me realize how much of a Romantic was hidden within that wonderful woman who made our home a place of joy and love. The other story came to me at Christmas 1941 when I received a copy of that year's *Chums Annual*, which featured a tale entitled "Forbidden Peaks," again set in the Himalayas on the borders of Tibet.

A leap forward in time to the afternoon of Sunday, October 26, 1980. Our cathedral is to host a Commonwealth service, an annual affair to which each of the many religions of the city—and therefore of the world—send a representative. This particular year is even more special than usual, because we will welcome the Dalai Lama. He and his entourage are staying at the Hotel Vancouver, right across the street. As dean, it is my duty to meet him on the steps of the cathedral. Little will he know that he is not being met by a cathedral dean. Rather, he is being met by a nervous small boy who thrills to this meeting with one who for him remains a mysterious figure from a faraway land. As I await this most distinguished visitor, His Holiness Tenzin Gyatso, fourteenth Dalai Lama, spiritual leader of the Tibetan people, images of soaring white peaks mingle with those of cliff-clinging monasteries in my imagination.

Then he appears. First his security entourage emerges from the hotel entrance: six stocky men in tight-fitting suits, looking as if they are not entirely at ease in these clothes. Two of them stare straight ahead toward where I wait on the other side of the street. One of them faces to each side. The last two look back toward the door as their illustrious charge emerges. The world of western suits is immediately banished. Tall and bronzed he comes, one strong bare arm emerging from a richly embroidered robe belted at the waist, heavy leather sandals on his feet. He does indeed look like a visitor from another world. I am so grateful. My boyhood illusions and expectations have not been shattered by mundane and boring western dress.

I prepare to meet him. The six security men walk imperiously out into the middle of Georgia Street and bring the traffic to a halt. Their charge walks across, then to my utter astonishment bounds up the steps, grasps my hand warmly, announces his intense pleasure at being my guest, takes me by the arm, and steers me back into my own cathedral.

In we go to the packed narthex, our guest clearing a path seemingly effortlessly, until we turn up the center aisle. The figure in the middle of all this excitement is obviously enjoying every moment. People almost climb over each other to see him. I finally deposit him among the delegates from the other great religions and they in turn introduce themselves and their tradition. Finally, he is seated in the large chair at the apex of the semicircle. I welcome the congregation and the ecumenical representatives, and try to convey what an immense privilege it is to have the Dalai Lama among us. Silence falls and the hour or so of readings and music begins.

In that hour came a memorable moment. One of the great common elements of all faiths is light. Light expresses so many levels of human thought. It banishes darkness and fear. It comforts and reassures. It speaks of the ongoing human quest for meaning, both personal and universal. We had decided to celebrate this universal symbol with a simple but profound ceremony. As they arrived, everyone in the congregation had been given an unlit taper. Now, cathedral servers handed each world faith representative a burning candle. The plan was that the representatives would move among the people, passing the light from one to the next. We had assumed that

the Dalai Lama, our guest of honor, would remain seated while this
was being done.

He would not hear of it. Reaching for a candle and asking for it
to be lit, he stood, and to everyone's surprise and delight set off, leading the way, plunging into the crowd, smiling, even laughing now and
then, lighting candles as quickly as he could—and of course everyone wanted their candle lit by him if possible. It was a marvelous
and unforgettable moment of hilarious spontaneity. On reflection, I
realize now it was far more than that. It was a moment when we were
shown the humility of true spiritual greatness.

## 22. ARM IN ARM
### English Bay, Vancouver, 1981

I'm sure you know those moments in life when, at the time, you
felt nothing in particular was happening, but when you look back later
you realize that a great deal had happened. I want to share two such
moments.

I was driving along Cornwall Street in Vancouver. It was about
noon on a lovely late fall day. I was driving slowly, the better to glance
between the houses at the ravishing views of the mountains and
English Bay. I became aware of two women coming down the sidewalk
together, arm in arm. One was in her early twenties, the other I esti-
mated as late seventies. Just as I passed they paused in their stride, their
heads went back almost in unison, and they laughed.

They were obviously members of the same family. I'm almost certain they were grandmother and granddaughter. They shared the same
styling of hair, one dark, the other silver, and the same face formation,
especially when they laughed. I felt that I had been given a glimpse
through a time barrier and had seen the same person alive at two different points in her life simultaneously. There looked to be between
them an intimacy and an ease that made years and decades seem irrelevant. I was reminded of the priceless gift that family, at its best, can
give us. The sharing of laughter, the linking of arms, the similarity of

face and stance, all made me aware that affection knows nothing of time. There can be in family ties such unity that when eyes look into eyes, they see neither age nor youth but a reflection of themselves.

The other moment came at the intersection of Davie and Denman in the West End on one of those long summer evenings. The hush in the air seemed to mute even the noise of the traffic that wound its way slowly along Beach Avenue. The yellow bulbs on the popcorn venders' barrows twinkled through the twilight. All around me were people of every age and description: family groups, couples, singles, all moving with a sense of weekend relaxation, everyone wishing to savor and extend this hour before nightfall.

I became aware of a couple walking together. They were elderly and slightly bowed. They moved slowly but in perfect unison, arm in arm, a rhythm that must have come from countless walks together. For a moment, the long golden road of the sunset eclipsed them into invisibility as they crossed between it and where I stood.

They came to a point where the sidewalk ended at the intersection. The step down to the street was a steep change of level. In their fragility, which they had long ceased to attempt to disguise, it was a formidable obstacle, even a moment of potential danger. He slowly stepped first into the roadway. When he was safely down, he turned to help her take the same step carefully, gingerly. Together, they set out on the journey to the other side of the busy boulevard. Once again, he stepped up on the sidewalk first, then turned to help her do likewise. Linking arms again, they continued their evening stroll, moving away from the beach and into the shadows of the surrounding apartment towers.

Out beyond the bay, the sun continued to disappear behind the islands. Children were unwillingly leaving the softly lapping water as parents called. It was important to be home before darkness fell.

In an unusually tender moment, the apostle Paul once wrote that there are three things that last forever—faith, hope, and love—but the greatest of these is love. I remember those two scenes by English Bay because there I had glimpsed two of the countless faces of human love.

## 23. THE PRINCESS
### Calgary, 1984

I had been the incumbent at Christ Church Elbow Park for only a few weeks when a senior member of the congregation asked if he could take me to see someone he was concerned about. As a senior partner in his accountancy firm, he had looked after her affairs for some years. Her name was Tania.

As Walter and I drove to pay our visit, he told me something of the story of the woman I was about to meet. Tania was a princess from an ancient lineage, a descendent of the Rurik dynasty, founders of the Tsardom of Russia in the ninth century. She and her sister had left Russia as young girls after the assassination of the Romanovs in Yekaterinburg in July 1918, emigrating first to Bulgaria and later to Yugoslavia. After the Second World War, Tania moved to Canada and began a new and utterly different life as the owner and operator of a ranch on the outskirts of Calgary.

As we pulled up outside her condominium block, I asked Walter how the ranch chapter of her life had gone. "Magnificently," he replied. "She took to it like a duck to water."

On the way up in the elevator, I asked another question, "Why do you think she wants to see me?" "She'll tell you," Walter answered cryptically. "You'll find her a wonderful person. I'll introduce you, make myself scarce for an hour or so, then come back to pick you up."

My initial impression of Tania Obolensky was her great beauty. Age and illness had worked their will, but they had not robbed her of her striking appearance, nor the warm, low timbre of her voice. She was seated in a chair designed for her needs, placed to give her a magnificent view of the mountains in the distance. Near her was some medical equipment to assist her from time to time with her breathing. In spite of this, one could hardly help noticing the long silver cigarette holder clasped gracefully in one hand.

As we got to know each other, the reason for her invitation emerged. She was under no illusions about either the state of her health or her life expectancy, and she had a deep concern. Although she had been baptized and brought up in the richness of Russian Orthodoxy, for many years it had become for her more a memory than an active practice. She wished to be able to share again the sacrament of bread and wine that her childhood faith called Eucharist, the Greek word for thanksgiving. Could I make that possible?

I assented without a moment's hesitation and we made an appointment for a few days hence. I suggested that she might like to invite a small group of friends to be part of the occasion. She was delighted to do so. In the ensuing weeks, we shared the sacrament more than once and we spoke of many things. In the telling of some of them there was much laughter, in spite of times when a cough interrupted or breath drew short.

Sometimes the conversation would turn to her family roots in imperial Russia. All around us in the apartment were small treasures of that vanished world. She never gave any hint of mourning its loss, speaking always of an extraordinarily rich, full life. When living on the ranch near Cochrane made her realize what Alberta sun can do to fine skin, she moved into the world of cosmetics, becoming an international figure in the field. Later, she and her sister opened La Boutique in Calgary. Travelling frequently to Europe, Tania was able to draw on her continental connections to bring in the finest fashions available.

Though time was kind to our relationship, the inevitable end eventually came. The celebration of her life took place in a packed church. It was a cosmopolitan crowd, including many from Tania's early years. At one point, I borrowed a moment from Shakespeare's *Antony and Cleopatra* to pay tribute to her. Two friends, Maecenas and Enobarbus, are chatting in a hallway in Rome. The subject of Antony, his involvement with Cleopatra and the politics surrounding their relationship comes up. Maecenas says, "Now Anthony must leave her utterly." Enobarbus replies emphatically, "Never; he will not." Then Shakespeare gives Enobarbus one of the great lines in the drama: "Age cannot wither her, nor custom stale her infinite variety."

Today, near where she lived in Calgary, a small public park over-looking the Elbow River is named in her honor. To sit for moment on a bench in Princess Obolensky Park is to look west to the mountains she loved.

## 24. A TALE OF TWO BOOKS
### Christ Church, Elbow Park, 1985

**Earlier in this chapter,** I mentioned that during my ministry in the Anglican Church of Canada, I saw not one but two prayer books introduced into this province of the communion. Canadian Anglicans know them colloquially as the "BCP" (Book of Common Prayer) and the "BAS" (Book of Alternative Services). The second of these was not without controversy when it came along in the mid-1980s, and though over time it has become widely accepted and used, to some extent it still troubles some traditionalists.

I had had some experience of the challenges of tampering with people's accustomed language for worship while serving as dean in Vancouver, when we attempted to respond to the quite appropriate social and political currents of the time by introducing more gender-inclusive language into our liturgical readings, hymns, and prayers. Now, as rector in Calgary, I was responsible for encouraging people to try out, and hopefully come to appreciate, their new prayer book.

By using the term "encouraging," I acknowledge that pastoral ministry is, or should be, a gradual and sensitive process, requiring the building of trust between priest and people. In my experience, how-ever, there is another essential ingredient that may surprise you: devi-ousness. My scriptural justification for this lies in our Lord's advice to be as gentle as doves, but also as wise as serpents.

My own deviousness was sometimes played out at parish funer-als. On many such occasions, the family would say to me, "Rector, we would like the service to be Prayer Book," and I would unhesitatingly accede to their request. At the time of the service, having recited the prayers of the familiar tradition, I would include one particular prayer from the Book of Alternative Services. It is a translation from the original Dutch, and it addresses beautifully the emotional needs of such an occasion:

> God of grace and glory, we thank you for *N*, who was so near and dear to us, and who has now been taken from us. . . . We pray that nothing good in this *man's/woman's* life will be lost . . . and that everything in which *he/she* was great will continue to mean much to us now that *he/she* is dead.

I began to recognize a familiar pattern. Invariably at the reception that followed the service, people would ask, "Rector, where did you get that wonderful prayer near the end of the service?" Then, if I knew my questioner heartily detested the new worship book, I would seize my moment and, with a pastoral twinkle, I would reply, "Know where I got it? In that awful green book." And invariably, we would laugh together as friends.

Let me share with you just four more treasured moments from the Book of Alternative Services, which I think illustrate the power of language—even contemporary or colloquial language—to rise to heights of inspiration and plunge to depths of devotion, to achieve eloquence, and to touch the heart.

A powerful, succinct summing up of Christian faith used in the Eucharist: "Christ has died. Christ is Risen. Christ will come again."

From the Litany of the Holy Spirit: "Come, Holy Spirit, breath of God, give life to the dry bones of this exiled age, and make us a living people, holy and free."

From the Blessing of a Marriage: "Let their love for each other be a seal upon their hearts, a mantle about their shoulders, and a crown upon their foreheads. Bless them in their work and in their companionship; in their sleeping and in their waking; in their joys and in their sorrows . . ."

And from the Commendation in the Burial Offices: "Give rest, O Christ, to your servants with your saints, where sorrow and pain are no more, neither sighing, but life everlasting. . . . All of us go down to the dust; yet even at the grave we make our song: Alleluia, alleluia, alleluia."

Five short passages from the BAS, out of many that I could have chosen. You, I hope, will have your own treasures from this book, and from many others. In my ministry, I have valued the resources to be found in the prayer books of The Episcopal Church and the Church of New Zealand, to name just two from a long shelf. Of the making of prayers, and prayer books, there is, thank God, no end, and there are many riches to be found in them: much beauty and much edification, in language both old and new.

## 25. MORNING ON THE PRAIRIE
### Southern Manitoba, 1986

Adlestrop is both the name of a small, now-closed railway station in the English countryside, and the title of a well-known English poem. The deceptively simple verses evoke a moment when a train stops at the station. The poet remarks on the fact that while nothing whatever happened—"No one left and no one came on the bare platform"—yet, precisely because of this, he was made acutely aware of the surrounding natural beauty of landscape and sky and birdsong.

I had a similar experience once while travelling in the predawn hours in the depth of winter across the seemingly endless miles of the Manitoba prairie. I had been invited to give a series of addresses over a weekend at the Anglican cathedral in Brandon. On Monday morning, I was to be driven by an obliging friend to the airport in Winnipeg to catch an early flight home to Calgary.

As I stepped outside at the appointed early hour, the car stood crouched against the snow banks, emitting great clouds of exhaust, as if it resented having to face the cold and darkness. I tossed my bag in the back and we moved off through the empty streets. Behind us, the west was still night. Before us to the east, a thin pencil of light promised coming sunrise. Eventually, we reached the highway. On either side of the car, the landscape stretched to the horizon. Dotted here and there in the darkness, the illuminated windows of early risers' houses shone like the lights of small ships on a great ocean.

By now, snow is whirling in parallel lines against the windshield and the edges of the highway have disappeared, so my friend needs to concentrate on driving. I am anxious about whether we will get to the airport in time. For a while, there is little conversation between us. Yet for some reason, the memory of those mercifully uneventful hours remains.

On and on we go, the car undulating gently along the eastbound ribbon of the highway, its surface rendered delicate and fluid by the drifts of light snow blown across it. Then, joy of joys, out of the slowly lifting darkness the lights of a roadhouse on the edge of Portage la Prairie lift the heart with a promise of breakfast and strong coffee.

Back in the car, feeling within us the life of a new day stirring, we begin to chat about this world in the middle of Canada, its layers of immigration, its history of depression, the promise of its rich resources. As we leave Portage behind, an industrial plant casts its harsh white light across the snow, its smokestack bidding farewell to the fading stars. Great hydro pylons march away to the northwest. They stand cold, angular, steel-limbed, yet they carry power that brings warmth and light. They look like enormous skeletons, yet they carry life itself across the miles.

We move across this winter land in our cocoon of warmth, the voice of a cheerful forecaster on the car radio reassuring us that the weather ahead is clearing. My companion asks if I'm aware of a famous Canadian poem by A. J. M. Smith called "The Lonely Land," written in the 1920s. Because I know he loves poetry, I ask him to quote it. He can't recall it all, but does bring to mind a powerful image toward the end. He recites it as we both gaze ahead into the distance:

This is a beauty
of dissonance . . .
This is the beauty
of strength
broken by strength
and still strong.

As I listen, I look out across the majesty of this prairie day now fully revealed to us, its sky cloudless blue, the sun cascading down on a world of pure whiteness. I imagine that we, in our tiny chariot, have been granted permission by some mighty emperor to move across this winter land, the domain of his jealous possession.

By the time this drive took place, I had lived in Canada for over thirty years. I had traveled the breadth of this country and to many places within it. It had become natural to think of myself as Canadian. Yet somehow in the course of this particular journey, I had a strange feeling that those mysterious powers we are learning to regard as the Spirits of the Land, by surrounding me in the darkness of predawn, by showing me the beauty of a prairie sunrise, by enveloping me in a world of blinding snow, and by communicating to me the vulnerability of my humanity on these endless plains, had somehow given me a new, deeper appreciation of being admitted fully to a vast family, my family, my Canada.

## 26. A DANCE OF JOY
### Christ Church, Elbow Park, Calgary, 1987

During my years of ministry in Calgary, there would be two L'Arche homes in the city. From time to time, I visited one of them, where two young professionals lived a common life with about half a dozen young men and women with intellectual disabilities. As time went on, it became apparent to me that these two staff members were moving toward committing their lives to each other in marriage. What I was not aware of was that they had reached a decision about their wedding day that would make it one of the most moving experiences in the lives of everyone who attended—including myself.

On the day of the wedding, I could see from where I stood at the chancel steps that there seemed to be an unusual flurry of movement and a mingling of voices in the narthex. At last, the procession formed and began moving up the aisle. As it got closer, it became clear that this was unlike any other wedding procession I had ever witnessed. I could see Jean and Bill bringing up the rear as bride and bridegroom. However, in front of them were five young people, not walking formally in procession as would have been normal, but milling about excitedly. They were dressed in festive yet simple clothes. The three young women held bunches of freshly picked flowers, which they waved at the congregation as they passed. They and the two young men turned again and again to look at Bill and Jean, as if to assure themselves that those familiar and trusted figures were still near them.

At times, their walk changed to a skip or a dance step. They made sounds that I recognized as laughter. I sensed that these young adults were expressing a quality of unadulterated joy that most of us know only in childhood. Utterly free of the slightest self-consciousness, they somehow knew that this was an hour of happiness beyond their understanding, but certainly not beyond their experiencing and sharing. As they came near to me, I realized I had tears in my eyes, as did many in the congregation. In a flash of spiritual intuition, I grasped the meaning of what I was seeing and hearing and welcoming. I understood that I was being given a rare glimpse of what our Lord Jesus means when he speaks of the kingdom of heaven.

The liturgy began, punctuated but somehow never intruded upon by the constant movement of the group. It was less a restlessness than a kind of spontaneous energy, a joy that communicated itself to everyone in the church. At every word and gesture of the bride and groom, at the saying of their vows and at their exchanging of rings, these young adults would become quiet for a moment and gaze avidly at the couple who lived among them and had now welcomed them into this most wonderful day in their lives. When Bill and Jean exchanged the ceremonial wedding kiss, the group's excited, joyous sounds were taken up and echoed in the loud clapping of the congregation.

When the liturgy was about to come to a close, Jean and Bill gathered their companions and showed them how to proceed down the aisle. Almost as if they knew the time for relative seriousness and decorum was ending, the young people moved eagerly from side to side of the aisle, greeting as many as they could reach, until they stepped out into the sunshine of the day.

Some years later, I would discover a passage from the poetry of W. H. Auden. It's part of his *For the Time Being: A Christmas Oratorio.*

He is the Way.

Follow Him through the Land of Unlikeness;

You will see rare beasts, and have unique adventures.

He is the Truth.

Seek Him in the Kingdom of Anxiety;

You will come to a great city that has expected your return
    for years.

He is the Life.

Love Him in the World of the Flesh;

And at your marriage all its occasions shall dance for joy.

Every year since that day, I receive a Christmas greeting from Jean and Bill. As I do so, I recall Jesus saying to those around Him who would listen and hear, "Except you become like little children, you cannot enter the kingdom of heaven."

## 27. THE LETTER

### Christ Church, Elbow Park, Calgary, 1987

It was that time of year when, inevitably, the parish treasurer knocks on the door of the rector's study, comes in, and announces—usually a little anxiously—that it's time to speak to the congregation about the finances of the parish. This encounter usually takes place sometime in November, as the end of the fiscal year looms. People's lives are busy, and even the most committed can forget that church income almost always lags behind church expenditure.

On this particular year, it was decided that everyone would be invited to participate in a meeting over a potluck meal. The need would be presented and responses would be invited. At some stage in these evenings, it's assumed that as well as the churchwardens presenting facts and figures, the rector will share a few thoughts on the theme of giving to support the needs of the church. I remember facing a blank sheet of paper, asking myself what I might say that had not been said many times before by previous rectors on such occasions: homilies about life being a matter of stewardship; quotations from Saint Paul reminding us of our Lord's maxim that it is more blessed to give than to receive. All of which is true and worthy, but all of which is also exceedingly familiar.

About three or four days before the dinner, the phone rang in the rectory. It was one of our daughters, requesting a small loan. She and her husband, newly married, really needed something for their apartment. As parents, Paula and I chatted a little about the request, but there was never any doubt that we would respond positively, which we did that very evening.

Perhaps it was because of the approaching dinner and its necessary short address about giving, that something came to mind that I had never thought of before. I realized that the very act of acceding to our daughter's request was nothing less than a deep, utterly satisfying pleasure. For the first time, something struck me about the ways in which we use money. If I had thought of it before, I had certainly not formed it consciously into a statement that could be shared with others. Now, the thought itself came fully formed. It was almost as if an inner voice said to me:

> You know, there are two things we can do with money. We can pay it to those to whom we owe it because we have to. That is to be a debtor.
>
> We can also give it to those whom we love because we want to. That is to be a lover. We have a choice. We can use our money as a debtor or as a lover.

Perhaps it was that word "lover" that triggered another memory. I realized that tucked away somewhere in my files was a portion of a letter written hundreds of years ago. I knew it would speak perfectly to the coming occasion. I did not have to worry about that blank page waiting for inspiration. I had received inspiration. All I had to do on the evening of the dinner was to tell the family story pretty well as I have written it here. And that is what I did. I told of my wondering what to say, of the request from our daughter, of the way we felt as parents, of our ready response, and of the reflection that experience engendered. Then I quoted from the letter I had remembered.

A very short introduction will give the necessary context. The date is September 11, 1522. Thomas More, then lord chancellor of England under King Henry VIII, is sitting down to write to his beloved daughter. She has moved to London for her studies and has recently written home, petitioning her father for financial assistance. More replies:

> You ask, my dear Margaret, for money with too much bashfulness and timidity, since you are asking from a father who is eager to give. . . . If my means were as great as my desire, I would reward each syllable with two gold ounces. As it is, I send only what you have asked, but would have added more, only that as I am eager to give, so am I desirous to be asked and coaxed. . . . So the sooner you spend this money well, as you are wont to do, and the sooner you ask for more, the more you will be sure of pleasing your father.

I don't recall now exactly how successful my appeal was that evening in Calgary. But I still treasure that long-ago letter.

The author in a characteristic pose, teaching at the College of Preachers in Washington, DC.

# CHAPTER FIVE

# America

*Growing up in the Republic of Ireland in a Church of Ireland family in the 1940s meant that one had a complex relationship with the concept of empire, especially the British Empire. I realize now that in some ways that relationship was remarkably like growing up in an Episcopalian family some 150 years earlier, after the Revolution that had severed the link with Britain and brought the United States into being. In both cases, a church tradition that had been deeply embedded in an imperial occupation had to find its place in a transformed political reality.*

*Having the opportunity to live for a short period in the United States, and to remain closely involved with the life of the Episcopal Church over a quarter of a century, I came to understand something else that I found intriguing and moving. Both in the Church of Ireland of my formative years and in the American Episcopal Church to which I came in mid-career, there lingered a complex, ambivalent nostalgia for the very empire against which both countries had fought to attain their independence.*

## 1. LAND OF LAST HOPE

### Ireland and America

**If you stand at the cliffs of Moher** in County Clare looking west, your guide (if you have engaged one) is bound at some point to say, "Well, the next stop is America." It's possible that in these days of great wings and daily flights your guide may refer to "the United States," but in my childhood it was always America. Two things would change this for my generation: the approaching Second World War and the increasing place of movies in our lives. But before these things affected us, the word "America" did not express a place as much as it did a dream, an aspiration, a great journey highly unlikely ever to be taken. To encounter someone who had actually been to America and returned could mean only one of two things: either that person was rich and could afford the return voyage or they had emigrated to America and, for some reason usually kept private, things had not worked out.

In the late eighteenth century and throughout the nineteenth, America attained huge significance in the Irish Catholic peasant imagination. By 1750, Catholic land ownership was down to five percent. Almost all land had been taken by English landlords. Peasant holdings were dirt poor. Death by malnutrition and starvation was commonplace. All hope of assistance from France or Spain, the great Catholic powers of Europe, had long faded. The last hope lay in faraway America: a hope so desperate that hundreds of thousands risked their lives and those of their loved ones on the dangerous voyage.

Nothing human, however grim, is without some element of humor. My mother used to tell a story that had gone the rounds in Castlecomer in her own teen years before the First World War: a tale of brave intention to set out for America, that ended within hours of an emotional leaving. The would-be emigrant had fortified himself in good company the evening before. Boarding the early bus for Cork and the westbound liner, he pointed to the fountain that stood in the village and loudly declared to all who had come to see him off on the great adventure, "Goodbye ould fountain, you'll be flowin' when I'm far away." With this highly alliterative flourish, he stepped aboard the bus. Alas, when the local bus from Kilkenny arrived in the town square the next morning, a chastened, embarrassed, and very sober emigrant returned home, never to set out for America, or anywhere else, again. All of which affords a laugh in a very different twenty-first century where long-distance travel is taken for granted by many of us.

But even in the early 1930s, it would still have been customary in some rural homes to hold a wake for the person leaving for America.

We might cynically think it was as good an excuse as any to shore up the emigrant with a night's drinking, but it was more than that. There still existed a folk memory since the days of the famine in the 1840s when it was assumed that no one would ever return from an infinitely distant America. My own experience of the United States would come in the very different world of the 1980s and 90s when on many occasions I found myself involved in the life of various Episcopal dioceses. Memories of life on an Irish farm were by that time distant, yet there were occasions when memory was awakened very vividly.

One evening after a clergy conference in the Diocese of Kentucky, I was about to address a large dinner gathering when the bishop announced that first, we would all sing "My Old Kentucky Home." As the voices sounded, to my intense surprise, I became a small boy on my grandfather's farm some sixty years earlier. On another occasion, having stayed overnight in the home of the then bishop of Virginia, I was being driven to Richmond on a glorious October morning, along a country road over golden leaves fallen from trees that formed a canopy of gold above us. Again, I found myself back on the farm in childhood years, listening to my mother's voice singing "Carry Me Back to Old Virginia."

The reason for my nostalgic sentiments was simple. One of my mother's brothers had left for America in 1932, to work on the farm of a cousin who had done well in Ohio. As a small boy, I was shown photographs of him: one portraying him bronzed beside a tractor, in another suited formally, even dashingly, one foot on the running board of a Model T Ford. For a small boy he was a figure of high romance, and he remained so when he returned to marry my aunt. It was he who had brought back the songs of a faraway land, songs that my mother would softly echo at bedtime on long summer evenings: the two I've already mentioned, and others like "Old Man River" and "Look Down That Lonesome Road." Most of them shared in common a certain melancholy tone. But this, too, is part of my Irish upbringing for, as the saying goes, "Being Irish, he had an abiding sense of tragedy, which sustained him through temporary periods of joy." That said, I was fortunate to be given the songs of early America in circumstances of comfort and security. I did not have to hear them as many did, as laments for a land they had left and would not see again.

## 2. THE PATRIARCH

### San Diego, 1980

In September 1980, there was a meeting in San Diego of the American House of Bishops. It is usual at these gatherings for an invitation to be extended to some speaker to give three morning addresses. That year I had the privilege of being that speaker.

It is also customary when the House of Bishops meets to have present as distinguished guests a small group of senior church figures from various parts of the world. Usually they are selected from churches that may be linked in some way with the Episcopal Church, perhaps through partnership in a major project.

The year that I was present, I noticed a venerable and colorful figure seated among the bishops. When I inquired about his identity, I was told that he was the patriarch of the Mar Thoma Church, an ancient Christian community centered in the state of Kerala on the Malabar Coast of India. There is a strong tradition that in obedience to the command of Jesus to go and teach all nations, the apostle Thomas arrived on the west coast of India about twenty years after the Crucifixion and Resurrection, and founded a Christian church there. Today, the Mar Thoma Church has over a million adherents, scattered around the world.

During a coffee break on the morning of my third address, the patriarch invited me to share a few minutes with him. In the course of telling me about his church, he dryly remarked that lest I have any doubts about its claim to the apostle Thomas as its founder, that tradition was at least as strong and credible as the claim of the Church of Rome to the apostle Peter as its founder. Touché, I thought.

Never before or since has a brief conversation over coffee taken me over so vast a geography—Western Asia, Africa, North America, the Middle East, north and south India—nor have I ever been invited to traverse such a vast and varied history that included such fascinating exotica as the links between the Babylonian patriarchy of the Middle Ages and the Malabar Coast via the trade routes across the Indian Ocean. It made me realize, not for the first time, how ethnocentric Western Christianity can be in its attitude to the rest of the Christian world. When I mentioned this to the patriarch, he smiled and said, "I wonder how many Western Christians realize that the faith in its Nestorian form was in Chan Ang in northern China only seventy-five years after it reached Canterbury in 597?"

I hesitated for a moment to seem to be setting up a competition in early Christian history, but I decided to draw a little on my own history of the Irish missionaries of the eighth century going down the Danube, encountering other missionaries coming north from Greece, eventually reaching Kiev, where they met with Viking trade delegations coming south down the rivers of Russia. I admit to a little satisfaction when I saw that I had piqued the patriarch's curiosity. It's even possible the ancient and cosmopolitan roots of my own religious tradition may have caused me to rise a notch in his estimation.

At one point in our fascinating conversation, my companion told me that every two years his church held a large gathering of some 150,000 people. Part conference, part festival, it was a vast celebration of the church's life in worship and word. On each of these occasions, a speaker from another part of the world church was invited to address the assembly. The patriarch indicated how pleased he would be if I would fill that role on the next such occasion, approximately a year hence.

When I learned the dates of the gathering, my heart sank. I had already accepted an invitation to an English diocese for the same time; those plans were already set in stone, and I could not change them at that point. With great reluctance I declined, making quite clear that I would have wished most heartily to be part of his church's life on that occasion.

By this time, our conversation was moving to a close. As it did, I could not resist one more question. "Your Holiness," I said, "you say that you expect 150,000 of your flock to attend. Where can you possibly gather that many people in one place?" He looked at me with a smile, which may have conveyed a certain amount of satisfaction that he now had the opportunity to blow the mind of this naïve Westerner. "Where do you think?" he asked rhetorically, then paused before answering, "In a dried-up riverbed, of course." I took refuge in echoing his "of course," as if nothing could be more reasonable. After all, other than in a dried-up riverbed, where else would you put 150,000 of your faithful?

## 3. THE COLLEGE

### College of Preachers, Washington, DC, 1982–1984

For two years, I had the privilege of serving in the position of warden of what was then called the College of Preachers. The college, a magnificent building in its own right, stood on the close of the immense Cathedral of St. Peter and Paul, also referred to as Washington National Cathedral. For more than half a century before I arrived, the college had offered courses in preaching to clergy from all parts of the country. It was regarded as a significant resource within the Episcopal Church.

The rhythm of its life was weekly. Each Sunday and Monday, clergy would arrive from across the church. Those coming for the first time would be curious and excited to be not only at the college, but also quite literally in the shadow of the National Cathedral, and within a short taxi ride of the heart of their national capital. There is a reason why I link these three aspects of those weeks for clergy. I will return to it later.

From Monday through the closing Eucharist on Friday, there was a pattern of homiletical instruction, sermon preparation, recreation, meals taken together, and daily worship. On two afternoons, participants shared their homilies in small groups and received feedback from their peers. This was frequently cited as the most rewarding part of the week.

For me, those two years as warden were a deep learning experience. Put simply, I realized that the college was far more than a place of teaching and learning. It was nothing less than a haven of healing in an age when clerical ministry was—as it still is—becoming increasingly stressful and demanding. The experience of attending the college alongside colleagues with similar challenges had the potential to be a part of this healing process.

One reality of contemporary life is the evidence of relentless disintegration at all levels of experience: societal, relational, personal. Traditions are challenged, ideologies clash, congregations become factional, a diffuse and unfocused anger pervades life. Resentment grows at both the status quo and attempts to change it. The fabric of both society and church wrestles with tensions and stresses. Such was the baggage brought by clergy to their week at the college.

In response, the institution offered some things that might assist with what could sometimes be a desperate search for integration of one's life and affirmation of one's ministry. For one thing, the college architecture itself, both interior and exterior, was gracious and traditional. To share a meal in the dining hall was to revive the memory of a less frantic and utilitarian world. The magnificence and scale of the adjoining cathedral could assuage a sense of personal vulnerability in one's ministry. In season, the Bishop's Garden offered its beauty and fragrance for times of quiet respite. A visit to the heart of the nearby capital provided opportunities to engage the great symbols and structures of the nation's life.

With all of this came the relationships that developed during the week: friendships—sometimes from the half-forgotten idealism of seminary years—renewed; conversations, sometimes one-on-one, at other times in groups; all serving to remind a vulnerable priest that he or she was not alone in their struggle to retain a sense of vocation. To add to all this, a priest could expect to receive insights about the homiletic task that would often reignite passion to replace what had too often become a disheartened and jaded attitude to the duty of preaching.

While I was warden for only two academic years, I remained part of college life for the next twenty-five years as visiting faculty. As those years went by, and the unrelenting tides of change continued to flow over church and society, I could see that the healing aspect of the college's work was becoming, if anything, even more significant and valuable. Ironically, even tragically, the need for this healing role became more and more obvious at the same time as the church's sense of the importance of the homiletic function was lessening.

In May 2008, the College of Preachers, which had opened in 1929, was closed. As I write, there is the good news that after some years of sitting vacant and deteriorating, it is to receive a new lease on life, thanks to some extremely generous benefactors who have contributed to a permanent endowment. It is scheduled to reopen in late 2020 as the Cathedral College of Faith and Culture. Programming will be broadened to encompass music, liturgy, and the arts, ethics and public engagement, and spirituality and leadership for both laity and clergy.

All this seems appropriate for such an institution in the twenty-first century. Permit me to express the hope that in all these changes and new possibilities, consideration will be given to its role as a place of healing and renewal for those who accept the fulfilling but demanding vocation of ordained ministry in our time—alongside their lay brothers and sisters who exercise the equally vital ministry of all the baptized.

## 4. AN IRISH EPISCOPALIAN IN AMERICA
### USA, 1982–2002

I alluded in the introduction to this chapter to some interesting parallels between the context of the Church of Ireland in the early days of the Republic, and the postcolonial traditions of American Episcopalianism. Because I was born in 1928, my generation was the first to grow up in the new Irish Republic. The echoes of the short-lived and swiftly aborted rebellion of 1916 were only a dozen years old, those of the tragic and vicious civil wars of 1921 and 1922 a mere six years behind us. The following decade would see a large exodus of

Church of Ireland families from the nascent Irish State, the equivalent of the exodus of those who became known as United Empire Loyalists from the United States to Canada a century and a half earlier. For those Church of Ireland people who stayed behind, as with those of English stock who stayed in the newly formed United States, there began a long process of adapting to radically altered circumstances.

If one were a member of the Church of Ireland, one had taken the links with the Church of England and with the crown for granted. I have spoken of this in earlier chapters. My parents had grown up in an Ireland where they went to church and asked God to save the king (or the queen, as may be). In the Great War that had ended in 1918, a great part of their generation had fought in the uniform of that same king. However, as we their children moved toward adulthood and were educated with the revised history texts of the new Ireland, we would be made ever more aware that the relationship between said king and one's country had for a long time been far from idyllic.

The realities of that relationship turned out to be rather chilling. They included what in today's world would be called ethnic cleansing—the indiscriminate slaughter of men, women, and children in the seventeenth century—followed in the eighteenth by the dispossession of those who remained from almost all the land that was rightfully theirs. Much of the nineteenth century saw the legal imposition of what today would be considered cultural genocide. Add in a political response to a half-decade-long famine in the middle of that century that today would be judged a crime against humanity. All these were valid reasons for the ambivalence that a member of a new generation of the Church of Ireland might feel toward the concept of empire.

Perhaps this was why something struck me rather forcefully in the first weeks and months after we moved to Washington, DC, in September of 1982, and I began my work as warden of the College of Preachers. My realization that I had come to a society that felt very differently about empire came early on, when I discovered that the weekly course schedule included no teaching sessions after lunch on Wednesday so that attendees could be free to make a pilgrimage that was very important to almost all of them, especially those who had travelled from parts of this vast country that were situated far from their nation's capital.

The pilgrimage had different emphases or priorities for different people, but almost everyone began at the Capitol Building, the seat of the United States Congress, and continued down the Mall to the various national institutions that lay along its long expanse. The personal pilgrimage usually ended at the Vietnam and Lincoln Memorials. I realized that for these men and women, it was a sacred journey linking them with their history and their love for their country.

It took me longer to grasp the rich irony that in spite of this very understandable display of national pride, very few of them actually thought about their country in terms of empire, even though by the late twentieth century their country had, thanks to its overwhelming economic, cultural, and military power, come to dominate every other society in the world. I realized that I was living in an empire that did not see itself as such. I was, as I whimsically expressed it to a friend one day, between the paws of a most reluctant lion.

I recall an occasion, two decades later, when this was brought home to me very explicitly at a large ecumenical gathering in Santa Fe. It was the first Lent after 9/11. The large Catholic congregation had invited a succession of weekly speakers to reflect on the theme "How then shall we live?" After I spoke, a man came up to me with his young son. He expressed appreciation for what I had said, but added that the one thing he would disagree with was my reference to the United States as an empire.

"Father," he said, "the reason I don't wish my country to be thought an empire is that the United States is fundamentally different from any of the great empires in history in that everything it does is for the good of others." I thought quickly and asked if he would accept the term "a great power" for the United States. He said he would. We parted friends.

Another memorable moment was in Washington itself. I was speaking to a board member of the college who was a senior figure in the State Department. To my surprise he said to me, "You know,

Herbert, I often think that if we had not chosen the way of empire, we would have become a society not unlike Canada." His tone was almost wistful.

My next learning curve was the degree to which the Episcopal Church, even though it made much of being a province of the Anglican Communion, and was immensely generous to other members of that communion—from Canterbury Cathedral to innumerable projects in the developing world—nevertheless tended to see itself primarily in national terms. The actual name of the great institution in which I was serving at the time is the Cathedral Church of St. Peter and St. Paul, but it is referred to far more often as the National Cathedral. Underlining this was the weekly sight of the flag of the United States carried at the head of the liturgical procession that began the Sunday morning celebration of Choral Eucharist.

I had come to realize that in both the country of my birth and the country that had welcomed me into its church life, there lingered, ironically enough, a nostalgia for the very idea of empire against which both countries had fought to attain their freedom.

## 5. THE BODY SNATCHER
### Washington National Cathedral, 1982

To stand in the south bay of the Cathedral of St. Peter and St. Paul in Washington is to realize that both space and time have voices that speak to those who care to listen. The first time I stood here was almost thirty years before the cathedral sustained considerable damage from an earthquake—damage which, as I write another decade after that disaster, is still only partially repaired.

I was being introduced to the cathedral by a friend. I could see at once that I had only to look in any direction to be made aware of the spaciousness of this magnificent building. The entrance to a nearby cloister beckoned my eye along the undersides of the many arches that form its roof. Beyond, in the main nave, a group of visitors were dwarfed by the immensity of it all.

It has been said that the great medieval cathedrals were built to make human beings look upwards. If you move to the main west doors of this cathedral, and watch people enter from the narthex, this old saying is immediately validated. Without exception, those who enter look up, their eyes drawn to the soaring roof.

As great space addresses the onlooker, so too does time and history. Even though one knows that this cathedral here on this hill is, in fact, a twentieth-century North American re-creation of all that is Gothic and European, one cannot help being taken back to the Middle Ages. But as well there is, particularly in this south bay, history of a different kind: the history of these United States, now a formidable global empire. One symbol of that history is the massive and ornate structure before us. We are standing in front of the tomb of Woodrow Wilson, president of the United States from 1913 to 1921, and therefore one of the victorious political power brokers who redrew the map of the world after the First World War. All of this one can hear retold if one pauses while a volunteer docent escorts a group of tourists through this area.

There is more than an echo of empire here in this solemn stillness. There are also traces of the varied humanity of the men who have held this office of president of their country. Among them is one who came to his predecessor's tomb—then located in the crypt of the cathedral before being moved upstairs to greater prominence here—and who displayed a quite different reaction to its solemnity.

Franklin Delano Roosevelt served as president from 1933 until his death in 1945. One day, FDR, as he was popularly known, had occasion to attend a service at the National Cathedral. The bishop made a well-intentioned but, as it turned out, unfortunate decision to take advantage of his leader's presence by making a point and pressing a case. Frances Perkins was secretary of labor at the time. In her book *The Roosevelt I Knew*, she recounts how the bishop earnestly and repeatedly encouraged the president to consider emulating his predecessor by planning to have himself likewise entombed in the cathedral. It seems the listening president had great difficulty in remaining polite; one can only assume and hope that he succeeded. As the visit drew to a close, the small group eventually arrived at the cathedral steps and the waiting limousines. In his best patrician manner, FDR expressed his thanks to the bishop, shook hands, turned and entered the limousine. As Perkins tells it, he had hardly settled back on the leather upholstery before giving vent to his pent-up feelings by exclaiming in a loud voice, "The old body snatcher!"

The story of this unfortunate interaction brings to mind another such incident involving church and state, this time in medieval Ireland. The Rock of Cashel is a vast outcrop that dominates the countryside of southern Tipperary. In the thirteenth century, a Norman landowner, for some reason enraged at the bishop of Cashel, burned to the ground the magnificent cathedral built atop the rock. His overlord was appalled at this act of sacrilege. When the perpetrator was brought to trial, his overlord demanded to know why he had set the cathedral on fire. The accused pleaded in his own defense that he had done so only because he thought the bishop was in residence in the cathedral at the time. After due consideration, the overlord declared that his fellow knight had sufficient good reason to carry out the burning and was therefore innocent of any wrongdoing.

It would appear that relationships between bishops and secular authorities such as kings and nobles—perhaps we could include even elected presidents—have had a long and checkered history across the continents and centuries.

# 6. MEMORIAL

## The Mall, Washington, DC, 1982

In Washington, DC, running west from the steps of the Capitol Building two miles to the Lincoln Memorial is a long pedestrian thoroughfare—really a public park—officially called the National Mall, but known as simply the Mall. If it can be said that America has a definable geographical heart, a central place or symbol that expresses the deepest level of its identity, the Mall is that place. I have mentioned before how important it was for the men and women who came to the College of Preachers for weekly seminars.

Let's imagine that, like many of them, you set out walking westward from the Capitol steps. On your way, to left and right, you are within a stone's throw of the National Gallery of Art, the White House, the Smithsonian, to name only a few great American institutions. One of the most recent additions since my time there, and a very significant one, is the National Museum of African American History and Culture. A little more than halfway along, you will pass within the shadow of the soaring obelisk that is the Washington Monument. Your pilgrimage will seem to have ended when you arrive in front of the vast and immensely impressive Lincoln Monument, with its large, rectangular reflecting pool.

But your experience is by no means complete. Facing toward the looming seated figure of Lincoln, turn and look to your right. You will see people moving toward a gently undulating grassy area that is in no way dominated by any soaring architecture, as so much of the Mall is. You would be wise to go in that direction, because what beckons you and others there is a place unique in American memory. It is a war memorial, but unlike any other war memorial in the world, for it memorializes not a great national victory, but a tragic and costly defeat. That defeat, some would say, shattered the resolve of the United States to remain entirely confident in its role as a great imperial power. To be sure, that power was by no means broken by Vietnam. Perhaps it would be true to say, however, that it created a deep wound in the American psyche, a wound that still remains, and that still affects and forms many decisions about American foreign policy.

The design for the Vietnam Veterans Memorial began in controversy and, for some, remains controversial. Traditional war memorials tend to soar aloft; not this one. You walk toward it until a simple sloping pathway begins to take you down into the earth. As you descend, a wall of marble rises on one side. On that wall, rank upon unending rank, are inscribed the names of those who died in the Vietnam War.

If you are going to the memorial merely as a visitor, you will notice something that will likely affect you deeply. All around you, people are stepping toward the wall, seeking a particular name. What is particularly moving is an almost universal gesture. When a name is found, if it is not too high up on the wall, the seeker always tries to touch the name cut into the stone, almost as if, even after many years, there is a desire to actually touch the loved one named in the sharp-edged letters.

There is something else that makes this Vietnam Memorial truly unique and deeply memorable. As I stood there and looked at the seemingly endless legion of names, I could see myself perfectly reflected in the highly polished black granite. It seemed to me as if I was within the wall and behind the names. The effect is salutary. You realize that no one can stand here in a detached way. Even if you are not in search of a loved one's name, you cannot but feel part of this tragedy, this awful loss of life.

I came away from the Vietnam Veterans Memorial feeling it to be a "thin place," not so much in the usual sense of that term—piercing the veil between the human and the divine—but in the sense of its being a place where the veil between past and present is made thin to the point that it allows us to voyage between the two, recovering into the present the pain and sadness of the past. A testimony to the power of this memorial is to acknowledge that even though I came to it as other than American, and therefore unable to claim it as a direct part of my own history, it nevertheless spoke eloquently to that sense of tragedy and loss that is an essential attribute of all humanity.

## 7. A COSTLY DISCIPLESHIP
### Civic Arena, Philadelphia, 1984

The Episcopal Diocese of Philadelphia celebrated its bicentenary in 1984. Between nine and ten thousand people gathered in the largest amphitheater in the city. I recall it was a warm summer evening. The mood, as you might expect, was festive. After all, it is no mean thing for an institution to have journeyed through two hundred years of a history that was at times stormy and divisive. Between 1784 and that evening of 1984, great tides of social change had swept through the church's life.

The eighteenth century saw a colonial society swept into revolution as some sought independence from the mother country while others regarded this same struggle as the betrayal of their deepest loyalties. The nineteenth century saw a country deeply divided over racial issues, an agony that tore the country apart in civil war. In the mid-twentieth century, the whole of Western society was affected by a vast tide of cultural change that affected society at every level: personal life, family life, community life, political life, not to mention the life of every institution, including the church.

All of this history was present as the hour for the celebration neared. Cars and buses unloaded their passengers from every corner of the diocese. Greetings were exchanged between people who had not met for years. Ushers did their best to direct people to their assigned areas of seating. Robed figures, mostly clergy, moved hither and thither setting final details to rights. The huge choir gathered for the occasion was beginning its last-minute rehearsal.

This celebratory service of Choral Evensong would have two homilies: one near the opening of the service and one near its close. I was responsible for the first. The second was to be given by Archbishop Desmond Tutu.

I had met Desmond some years before he became the world figure he now was. As dean of Christ Church Cathedral in Vancouver, I had invited him to be our preacher while he was visiting the city. Since then, he had taken a leading role in the struggle against apartheid in his homeland, often at great personal risk. For his courage and commitment to that great cause, earlier in this very year he had received the Nobel Peace Prize.

Meeting Desmond again in Philadelphia was just as pleasant as our former encounter in Vancouver; he was one of the easiest and warmest people to engage, always ready to lighten the mood with quick repartee and ready laughter. At the same time, I was aware that for this huge gathering, his was the significant voice of the evening. I hoped that what I had prepared for my contribution would be worthy of the occasion.

Time has drawn a veil over the details of what I said that evening. The reason the evening has remained memorable for me is not only because I was given the privilege of sharing it with Desmond Tutu, but for two particular moments in his presence.

The first is typically Desmond. By the time he stepped to the microphone to speak, the arena had become very warm. As is his wont, Desmond decided to do something totally unexpected. In a hushed and solemn tone, his very first words were, "My friends, I wish to tell you a story about a clergyman who was in bed one night with his wife." To say that Desmond got peoples' attention is an understatement.

The single statement was so utterly unexpected, coming from so eminent a figure on such a solemn occasion, it is not exaggerating to say that it electrified the arena. In the pause that followed, you could also feel a ripple of discomfort. Was this visitor going to spoil this special evening? How could this levity possibly be appropriate? With impeccable timing, Desmond then added, "She turned to him and said, 'Darling, I can't get to sleep; preach me one of your sermons.'"

The place exploded with laughter. All was well. Everyone relaxed, and most important of all, Desmond had this great crowd in the palm of his hand. It was masterly. He proceeded to give a magnificent plea for the life of the church to be characterized by its commitment to justice of every kind in contemporary society. His words were greeted with rapt attention.

The second moment is a more personal treasure. Because of the size of the arena, the flight of steps from the specially built sanctuary area was very high above the arena floor, so those leading the service could be clearly seen. As the procession came down those steps at the end of Evensong, Desmond and I were walking together. He turned to me, expressed warm appreciation of what I had said during my homily, and requested a certain quote that I had used. I said he was most welcome and I would give it to him in the robing room, but I was suddenly moved by the simple fact of being in his presence.

At that time, there had been many news items on every form of world media about Desmond's South African struggle. It was well known that especially in the volatile streets of Soweto, Desmond had on more than one occasion risked his life to stop what had become known as "necklace" lynchings, a style of execution where a car tire filled with gasoline and set on fire would be thrown over the victim's head and shoulders.

Acutely aware that I was walking beside a person of such courage shown in the name of Christ, I said, "Desmond, I speak in a world very different from the world you know. For the most part I receive appreciation. You sometimes speak at the risk of your life. For all of us, thank you, my friend. Thank you."

For a moment, he put his hand on my shoulder, and then we came down together.

# 8. PETER
## Washington, DC, 1988

Peter was the rector of a large urban congregation in San Francisco. He had been there some seven or eight years, and had developed a good relationship with his people. They appreciated his ministry and he was happy among them. There was, however, an aspect of his ministry that Peter felt should be improved. He had become dissatisfied with his role as preacher. One aspect of his preaching that particularly concerned him was his difficulty in speaking without notes when the occasion required it.

It is easy to forget that the responsibility of communicating the faith extends far beyond the Sunday sermon. Those tend to be fairly formal affairs, prepared for carefully and most often using a written text. But there are many other occasions in the ongoing life of a parish priest which demand that he or she be able to speak naturally and spontaneously. Peter felt he needed help with this aspect of communicating, so he decided to come to one of the week-long seminars on preaching held in what was then known as the College of Preachers in Washington, and where I was by now an adjunct faculty member.

One part of the seminar format was, paradoxically, sometimes dreaded by participants but very often appreciated by them afterwards as the most helpful part of the week. The seminar would split into groups of six. Each group would be assigned its own room. One by one, each member of the group would address their colleagues in a way of his or her choosing. All were encouraged to use their time as they wished, but to consider branching out and trying some method new or unfamiliar to them, or in which they felt the need for practice and improvement.

In his particular group, Peter was determined to speak freely and spontaneously. It became obvious that this would call for great courage on his part, but he was determined. I have never seen a speaker as nervous and as stressed. However, he chose a passage from the ministry of Saint Paul and said that he wished to say three things about his subject.

All went well as he moved through his first two points. One could see that he was gaining confidence. Because he had no notes, he was beginning to have more eye contact with the group. Suddenly he froze. He simply could not continue. It was then that a memorable, even beautiful thing happened. In the intimacy of the small group, his listeners were able to offer him help. One said, "Peter, if Paul made those two points you've just told us, he probably would have . . ." Just at that moment Peter interrupted excitedly, "I have it! I know!" And he went on to complete his short address very effectively.

If his earlier stress could be said to have been extreme, it was nothing compared to his joy now at succeeding. It was moving to see. He was delighted, relieved, elated, and he showed it. The positive mood enveloped the whole group, because everyone felt involved in Peter's breakthrough. What was most remarkable was the way in which the experience changed Peter for the rest of the week's sessions. He was much more alive and engaged, participating much more fully than he had been before.

The sequel came some weeks later. I was back in my own parish in Canada, Peter in his in San Francisco. One day I received a card. It had five very short lines on it, all but the last of them followed by exclamation marks: "Herb, I tried it! It worked! They loved it! Thank you! Peter."

I still treasure that card among my memorabilia. It represents something far more significant than an individual achievement. It points to how much the role of preaching in ministry is bound up with personhood. It reminds us that preaching—indeed all public speaking—is far more than part of one's job, far more than a mere duty or function or activity, or indeed anything in any way merely utilitarian. It is nothing less than an *art*, and therefore integral to who we are, and to how we feel about ourselves. The College of Preachers was never merely a place for improving one's preaching skills. It was a place for nurturing the art of preaching.

## 9. THE MOTEL

### Lorraine Motel, Memphis, Tennessee, Spring 1988

For about a decade, from 1978 to 1990, I was a regular Lenten speaker at Calvary Episcopal Church in downtown Memphis. One year, the rector, Douglass Bailey, by then an old friend, said that he would like to show me where Martin Luther King Jr. had been assassinated.

That terrible event took place a few minutes after 6 p.m. on April 4, 1968—almost exactly twenty years before our visit. King had come to Memphis to lead a large public protest against racial discrimination. On the eve of the planned demonstration, he checked into the Lorraine Motel before meeting friends for dinner. While he was preparing to go out, a crowd of his supporters gathered in the parking lot of the motel and began to call for him to appear so they could welcome him to the city.

When he emerged from his second-floor room onto the balcony, King barely had time to utter a few sentences before a bullet fired from a window of a neighboring rooming house shattered his jaw. Within an hour, he was dead. Anger at the killing of one in whom the hopes of millions were invested was intense and spread nationwide. Incidentally, my host's downtown congregation had its life and role utterly changed as a result of the fierce rioting that took place in that city during the days following the murder.

Today, King's death is a national holiday and his life and work are remembered as a permanent milestone of American history. The Lorraine Motel has become a shrine to his martyrdom; the building razed and replaced by the National Civil Rights Museum.

When we came to it that spring day in 1988, however, none of this had yet happened. The area was surrounded by barbed wire, and two armed guards were on duty. We were given permission to drive into the parking lot area, but were not allowed to leave the car. As the gate opened, I became aware of a woman's voice singing somewhere very nearby. We could not see the singer, but the voice was that of an older person. Unaccompanied by any instrument, she sang a slow and infinitely sad melody. Within a few minutes her singing ceased, but the echo of her voice gave a deep poignancy to the rest of our visit.

The whole occasion was memorable, in part because I learned there something about how history is formed. I thought I understood the process by which oral traditions change as they are passed on, but I was about to actually experience it.

As we sat there, Doug told me something I have always remembered. First, he pointed up to the balcony on which tradition says that King was standing when he was shot. He said, "See that second door? That's the room he came out of." Then Doug paused and added, "But there are some who say that it was not that second room, it was the third room." And he pointed again.

I was about to reply but Doug continued, "Hang on, there's more." He then gestured across the parking lot to a large red brick building that looked closed and shuttered. Doug asked, "Do you see that end window on the second floor?" I nodded. "That's the window from which tradition says that James Earl Ray fired the shot that killed Martin." Then he paused again before adding, "But there are those who say that it was not that window, but the next one over."

We both sat quiet for a while. Then Doug said, "I brought you here to show you this and tell you the story. I'm sure I don't have to explain why." Then we began to discuss the way in which traditions develop in communities. Here was the story of a well-known event that many people had witnessed, yet here it was changing, within a scant twenty years after the fact. We went on to speak about how the Gospels and their stories were formed in the various communities that sprang up after Jesus's crucifixion and resurrection. Just as this story about an event in our own lifetime was already changing in its details, so the stories about our Lord also changed in the telling by different writers.

Even when Christians decided that four of the many Gospels written in that first century would be declared official, succeeding generations would reinterpret the stories in endless ways that reflected and responded to changing customs and changing ways of seeing the world. And so it continues. The event itself remains in memory; its details change in the remembering and the retelling.

That afternoon spent with a friend at a great historic landmark encouraged me even more to explore the Gospels to find ways in which I could make these timeless, universal stories speak to my own world and time.

## 10. BEAUTIFUL UPON THE MOUNTAINS
### Santa Fe, New Mexico, 1990

It was a day in which nothing very much happened, yet so much happened that it remains a shining memory. Sometimes I think that day was affected by the experience of the evening before—but I am getting ahead of myself.

It all happened because the rector of the Episcopal parish in Santa Fe, New Mexico, invited my wife, Paula, and I to visit, so I could deliver a series of addresses to her congregation. Those duties over, she announced that she had purchased tickets for Friday evening's production at the Santa Fe Opera of Mozart's *Don Giovanni*. After that, on Saturday she had arranged a very special trip to Taos Pueblo.

We had heard of Taos, the massive tiered pueblo building built in the high desert in the north of the state. Native Americans from the Tiwa tribe built it and have lived there for millennia; it is considered to be one of the oldest continuously inhabited communities in the

United States. Of Mozart's *Don Giovanni* I knew little, other than a vague memory of the story of Don Juan, a figure of unrelieved wickedness and debauchery who gets his just deserts by being seized by the Lord of Wickedness and consigned to the nether regions.

What I certainly didn't know was that I was about to see *Don Giovanni* in a way that could only be experienced in that particular opera house, in that part of the world. Over the last six decades, there have been three theatres built on the same site, looking westward from the high mesa north of the city of Santa Fe. The one standing when we attended was the second in the series, all of which share a common design feature. At least a third of the roof, as well as the sides of the auditorium and the rear of the stage, are open to the August sky, allowing visitors, as the performance begins, to witness a scarlet sunset sinking below a range of mountains whose very name—Sangre de Christo: Blood of Christ—pays tribute to that sunset. As the production unfolds, this amazing sight gives way to the emergence of a glittering ocean of stars.

All this we experienced while at the same time being riveted to our seats by the climactic thundering orchestration of the terrors of Don Juan, as he is literally dragged from this world and hurled into hell. For some minutes, art and nature blended in one's consciousness to engender a sense of awe and even terror at the ultimate price of human wickedness. Such for me was the experience of that Friday evening: a heightening of consciousness that remained even in the bright sunlight of the following morning.

There was another surprise before we set off in the rector's car. She informed us that Robert Runcie, then the archbishop of Canterbury, happened to be on a visit to friends in the city. She had invited him and his wife to travel with us, and they had accepted. Thus it came about that we found ourselves in exalted company, preparing to share what promised to be a magnificent journey.

Taos was all that we could have hoped for: exotic, ancient, mysterious. To experience it was more than sufficient to make a most memorable day in itself. But then our hostess proposed something else. She told us that in the 1920s, the English writer D. H. Lawrence had bought some property in these hills, and lived in New Mexico for a time before returning to England. There was a nearby memorial to his memory, referred to by some as a shrine, which she felt we might like to visit.

We drove a certain distance up the mountain, then began to walk the last quarter of a mile or so toward the memorial. About a hundred yards below the actual site, there was a bench for weary travelers. After wandering and climbing around Taos, we were very glad to sit for a while. The view was glorious. Once again, the distant peaks of the Sangre de Christo Mountains glittered in the clarity of the air in this high country.

It was at this point that the last incident of this wonderful day took place. Two men approached where we were sitting. They gave us a nod of silent acknowledgement, as one does to be polite to strangers, and kept on walking. At least, one of them did. The other stopped, turned, looked at the archbishop, and said in a wondering voice, "It can't be, but it must be!" Hearing his voice, the archbishop looked again, blurted an astonished "My God, it's . . ." and uttered a name that I have forgotten, whereupon they shook hands vigorously and launched into a hearty conversation. The whole moment was quintessentially English.

It turned out that the archbishop of Canterbury and the secretary of the General Synod of the Church of England had stumbled upon one another halfway up a mountain in the high wilderness of the American southwest. I am sure they both dined out on the encounter on many subsequent occasions. After a few minutes, we all walked to the memorial and chatted about D. H. Lawrence, his life and writing. Half an hour or so later, we arrived back down at the parking lot and parted ways, the archbishop and his friend and colleague still expressing their surprise and pleasure at the encounter.

I have always recalled that Friday evening and Saturday as a magic time. True, nothing of any great significance happened, no matters of great moment were discussed. But for some reason, things combined to create a special and memorable experience. The grandeur of the opera, the glory of the sunset and the stars, the sad beauty of Taos and

its long-vanished past, the company of charming friends, the wild surprise of English voices meeting on an American mountain top—all
this against the vast backdrop of what must surely be the most roman-
tically named mountain range in the world.

So wonderful a day was it that as I cast about for a title for this
piece of memoir I found myself reaching out to that incomparable
lyricist, the prophet Isaiah: "How beautiful upon the mountains are
the feet of the messenger . . . who says to Zion, 'Your God reigns.'"
Certainly, the beauty of that remembered day assured one that indeed
a Creator God does reign.

## 11. THE OLD MAN AND THE YOUNG
### Princeton Chapel, Summer 1995

This is the story of my relationship with a passage of the Book of
Genesis to which I was introduced as a small boy in Sunday school in
the Church of Ireland. Because it is perhaps the most mysterious and
potentially terrifying passage in the whole record of Holy Scripture, I
was fortunate that the person who first told us the story did so in a way
that was reassuring even as it was fearful. The narrator was the rector's
wife, a kind, soft-spoken person to whom I realize now we looked as a
motherly figure.

The passage in question occurs in the 22nd chapter of Genesis
when God approaches the patriarch Abraham and makes a terrible
demand. Abraham is to take his son Isaac to a mountaintop. There
they will together build an altar. Abraham is instructed to take his son,
place him on the altar, and, having ritually killed him, burn the body,
as a sacrificial offering to God.

By this point in the telling, we would have been riveted by our
teacher, hanging on every word, thrilled and terrified. Fortunately, at
the same moment, it was possible for her to begin to ease our terror.
Just as Abraham is about to kill his son, he is confronted by an angel
who forbids him to proceed. The angel points to an animal caught
in a nearby bush. Isaac is unbound and taken from the altar, and the

animal is sacrificed instead. Isaac goes free, and eventually father and son descend to make the journey home.

Such was my introduction to a story that would remain in my imagination as something dark and fearful through my growing years, first in primary school, then in secondary. I was about sixteen when a very fine teacher of English literature used the solemnity of a school Remembrance Service to read what is possibly one of the most bitter condemnations of war ever written: Wilfred Owen's "The Parable of the Old Man and the Young." In fourteen devastating lines, Owen places the story of Abraham and Isaac in the setting of the trenches of 1914–1918. His Abraham is a callous army general, his Isaac is the whole generation of European youth that died in those trenches. For me, as I listened that morning, the fusing of the childhood memory with the fact that even as we worshiped, the Second World War was in full fury in Europe, made the moment deeply moving. I realized that this ancient primitive story was no longer ancient; here it was in my own lifetime. A subsequent conversation about this with our English master would give me the concept of opening up literature to more than one level of meaning, thus introducing me to the world of myth.

A few years later, at a morning lecture in the Divinity School of Trinity College Dublin, we were reading this same Genesis passage. This time, the lecturer used the Abraham and Isaac story in a different way. He pointed out that the story became significant in the history of Israel at a time when Hebrew thought was beginning to reject child sacrifice, a custom still practiced by surrounding societies.

Rich in meaning as the story was by now for me, in later years it would become even more so. In the early summer of 1995, I had the privilege of taking part as faculty for a summer preaching school at Princeton. While there, I encountered this same passage. This time, I was given an unforgettable example of its mythic power.

In the course of the seminar, a midweek service was held in the magnificent chapel of the university. As we exited the main doors at the end of this act of worship, I noticed an object ahead of me. Memory says that it was about six feet high. I was intrigued and went over. There on the top of a rough-hewn stone plinth stood two human figures, wearing contemporary clothing, cast in bronze. One, clearly older, stands and looms threateningly over the other, who is kneeling, shirtless and tied with rope, in an attitude of beseeching. I realized I was looking at the story of Abraham and Isaac.

The thought occurred to me that there must be some reason for this choice of subject, but lunch hour was nearly over, colleagues wanted to discuss the afternoon session, and so, distracted, I left. Later, a friend asked me if I would like to return to the sculpture. When once again we stood there together, he said quietly, "Yes, it's Abraham and Isaac, but it's far more than that. It memorializes the Kent State Massacre." I was astonished. I knew what he was referring to: that tragic day of May 4, 1970, when the campus of Kent State University was the scene of a confrontation between students and members of the National Guard. Four students died, nine were injured. My friend explained that Kent State had originally commissioned this sculpture but then rejected it as inappropriate. Hence it stands in Princeton, a searing memory of the day when, as a commentator of the time said, "America began killing its young."

I was impressed at how well the artist had succeeded in flawlessly and effectively weaving together scripture and history. I realized yet again how powerfully the mythic depths of scripture can speak. Encountering this piece of sculpture has ever since been a major influence on my reading of scripture, and my efforts to reflect on its endless meanings.

# PART THREE

# To Be a Pilgrim

The Church of the Beatitudes, near Capernaum. This is the door out of which the stern nun emerged to hush the singers in one of the stories in this chapter.

# CHAPTER SIX

# Holy Lands

*T*o *be a pilgrim in the Middle East is to discover that while one cannot be in two places at one time, one can be in two times—the present and the past—at one place. To look down the length of the Lake of Galilee, to go deep into the foundations of the Church of the Holy Sepulchre, to stand outside the entrance of the great crusader church of St. Anne and, from where you are standing, to see not only a fourth-century Byzantine mosaic floor but a much more ancient Canaanite shrine, is to walk in a multilayered world and to tread corridors of time. To walk the streets of Jerusalem is to feel the vibrant pulse of a modern society. To move through the barriers that divide two ancient peoples is to feel the complexity and tragedy of history, its seemingly intractable alienations, divisions, and occupations.*

*I had the opportunity—the privilege, really—to have these experiences on a number of occasions, first as a pilgrim myself, and then as a guide to others, often attached as visiting student, teacher, or scholar to St. George's College, an Anglican community of education, hospitality, pilgrimage, and reconciliation in Jerusalem.*

## 1. MARY

### Kidron Valley, Jerusalem

I have been on many pilgrimages to Jerusalem over several decades. As often as possible, I visit the Church of the Sepulchre of Saint Mary, at the foot of the Mount of Olives. The upper church built by the Byzantines has long gone. In its place are the remains of the Crusader shrine. We move down steps that are wide and shallow. They begin in the blazing sun and deposit us in candlelit gloom.

Around us in the earth lies the dust of Crusader queens. A little further down we stand in the older walls of Byzantium as we approach the tomb itself. Centuries ago, the Crusaders placed a band of script that is now all but worn away:

> This is the Vale of Jehoshaphat,
> Where begins the roadway to the stars.
> Mary, favoured of God, was buried here,
> And incorruptible was raised to the skies.
> Hope of captives,
> Their path, their light, their Mother.

To grow up in the Ireland of my childhood was to be surrounded by a world of folk Catholicism. Nowhere was the difference between Roman Catholics and members of the Church of Ireland felt more strongly than in the place occupied in people's lives by the person of Mary, mother of our Lord.

As a Church of Ireland child, I was taught that because our Lord's mother is named in the Creeds I was to give her much respect for her role in the great story of Christian faith. As a choirboy in our parish church, I became aware of her feast days in the Book of Common Prayer: Nativity, Annunciation, Purification. But I was also taught to give precedence to our Lord and always to pray to him rather than to her.

Nevertheless, Mary was everywhere in my childhood and student world. The image of the Blessed Virgin Mary was in every Irish Roman Catholic home. Her statues stood outside every Roman Catholic church, and in small shrines along country roads. Much of the prayer life of the church was directed to her. Retreats and novenas were frequent. The spiritual practice of reciting the Rosary centered on Mary. Particularly in times of pastoral need, sickness, and death, it was to our Lord's mother that most public prayer was directed. She bore many names: Our Lady of Perpetual Succour, Our Lady of Lourdes, Our Lady of Sorrows, Stella Maris or Star of the Sea, Queen of Heaven. All these things helped to make Mary ubiquitous in my world growing up.

From early years, I became aware of the infinite variety of this woman who exists in the memories and imaginations of Christian believers on more than one level. She lived in a small village. She was the mother of Jesus. That was the human reality. But then there are those other layers of reality in which she becomes mysterious and majestic and timeless. As a student in Dublin, I witnessed the vast crowds that gathered in 1950 to celebrate the Pope's declaration of Mary's Bodily Assumption to Heaven. From time to time would come news of her appearance to contemporary men, women, and children: phenomena that have resulted in huge shrines that attract vast numbers of pilgrims.

As an adult, I came to realize that there is a paradox about Mary. It is as if the very limited scriptural references to her have had the opposite effect to what might be expected. The very slenderness of the biblical material seems to haunt and tantalize us century after century, encouraging more and more reflection about the myriad ways in which she speaks to various facets of our human experience. Eventually, I would come to write a book, called *Portrait of a Woman*, in which I too would seek to imagine and explore the relationship between this long-ago woman and her son, Jesus.

Much Irish poetry is deeply religious and much of it sings of Mary. When I came to learn Irish poetry in its original Gaelic, I learned by heart lines that in English translation say this:

O Mary of Grace, Mother of God's Son,

Direct me on the road towards goodness.

Save me from every evil,

Save me both in Soul and in Body.

May God of the angels be over my head;

May God stand before me; may God be with me.

Some years ago, ongoing conversations between Anglicans and Roman Catholics resulted in an extensive document entitled *Mary: Grace and Hope in Christ*. While much of its language is densely theological, some of it rises to poetry:

The scriptural witness summons all believers in every generation to call Mary "blessed": this Jewish woman of humble status, this daughter of Israel, living in hope of justice for the poor, whom God has graced and chosen to become the virgin mother of his Son through the overshadowing of the Holy Spirit. We are to bless her as the "handmaid of the Lord" who gave her unqualified assent to the fulfilment of God's saving plan, as the mother who pondered all things in her heart, as the refugee seeking asylum in a foreign land, as the mother pierced by the innocent suffering of her own child, and as the woman to whom Jesus entrusted his friends.

All these words and images and memories and reflections crowd into one's mind as one stands in the rock-cut cave at the bottom of the twelfth-century stairs, gazing on the Tomb of Mary. Other claims are made for the place of Mary's resting. A great part of Christian faith celebrates her bodily assumption from earth to heaven. One thing we do know for certain: that we possess here a tradition that not only refuses to be diminished by time, but grows even stronger with its passing. Such a tradition has at its heart Mary, the woman who is forever both Galilean girl and *theotokos*, Mother of our Lord and Queen of Heaven.

## 2. THE GARBAGE DUMP
### Kidron Valley, Jerusalem, 1970

It is late October. A long, sunny afternoon is getting on for the hour when it is time to head back to the hostel for supper. It is also the hour when the lowering sun shows the golden shadings in some of the stone walls of the old quarter of Jerusalem. I have just left the south end of the temple area, the great ruined steps that once carried crowds of pilgrims from all over the known world of that time, all of them making what was for some of them their once-in-a-lifetime pilgrimage to the temple in Jerusalem, the very heart of their Jewish faith.

Reluctantly turning away to begin the return journey, I walk toward the nearest city gate, the ancient Dung Gate, under the shadow of the city walls, then out and down along the road toward the Kidron Valley. To my left, further up the hill, the great walls continue north. I can see where the next city gate—the Eastern Gate—was blocked up centuries ago to prevent pilgrims trespassing into the temple area itself. If I look to the right, I can see the slope of the Mount of Olives. Somewhere on the lower part of that slope is my hostel. But first I have to follow the narrow road as it turns east and angles down toward a small bridge. By the time I reach the middle of the bridge, I can see up and down what is obviously a dried-up river bed.

At this moment, two very different things strike my consciousness simultaneously. First, I am aware that this is the same Kidron Brook which, ever since I was a small boy in my parish choir, I have associated with the terrible night that Jesus spent before he was taken, tried, and crucified. All these years, I have thought of this place in terms of solemn hymns and psalms, glorious but sad music, passages of scripture that tell the story of our Lord's passion. But then I become aware of something which seems utterly at odds with these reverent associations. There in the dry bed of the river, stretching away from both sides of the bridge, is a huge city garbage dump. Strewn everywhere are old automobile tires, bits of broken furniture, battered stoves and refrigerators, discarded clothes, everything you can think of in such a place.

It is as if two orchestras have begun to play two clashingly dissonant pieces of music in my ears. I am much more than surprised. I am shocked, and I am saddened. What suddenly seems a naïve illusion—the faith of boyhood years—has been shattered by a reality I find appalling. I feel somehow mocked for my naïveté. My treasured memories of the Gospel accounts of such things as the Last Supper, the trial, the condemnation, the execution of Jesus, are all being brutally challenged. Something about the scene is tempting me to dismiss them as fables for children, simplicities that have no place in the so-called real world.

Just then, at the lowest point of those feelings of hurt and disappointment, something wonderful happens. It is as if a voice speaks deep inside me and utters a single unforgettable sentence.

The voice says quietly, "But I came to you into a world of garbage." In that moment, disillusion and despair fade away. It is as if a great shadow withdraws.

Years later, I would read a French scholar, Paul Ricoeur, speaking of the necessity in our faith journey to pass from what he calls first or early naïveté to second, mature, adult naïveté. I would know exactly what he meant, and I would realize retrospectively how symbolic it was that I had been standing on a small dusty bridge when I had precisely that experience. For me, this was a crossing over from that early naïveté to a mature naïveté that has held me firm in faith to this day.

Four decades after my Kidron experience, I was commissioned to write the words for a new Christmas carol, to be set to music by my dear friend and colleague, the late Patrick Wedd. Again, I felt vividly the same beautiful paradox I had experienced on that bridge: that God, the mighty ruler of both time and space, chose to come into the world in the most unlikely of places: a rude stable, perhaps a cave, a place of shadows, comfortless and cold—a poor place, in every sense of the word (to use the phrase that became the title of our carol). In the final stanza, I tried to capture the profound truth that it is in precisely such poor places that God always chooses to come.

A poor place this, the world of these our days,
So poor in justice, poor in joy and peace;
Where children starve while every evil pays,
And empires clash in wars that never cease.
Yet still the Holy Child is brought to birth;
The grace he gives far more than we can tell.
His loving hands enfold the wounded earth,
And all is well, and all things shall be well.

# 3. THE PITY OF WAR
## Dog River Pass, Lebanon, 1970

**I have seen war memorials in many places,** but I have never been presented with so much evidence of the futility of war as when, while driving up the coast highway just north of Beirut, I saw the cliff carvings at Nahr el-Kalb. Rather than merely describing the area and its wall tablets, I think it best to share the story of the place.

In 1697 Henry Maundrell, academic of Exeter College in Oxford and priest of the Church of England, was acting as chaplain to the new Levant Company based at Aleppo, Syria. Perhaps realizing that his term as chaplain might soon end, he obtained permission to assemble a small expedition and set out on a journey south to Jerusalem. With him were fifteen companions.

As they travelled down the coast, they eventually came to the north bank of the Dog River—its Arabic name Nahr el-Kalb—where it entered the Mediterranean. An ancient bridge linked the two high, dark walls of a steep-sided gorge. As they crossed the river, Maundrell noticed that there were large stone plaques built into the walls of the gorge, accessible only by a narrow, obviously ancient path. They camped on the south bank and investigated. To do so was not without danger. Maundrell has left us a vivid record of the area:

> You have a path of about two yards wide along the side [of the cliffs] at a great height above the water, [this] being the work of the emperor Antonius. . . . In several places we saw strange antique figures of men, carved in the natural rock, and in bigness equal to the life.

What Maundrell discovered when he and his companions explored that path is perhaps the world's most sustained record of conflict between warring empires, and is today a UNESCO World Heritage site.

The earliest plaque told the travelers that an army of Ramses the Second of Egypt had passed through over 3,500 years earlier. It had come to establish Egyptian dominion over this area, and to define the northern border of Egypt's imperial territories. North of the river, the Hittite Empire stretched far away to the coasts of the Black Sea. Ramses used these great natural walls to boast of his conquests in many wars. In doing so, he set the tone for a series of *stelae*, or stone slabs, that would tell the story of war for the rest of the historical record, down to very recent times. Century after century, successive armies would march through here, pausing to order their engineers to cut into the cliffs a record of their passing, marking their ephemeral victories.

Millennia after Ramses, in the seventh century BCE, Esarhaddon, ruler of the powerful Assyrian Empire, left his mark as he passed by. In that same century, Nebuchadnezzar, monarch of the newly victorious Babylonian Empire, already the conqueror of both Assyria and Egypt, returned north through this place to his imperial capital of Babylon. He was so proud of his conquests that he installed his plaque on the north side of the river, opposite that of Ramses, to send the clear message that he had humbled the power of Egypt.

On and on the inscriptions go, each showing in its own degree of wear the ravages of time and weather. Antiochus of Egypt, general in the armies of Alexander the Great, came through, leaving a plaque celebrating victory in the Sixth Syrian War. In 215 CE, the Roman Emperor Marcus Aurelius marched by in his turn, travelling from Antioch south to Alexandria. In 1861, Napoleon the Second's regiments crossed the bridge to intervene in the Lebanese civil war, once again recording the event on the cliff face. In 1918, in their final drive to end the Ottoman Empire, British and French armies marked their triumphant passage on the walls of the pass. Yet another plaque tells us that in 1919 the British Desert Corps took Damascus, Homs, and Aleppo. In 1941, troops of the Free French, fresh from liberating Damascus from the forces of Vichy France, inscribed their victory on these ancient stones.

There are others, but these will suffice to make the point. Why tell this story? The English poet Wilfred Owen gives us a reason in four short words. In the preface to his 1920 collection of poems, he writes of what he terms "the pity of war." In a memorable verse from that volume, written after a gas attack on the Western Front, Owen quotes sarcastically the Roman poet Horace's assertion that it is "sweet and fitting to die for one's country." He speaks scathingly of those who

> . . . tell with such high zest
> To children ardent for some desperate glory,
> The old Lie: *Dulce et decorum est*
> *Pro patria mori.*

The rock reliefs of Nahr el-Kalb are mute testimony to that all too human instinct.

## 4. A PILGRIM'S QUESTION
### St. Gabriel's Church, Nazareth, 1976

From where I am standing at a pedestrian crossing, I can see that the south end of the main street in Nazareth is hectic. Cars, buses, taxis, here and there a donkey with its small cart and usually elderly driver, the obligatory tourist camel offering rides, a host of pedestrians hurrying every which way, all mingle together in barely controlled confusion.

I am with a group of Canadian pilgrims, all of whom have grown up in Christian faith and who worship in their various churches. As we wait for the light to change, a voice in my ear, struggling to be heard over the cacophony, asks the question that is probably echoing silently in all our minds, "My goodness, is this really Nazareth in Galilee?"

I know my friend realizes that this is indeed Nazareth, but I also know why he expresses puzzlement. For him, as for the rest of us, everything we are seeing and hearing clashes with every image that has ever entered our minds about Nazareth. We cross the street when it looks reasonably safe to do so, enter through a gate between high railings, and find ourselves in a quiet courtyard. We walk across the area, take two steps down to a closed door, push it partially open to see what is going on inside, then wait for a few minutes until the mid-week Eucharist ends and we can be invited in.

This is the Greek Orthodox Church of Saint Gabriel, otherwise known as the Church of the Annunciation. Very much alive today as an active parish church, it offers itself as a kind of oasis amid the roar and bustle of modern Nazareth. Only when the visitor is told of the significance of the site can he or she recognize that this quiet courtyard is a doorway that opens on a long corridor down the ages of the faith.

The church is built over a grotto containing an underground spring that fed the little village of Nazareth in ancient times, and still runs with water today. The building—erected in the eighteenth century, and the most recent of several churches on the site—hallows the spot where tradition has it the Virgin Mary was drawing water when the angel Gabriel appeared to announce to her the miraculous news that she was to give birth to the Son of God. Nearby can be found the old village well, known as Mary's Well, fed by the spring. Today, the well is enclosed by a nondescript yellow building, doubtless to preserve the spring water from contamination by countless eager pilgrims wishing to fill bottles with the water that once nurtured the boy Jesus, his mother, and their family. Most recently, it was reconstructed for Nazareth's millennium celebrations in 2000.

St. Gabriel's beauty is in its walls and, as always in this Orthodox tradition, especially in its glittering iconostasis, the wall of religious paintings that separates the sanctuary from the nave. Looking around, we see that art covers almost every inch of surface. I'm looking particularly at a magnificent fresco depicting the resurrection of Christ. In it, Jesus steps out of the darkened tomb. It frames his sunlit form. White linens used for his binding are falling away. Only when my gaze is drawn to his hands do I see something deeply moving, something I have often been told to search for in Orthodox iconography. As Christ rises, his outstretched hands grasp the hands of two smaller figures. As he lifts them from their tombs, Adam and Eve, father and mother of humanity, gaze at Jesus in gratitude and wonder.

There is something immensely thrilling about seeing these images. Their message is clear and insistent. Human nature is transformed by being grasped and taken up into the divine nature. Not only, are we being told, did God in Jesus come down to us. We are also being told that in everything he did, by his embracing of our human nature and by sharing our experience of life to the full—even to the death—Jesus lifted that human nature to its highest level.

Over the years I have been taught this, but the images on the walls of St. Gabriel's in Nazareth bring it home in a deeper way than I have ever experienced before. I realize that if what I am seeing in this image of the rising Christ is true, his hands lifting Adam and Eve are also lifting me and the whole of humanity from darkness to light, from death to life. There is a magnificent prayer that expresses these truths:

> O God, who wonderfully created, and yet more wonderfully restored, the dignity of human nature: Grant that we may share the divine life of him who humbled himself to share our humanity, your Son Jesus Christ; who lives and reigns with you, in the unity of the Holy Spirit, one God, for ever and ever.

We eventually leave St. Gabriel's, but not before we have been warmly welcomed by its priest. We have many questions for him, and he in turn wishes to ask us a few questions about Canada, because he has family members who have emigrated there. By directing our minds back homewards in space, he also succeeds in returning us firmly in time to the present. He helps us to realign our images of Nazareth from ancient to contemporary.

## 5. THE LAKE

### Galilee, 1983

Her name was Egeria. She must have been an extraordinarily courageous, even audacious person. In the last quarter of the fourth century, she went on pilgrimage to the Holy Land—alone, to the best of our knowledge—and wrote to her friends and spiritual companions back home an account that has lasted across all the centuries between her lifetime and ours. Sometime in the year 381 CE, she would have found herself in Galilee, walking in the vicinity of the northwest corner of the lake.

Today, if you drive north from Tiberias along that same but now very different road, there comes a point when it gradually turns eastward along the lake. On your right are the properties of the Franciscans and the Benedictines, both running down to the shoreline. On your left, a hillside slopes up from the road; at its summit is the very graceful Church of the Beatitudes. Near that church there is a cave. Long tradition says this is where Jesus gave the instruction ever since known as the Sermon on the Mount. It is not the first church to mark this spot. When Egeria came here some sixteen hundred years before I did, she visited the Church of the Loaves and Fishes, and wrote that "near there on a mountain is the cave to which the Savior climbed and spoke the Beatitudes."

Today, if you stand on the summit of the hill, you can see a winding path work its way down toward a small surfaced area where groups pause to look out over the lake, sometimes to listen to a short devotional reflection. I stood there one cold, bright midmorning in March of 1983. From here, one can see the full length of the lake, a distance of about twenty kilometers. One can also discern its shape, and I think this is the reason why I found myself being given a gift, one that I tried to communicate spontaneously to the group of clergy folk I was accompanying from the College in Jerusalem.

The lake has had several names throughout history: the Lake (or Sea) of Galilee, the Lake (or Sea) of Tiberias, the Sea of Minya, Lake Gennesaret (or Ginosar), Lake Kinneret (or Kinnereth, or Chinnereth). These last five names are all variants derived from the Hebrew word "kinnor," meaning a harp or a lyre. And indeed, when you look south from this hill that is what you see: the shape of a harp, wider at this northern end, narrowing as you follow the coast south. Perhaps it was because of this that I felt as if the lake was, as it were, singing to me, communicating levels of meaning about itself that had never occurred to me before. These thoughts I tried to communicate as they came to me. Sometimes I would hesitate to form a thought or grope to express an image, but if anything, the spontaneity of the moment seemed to help, rather than hinder, my efforts.

There came to me the image of the lake as a great deep womb, from the waters of which had come the faith we all shared in that small group, and that was shared by untold millions across the planet. The idea of Christian faith's birthing in this lake came from the fact that so much of the Gospel story is linked with this coastline and these waters.

That image faded and another took its place. I saw the lake as a great font in which every one of us, and indeed all Christians, had been baptized. When I said that, one member of the group suggested that we might there and then reaffirm our baptismal vows in some form, which we did. Naturally there was a short silence shared before we moved on down the hillside towards the Benedictine Church at Tabgha, and thence onward to Capernaum—walking all the while in Egeria's footsteps.

For me, that fleeting time above the lake has remained a vivid memory. Never again would the words "Sea of Galilee" be merely a geographical term. In that short interlude, the lake had become for me—and I think for some others—a "thin place," where worlds intersected and a presence made itself felt. To this day, as from time to time I read a Gospel passage linked with the lake, again and again that harp-shaped body of water comes to take me back to the view from that morning hillside where once it sang to me.

# 6. ALLELUIA!
## Bethlehem, March 1984

As I now remember her, I would say that Noor was in her early sixties. She was a grandmother, one of three members of a family who were on the support staff of the college. Her responsibility was the college laundry. For this she had resources. The laundry room was equipped with two state-of-the-art machines, as well as an ironing board and irons for such things as the altar linens for the chapel.

Because Noor spoke little English, communicating with her was necessarily limited for many of us visiting students or members of the academic staff. However, we found our own ways of expressing appreciation for her work, which was always meticulously carried out. Noor smiled a lot and, like many Palestinian folk, she smoked a lot. Because Jerusalem stands at a high altitude, winter can be very cold. Skies can be grey. Light snow can fall. At some stage in the winter of 1993, Noor became ill. A cough that began mildly turned incessant. Through the weeks of January, she had been absent from time to time. By late February, she had ceased to come to work at all. Word came that she was ill, but looked forward to resuming her duties. More time passed, until eventually word came that Noor had died.

Sometimes, when somebody dies, we realize that there are many things we don't know about them. For instance, many of us did not know that Noor's home was in Bethlehem, south of Jerusalem. Nor did we know that she had been a faithful parishioner of the town's Syrian Orthodox church.

When a date for Noor's funeral was announced, it was decided that the permanent members of the college staff, along with three of us visiting lecturers, would attend. We would drive through the Occupied West Bank in the college van, and we would wear our black cassocks as a mark of respect.

When we arrived at the house where Noor had lived with her daughter's family, it was already crowded, particularly in the large front room where Noor's body lay in its small open coffin. We were greeted warmly and offered simple hospitality: a mug of tea, a small sweet cake. We found places along the back wall, where we could remain discreetly out of the way, for in no way did we wish to intrude.

Time went by as family and friends chatted. Those closest to the coffin, including some obviously elderly contemporaries of Noor, expressed their sorrow quietly. After about half an hour or so, the low buzz of conversation dwindled into silence. One by one, Noor's immediate family members reached into the small coffin to briefly touch her folded hands. Then, again, the room fell still.

At this point, something took place that was so sudden and unexpected that I have never forgotten it. It happened very quickly, which only served to add to its power. The door to the crowded room suddenly flew open. Six young men of the family strode in. One went over to where the lid of Noor's coffin was leaning against the wall of the room. Two others laid it over her body and proceeded to fasten it down securely. Then all six took up their positions, three on each side of the coffin. Pausing for a moment to gather themselves, at a silent shared signal they straightened as one and lifted the coffin.

All this was familiar to us as Western clergy, especially those of us with experience of rural ministry. But none of us anticipated what would happen next. With a loud shout of "Alleluia!" the six young men proceeded to throw the coffin aloft toward the ceiling, catching it again as it came down. Three times they did this, each time heaving the coffin on high, each time catching it again, each time giving their shout of "Alleluia!" As they caught the coffin for the third time, one of them signaled that the door of the room should be opened, and with continuing shouts of "Alleluia!" spreading amongst the crowd, all poured out into the street to witness Noor's coffin being placed inside a waiting hearse. As the hearse slowly moved away, a procession formed and we from the college joined it.

The Eucharist with its rich, sonorous Eastern liturgy was solemn and beautiful, but what has always remained in my memory is Noor's small soaring coffin rising triumphantly into the air before returning to be cradled in the arms of those who loved her.

## 7. AN EVER-CHANGING TEXT
### Qumran, 1990

It was at Qumran that I realized something about translating the scriptures. We had driven down from Jerusalem and arrived at the ruins before dawn. We waited for the sun to rise out of the desert, shimmering on the utterly still surface of the Dead Sea: an indelible memory in itself.

The Essenes, a reform monastic movement, came here from throughout Judea to try to create an ideal society in what they saw as a dark age for Israel. They were a highly disciplined community, one of whose main activities was to study and copy the sacred scrolls. You can still see the scriptorium rooms where they did their work, and in the Shrine of the Book in Jerusalem you can see their massive scroll of the book of Isaiah.

After we had left the site and were heading further south to Masada, I found myself thinking of those times in history when people felt called to delve into the scriptures, seeking meaning from them for their time. Qumran and the Essene community were one example. (By the way, that community was working on the scrolls at the same time as a young rabbi in Galilee was calling his disciples.) There have been many other such times. Following the collapse of the Western Roman Empire in the fifth century CE, monastic communities of Celtic monks in the islands of the north Atlantic spent countless hours creating some of the most beautifully illustrated scrolls we possess. In the early years of the seventeenth century, at a time of deep religious tensions, the monumental translation of the Bible known as the King James or Authorized Version was produced in England.

In the mid-twentieth century, there began a flood of Bible translation that still continues in our day. In 1949, in my early months at Trinity College Dublin, there was great excitement about the publication of a new translation in contemporary English of the Epistles of the New Testament. The author was a Church of England priest named J. B. Phillips. The title he gave his translation was *Letters to Young Churches*.

At the time, many felt that this new translation fell far short of the magnificent language of the Authorized Version. An acknowledged authority of the time, C. S. Lewis, surprised many by his stance.

> We must sometimes get away from the Authorized Version, if for no other reason, simply because it is so beautiful and so solemn. Beauty exalts but beauty also lulls. . . . Through that beautiful solemnity the transporting or horrifying realities of which the book tells may come to us blunted and disarmed and we may only sigh with tranquil veneration when we ought to be burning with shame or struck dumb with terror.

Lewis was by no means dismissing the Authorized Version. He was applying criteria for the use of scripture other than that of language, however beautiful.

One evening, at a meeting of the Theological Society of the University, one of the faculty pointed us to something I recall very clearly. He began by reading us a few sentences of Phillips's own comments on his work:

> I began the translation in 1941 for my youth club and members of my congregation in much-bombed south-east London. . . . I felt that much of the New Testament was written to Christians in danger, and we for many months had lived in a different but no less real danger. I began with the Epistles. . . . I wanted above all to convey the vitality and radiant faith as well as the courage of the early church.

To illustrate the point, we listened to a passage from Paul's letter to the Christian community in Rome, first in the King James Version:

> For I reckon that the sufferings of this present time are not worthy to be compared with the glory which shall be revealed in us. . . . For the creature was made subject to vanity, not willingly, but by reason of him who hath subjected the same in hope, because the creature itself also shall be delivered from the bondage of corruption. (Rom. 8:18–21)

Then we heard J.B. Phillips's translation of that same passage.

First, imagine yourself back in 1941 London. Many parts of the city lie in ruins. Every night, more are killed by heavy bombing. Your vicar is reading his new translation of a letter to a long-ago Christian community in Rome, living in dangerous and unpredictable times. He is reading it to a group of young Christians in a time that is once again dangerous and unpredictable:

> In my opinion, whatever we may have to go through now is less than nothing compared with the magnificent future God has planned for

us. . . . The world of creation cannot as yet see reality . . . yet it has been given hope. And the hope is that in the end the whole of created life will be rescued from the tyranny of change and decay.

Thirty years have gone by since I stood looking down into the ruined foundations of Qumran, imagining the rooms they once supported, as if waiting for the return of those who lived there, seeking ever-new insights from the ancient scrolls. What I realized that day was that the work of those long-gone Essenes has, in fact, never ceased. In modern laboratories, minuscule scraps of ancient papyrus are probed by powerful lenses, sometimes to gain new meaning from a single word. In libraries and studies, present-day scholars continue to wrestle with language, seeking new ways to express eternal truths.

The small Essene community who first gathered these scattered stones and built these broken walls would delight in the knowledge that their quest for understanding continues. They would lift their voices in praise and thanksgiving, that Quamran lives.

## 8. THE SONG AND THE SINGERS

### Galilee, 1993

The name of the village was Kfar Nahum, the village of Nahum. It stood very near the northern shore of the lake. The majority of its people depended on the lake for their livelihood, many of them as fisher folk.

The role of Kfar Nahum in the long story of Christian faith begins when a young man from the nearby town of Nazareth, freshly returned from his journey from the southern reaches of the Jordan, arrives to find lodging in the village. After he has acclimatized himself and has got to know some people in the village, he will begin to walk the beach where young men like himself come in to the quayside with their catch. One day, he will approach two of them and they will begin to chat, perhaps about the state of fishing on the lake, perhaps more circumspectly about the Roman occupation of their country, perhaps about many other things.

Because of these conversations, a relationship will begin to form. One day, some of these young fishermen and their womenfolk will look back on those conversations and realize that their newfound friend from Nazareth had been drawing their lives irrevocably into his. In such ways does Kfar Nahum become the birthplace for a fellowship that would grow into nothing less than the worldwide faith of Christianity.

Many centuries later, but in the fellowship of that same faith, a group of us, all clergy, found ourselves walking in the ruins of what today is called Capernaum. It was not the first time I had been there, nor would it be the last, but because of an incident that took place that morning, it would be the most memorable.

About thirty years ago, a large modern sanctuary was built in the ruins of Capernaum. Many feel it sits uneasily and intrusively among the foundations of the village, but there it stands. On this particular morning, our group was walking slowly in the vicinity of this building, conscious of how it looms over, even dominates, the remains of the village. As I recall, it was a beautiful morning and there were a number of other groups moving around the area, many of them listening to their guides telling them about the history of the village, its place in scripture, and so on.

Suddenly we became aware of voices lifted in song. So striking and captivating was the sound, so beautiful the melodies, so rich the harmonies, that gradually all other voices fell silent. Many began to look around for the source; some began to move toward it. By chance, it came from a spot quite near us, and when the group came into view we could see that it was composed of about fifteen men in United Nations uniforms. They were Fijians, part of a police contingent enjoying a few days' leave in the Holy Land. This we learned from our own guide who made enquiries after the singing was over. However, what was most interesting was the choice these men had made. Because, their leader explained, they did not feel entirely at home in any of the languages spoken by the eclectically polyglot guides, they decided to express their gratitude by singing the wonderfully tuneful gospel hymns of their tradition in all the sites they visited.

The sequel followed just before noon that same morning. Our group was standing near the Church of the Beatitudes, built on the crest of the hillside above the lake. Once again, there were various groups with their guides; once again, we heard the Fijian voices breaking into song. Looking around, we saw that they had chosen the shelter of a large tree a considerable distance from the open church door. I mention this because of what happened next.

They had sung no more than part of a hymn when a small, elderly nun appeared from the church porch. She paused, looked around to see where the sound was coming from, then set out toward the group as quickly as she could walk. I recall how the headpiece of her robes billowed behind her in the slight breeze on the hilltop. Before she had even reached the group, she began to wave her hand in brusque dismissal. There was not the slightest element of welcome, nor the slightest effort to engage them in anything approaching an understanding or empathetic way, and most certainly there was no appreciation for the magnificence of their singing. Within the church it was time for the noon mass, and nothing, not even an obviously genuine expression of deep faith, could be allowed to impinge on that observance.

The wonderful singing ceased abruptly and the group moved on. The elderly sister stood some distance from them as if to make sure of their departure. Not one word of greeting or parting was exchanged. As a priest of the church, I found myself cringing at the encounter. Ever since, I have recalled it as an example of the mistrust, even rejection, that the institutional church can sometimes show to genuine folk religion. However, what remains most memorable for me, and always will, is the singing.

Looking back, I think I know someone who would have understood, someone who would not have silenced the song but might even have joined in its harmony. I don't know his name. I know him only as "the psalmist." Many centuries have passed since he wrote, and perhaps even sang, his own newly written song:

Come, let us sing to the Lord; let us shout for joy to the rock of our
salvation. Let us come before his presence with thanksgiving, and
raise a loud shout to him. For the Lord is a great God . . . (Book
of Occasional Services)

I think he would have welcomed both the singers and their song.

## 9. CALVARY
### Jerusalem, April 1993

We had come to Jerusalem in January, knowing that we would
be there for almost four months, an academic term in the life of St.
George's College. My responsibility was to travel around the area
with groups of clergy from many places in the Anglican communion,
linking various places with the Gospel passages where they are mentioned, and suggesting ways in which their preaching might feature
these places.

You can perhaps appreciate how and why I treasure those few
fleeting months in my life. However, as with everything in life, the
time came for it to end. It was a Sunday afternoon; all our things were
packed, ready for an early departure the next morning. We had some
free time before the evening meal. How would we spend our last few
hours in this ancient city?

The decision was not difficult. We walked from the college down
the Nablus Road to the Damascus Gate. Entering the Old City, we
found ourselves in the labyrinthine network of streets that forms the
*souq*, or market until we suddenly turned into the open area that fronts
the entrance to the huge Church of the Holy Sepulchre. We stood for
a moment at the slab of stone where long tradition says that Joseph of
Arimathea and others anointed the body of Jesus for burial. Then we
climbed a flight of stone steps to the place where we wished to spend
our last afternoon in Jerusalem.

I had been in this place many times with clergy from the college.
It had come to captivate my wife, Paula, and me more than any other

place in our travels around the Holy Land. To explain why, I need to share with you something of the long story of this place, and to describe our surroundings.

Long before the towers of Canterbury stood above the fields of Kent, long before the Dome of the Vatican dominated the cityscape of Rome, the Church of the Holy Sepulchre stood here as witness to the imperial instincts of Constantine and the piety of his mother, Helena. In the fourth century, she had come with all the authority of her position and title to seek for the sites of the death and resurrection of Jesus. What she encountered was the local Christian community. They had preserved the memory of where the Lord had been crucified, and the location of the tomb from which he had been raised.

Actually, there had been an earlier visitor on the same quest. In the year 160 CE, a bishop named Melito had come from the city of Sardis to verify the places in the Gospels. He too had been led by the local Christians. Two centuries later, when Helena in her turn was shown the venues sacred to Christian memory, she brought to bear the vast resources of her son's empire to build this massive shrine over them. Ever since, this huge church has been an irresistible magnet of memory and pilgrimage for most of the Christian world.

We climb the flight of stone steps and find ourselves in a small, highly ornate, dimly lit chapel. The focus is the altar. Here, day after day, year after year, pilgrims come from far and near. On one wall of the chapel, there is a stone ledge that can serve as a seat. So we sit and observe people doing the same simple actions that we ourselves have done in this place. We watch as people drop to one knee, making the sign of the cross. We watch as a mother lifts a child to kiss the icon near the altar and then kisses it in turn herself. We watch as pilgrim after pilgrim kneels on the floor before the altar, then moves forward underneath it and extends an arm down through a small opening to touch a rock beneath.

No ordinary rock, this is the top of an outcrop that rises from the floor of the stone quarry that lies far beneath this great basilica. Into its surface, the upright of our Lord's cross was embedded. Here the crosspiece that he had carried from the nearby city gate was fastened. Here our Lord died.

This is where we wish to be on our last day in Jerusalem. When the last pilgrim of the day has passed through, we stand and move to the altar to do again what we wish to retain as a lifelong memory. Taking turns, we kneel on the floor, stoop under the altar, lean forward, and extend an arm into the small opening until we can feel the hard surface of the rock.

So much pours into the mind at such a moment that words cannot do justice to the experience. We get up, turn, cross the chapel to the stone steps, and leave. Yet there is a sense in which we have never left this holiest of places.

The author blessing the cup in the tiny twelfth-century St. Oran's Chapel, the oldest building on Iona.

# CHAPTER SEVEN

# Celtic Lands

*I*n *my childhood and student years, the new Irish Republic set out to make us the first generation clearly aware of our country's long history. From mythic early invasions, through millennia of Druidic spirituality, to the coming of Christianity and repeated invasion by Norsemen, Normans, and English, we were told the proud story of our country.*

*Only in later life did I realize that at no time did that education include actual encounters with the tangible evidence of that great heritage. The simple reasons for this were the very limited resources of the new country and the absence of all but local travel in the lives of most people. Until I returned to Ireland with pilgrim groups decades later, I had not stood under the looming grandeur of a High Cross, nor paused at the dark entrance to the great megalithic tombs of the Boyne Valley, nor stared across the grey chop of the Atlantic to Skellig Michael rising from the ocean.*

*When I did come to more fully experience this rich history, I also began to more deeply appreciate the immensely significant role Ireland played in the formation and rebuilding of Europe, particularly in the period between the fall of the Western Roman Empire and the emergence of the early Middle Ages.*

## 1. THE VALLEY OF TWO LAKES
### Glendalough, County Wicklow, Ireland, 1998

The hills around the valley are steep and heavily wooded. For about thirteen hundred years, this has been a place of Christian pilgrimage, ever since Kevin, a sixth-century monk, walked over the pass in the

Wicklow Mountains and found himself beside the larger of the two lakes that give the valley its name.

On the high ground above the upper lake Kevin built his hut, gradually gathering around him those who wished to be in the company of a holy person. Some stayed, joining the community in its life of manual labor, farming, prayer, worship. At some point, the community moved down the valley to the smaller, lower lake.

Eventually there developed what became known as a monastic city, cradled by the two arms of a small river. Protected also by its surrounding earthworks, at its center a place of worship, the community grew and diversified, an island of civil society in a surrounding violent world. Almost all building was of wood. With the passing of centuries, a few communal buildings would be rebuilt in stone. In the turbulent ninth century, a round tower would soar above the area to provide advance warning of the coming of Norse marauders and to offer some element of refuge.

Even today in an age of unrelenting change, little has changed here. The valley has been designated a national park. The monastic city itself has become a vast graveyard, used by local people for over a thousand years. A small cluster of houses stands nearby, among them a family hotel and behind it, an education center for visitors.

My destination on this walk is not toward the lakes but eastward along the southern slope of the valley. On my right is the steep slope of the Derrybawn (White Oaks) Mountain, on my left the slope of the valley falling away toward the river. After about twenty minutes, I climb a low stone wall and move down among the trees. It is silent here, no breeze stirring. I pass out of the trees toward another low wall, and there within its stone enclosure is the ruin of Saint Saviour's Church. Just beyond it, I can hear the low murmur of the river.

Saint Saviour's was built here six hundred years after Kevin founded his community. There is a certain sadness about the reason it was built. A reforming abbot named Laurence O'Toole decided to bring in one of the new monastic orders flourishing in England and on the Continent: Augustinian Fathers from Canterbury. O'Toole hoped that their sterner monastic discipline would renew the life of an Irish church he saw as tired and depleted from age and isolation.

For me, this is a place of particular peace and beauty. There is the presence of time: untold millennia in the natural surroundings, at least eight hundred years in these low walls that now hold little more than rain pools and tufts of grass. I sit on a low stone bench that juts out of the wall.

I have always known something of the story of Irish Celtic Christianity. Growing up in this country made sure of that. I knew the stories of the spiritual giants: Patrick, Brigid, Columba, Kevin. While I never dismissed them, I realize now that I took them for granted. I had to go away before I could return to meet them again.

Something extraordinary has happened since I left Ireland in 1954. The spirit of community life in this valley during those later years of Kevin's lifetime excites and intrigues Irish Christians today in a way that the tradition of the continental reformers who built Saint Saviour's never has, even though it is their form of institutional Catholicism that has dominated Irish religious life down to my own lifetime.

I glance over at the archway that once held the door to the refectory where those twelfth-century Augustinians ate their meals. I can so easily imagine their contemptuous dismissal of the Irish Church foundations further up the valley. Yet those Augustinians are largely forgotten, while the memory of Kevin and his companions lives on and beckons to Christians today. I find myself asking what it was about the simplicities—even crudities—of those sixth-century Christians that speaks so eloquently in my lifetime.

Many today feel that a certain simplicity of Christian faith and practice ended with the passing of the Celtic Way. I use the word "way" rather than the term "church," because it is quite wrong to think of Christians such as Kevin and Patrick and Brigid and Columba as in any way perceiving themselves to belong to any church other than the One Holy, Catholic, and Apostolic Church. They might have resented it at times, criticized it, railed against it, but they would have always seen themselves as of it and within it.

Between the time Kevin walked into this valley in the sixth century and the time Laurence came to guide the community more than half a millennium later, much had happened in the great outside world. Belief that had been held with simple joy and passion had become a system of intellect and sophistication. Sitting here today in Saint Saviour's, looking back a thousand years to Laurence and his world, I am of a church and a time that has become weary and mistrustful of sophistication and intellect in matters of faith, longing again for simplicity, for what Paul Ricoeur called "second naïveté."

The clouds are coming in over the valley from the west and I must leave. I stand for a moment, facing the ruins of the sanctuary. I try to imagine being among the canons as they celebrated mass, full of good intentions for the edification and improvement of what they saw as their dreamy, lazy Irish brethren in their shabby monastic city further up the valley, not to mention their brazen women who had scant respect for foreign cowls and accents. These men must have been confident that they embodied the future. They would never know that it would be those whom they dismissed who would speak to a faraway future world hungrier for the things of the spirit and imagination than for the things of the intellect and reason.

I climb the low wall and step back into the shadowed world of the trees. The first drops of an evening shower begin to fall.

## 2. A SPIRITUAL GIANT

### Iona, off the Coast of Mull, Scotland, 1997–2013

**The journey to Iona happens in stages.** First there is the train or bus or car from Glasgow to Oban on the west coast of the mainland, then the ferry from Oban to Craignure on the east side of the Isle of Mull. The road across Mull is winding and narrow—basically a single lane. There are frequent lay-bys to allow oncoming traffic to pass. After about an hour's drive westward, there is a last slope up to the brow of a hill, and there on one's left is the tiny village of Fionnphort, clinging to the rocky shoreline. Ahead across the narrow sound lies the long low outline of the island, the village along the shoreline, the abbey beyond. A brief wait for the ferry, a fifteen-minute crossing, and you walk up the steep concrete wharf. At last, you have arrived at Iona. Why the anticipation of returning? Because it is lovely and peaceful and quiet, at least in the face it presents to the visitor? Perhaps, but that's not all. There is more; there is a palpable sense of permanence, of endurance. After fifteen hundred years of peace and of turmoil, times of being under fierce attack, in spite of the world changing all around it, in spite of day trippers coming and going on the ferry—in spite of everything, Iona has remained a place of Christian pilgrimage.

People living on Iona—about two hundred of them in all—come and go with their varied lives, whether it's running one of the island's few shops, driving the single taxi, operating the boat service, or staffing the two small, friendly hotels. Visitors disembark from the ferry. Some sightsee before lunching in one of the modest restaurants available near the dock. Others explore the Abbey and its gift shop, now run by Heritage Scotland, or the bookstore that sells the publications of the Iona Community.

All this quotidian activity proceeds perfectly normally, but you have a peculiar sense that there is something more going on here. One aspect of that "more" is that for fifteen centuries people have come here to pray, to worship, and to work together, to seek the foundations of their faith in Jesus Christ, or—as it is with all of us sometimes—to search for faith itself.

The heart of the island's life is the abbey and its residential buildings, which house the programs of the community, attended by young people from many countries, and focused around peacemaking, social justice, and environmental concerns. The abbey itself is the worship center of life for anyone—community member, local resident, casual visitor, or pilgrim—who happens to be on the island at any given time. In the various times I was privileged to worship in the abbey, I was struck by the way in which the language mingled both beauty and simplicity, and was deeply grounded in the realities of daily life.

One prayer in particular has stayed in my mind. It is said very often in the abbey's worship life. It's a response of the congregation, a promise made to God, using words which scripture tells us were first spoken by King David—blunt, plain, challenging: "We will not offer to God offerings that cost us nothing."

Scattered throughout the worship of the Abbey are blessings that are, as I say, beautiful yet simple. This effect is achieved by the use of vivid images:

> May God's goodness be yours,
> and well, and seven times well, may you spend your lives:
> may you be an isle in the sea,
> may you be a hill on the shore,
> may you be a star in the darkness,
> may you be a staff to the weak;
> may the love Christ Jesus gave fill every heart for you;
> may the love Christ Jesus gave fill you for every one.

The memory of a spiritual giant pervades this island. Columba and his companions came here from Ireland in 563 CE, exposing themselves to the unimaginable risks of their watery journey into the unknown. Here on this three-mile-long island they founded their community. Columba was an immensely versatile man: natural leader, diplomat, peacemaker, poet, pastoral caregiver, wise administrator. So successful did the pattern of life on Iona become that other communities began to replicate it, both in northern Scotland and back in Ireland.

The story is told that when the boat carrying Columba and his monks landed at the south end of the island, their leader leaped out and began to walk up the sloping shingle beach. One of his young followers, probably exhausted from the endless hours of rowing across what is still today one of the most dangerous tidal channels of the North Atlantic, called out to his leader, "But father, the island is so small!" Columba, so the story goes, turned and called back, "My son, it is indeed small, but it will be great."

There is a blessing attributed to Columba that has come down through the centuries. I have often used it in public worship or at a conference or seminar. It never fails to move those who hear it. Whenever we would prepare to leave the island after a pilgrimage, we would gather at the ferry dock, all of us weighed down with our baggage. Putting down what we could, we would join hands, and I would share Columba's blessing as Iona's parting gift.

> Deep peace of the running wave to you.
>
> Deep peace of the flowing air to you.
>
> Deep peace of the quiet earth to you.
>
> Deep peace of the shining stars to you.
>
> Deep peace of the Son of Peace to you.

## 3. THE VISIONARY

### Lindisfarne, off the Coast of Northumberland, England, 1997–2013

If you journey to the Holy Island of Lindisfarne, you must hope that the tide will allow you to cross over before nightfall. So it has been for everyone before you for more than a thousand years of pilgrimage.

Today the heart of the island is the small, picturesque village. Most of the shops respond to the varying needs of visitors: pilgrims who flock here from all over the world, locals from nearby towns and cities who crave a few hours of simplicity and quietness, tourists who show up out of simple curiosity. The population of the island lives by the rhythms of the tides. I recall watching a young mother with her child in his car seat. She stopped at the main interesection in the village, ran to consult a tide table posted on a nearby telegraph pole, jumped back in her car, and set off for the causeway to the mainland, which she now knew would be open.

All around the village are signs of a long history: the parish church with its Saxon and Norman elements, the ruins of the medieval priory, the heritage center telling the story of the eighth-century illuminated manuscript known as the Lindisfarne Gospels, and, in the center of everything, the tall, more-than-life-size statue of Aidan, the founder and first bishop, from whose ministry the island would achieve its lasting fame.

Aidan came here in the year 635 at the invitation of a king. The decisions and actions they took together play a large part in the formation of what is today the Church of England. At the time, the Kingdom of Northumbria was in danger of becoming deeply divided. Two different cultures—one Celtic and older, the other Anglo-Saxon and newly arrived—were demanding that people choose their loyalties. King Oswald took a decision. In his boyhood, he had been sent to Iona to be educated, so he favored the older Celtic tradition. He wrote to Iona and requested a teacher.

The small group of Celtic monks who made the long, dangerous journey east was led by Aidan. When they arrived safely at Oswald's fortress castle of Bamburgh, the king could not do enough for his guests. He extended to Aidan every resource he could possibly need, even offering him living space in the castle, should he wish it. Legend has it that while Oswald was speaking, Aidan looked out from the castle battlements. A small, narrow island to the northeast caught his eye. He could see that it would be cut off daily by the deep tides. "There," he indicated to Oswald. "I would like that island."

And so began one of the great and beautiful chapters in our Christian story. Over the next sixteen years, Aidan would become a powerful, but gentle and beloved, figure known far and wide over the Kingdom of Northumbria. A brilliant teacher, yet utterly unassuming and approachable, walking almost everywhere; his name is recalled with affection to this day. Lindisfarne would become a powerful force in the development of the faith.

Throughout Aidan's ministry on and off the island, tensions grew between the older Celtic tradition centered in Iona and the newer Anglo-Saxon way coming from the south. Aidan, well aware of this, proved to be an extraordinary visionary—one with the courage to act on his vision. Even though he himself had been formed in the old Celtic way, Aidan could see that the future lay with the Anglo-Saxon understanding of Christianity. He devised a far-sighted plan: he would seek out a new generation of Anglo-Saxon Christians and form them to be the leaders of the future. And he would do even more: he would seek out both young men and young women—a truly radical departure in the world of that time.

All this Aidan did, and the names of his students still resound in Anglican history. To name only three: Chad would become bishop of Lichfield in the Midlands, his brother Cedd would form the East Saxon church, and Hilda, a niece of the royal family, would become the brilliant abbess of the large double monastery of Streoneshalh near Whitby, a mingled community of men and women.

Why do I tell this story? Partly because of my grateful memories of several opportunities to visit Lindisfarne, but also partly because I suspect there are questions Aidan might wish to ask us today, questions about our own commitments to the future, and about the efforts we are prepared to make to attract a future generation and form them in Christian faith. Aidan would easily recognize the issues we struggle with. After all, he grappled with them in his own time and in so doing, made a massive contribution to the future Church.

## 4. A LONGING FOR SOLITUDE
### Inner Farne Island, North Sea, 2001

On one of our pilgrimages to Northumbria and Lindisfarne, it was suggested that we might take our group to the Farne islands off the North Sea coast. We were told that the area was one of the largest bird sanctuaries in Europe. For us, however, there was another reason to visit, so driving south to the town of Seahouses, we rented two large powered craft and set out for one of the islands, Inner Farne.

The moment we stepped onto the small stone wharf, we were surrounded by innumerable Arctic terns. The birds seemed to have no fear of people. Our visit was happening during their nesting season, and they fiercely protected their nests hidden in the carpet of green growth covering much of the island. Through this growth, wooden boardwalks have been carefully constructed. Notices remind visitors to remain on the boardwalk as they pass through the area. The adult birds ceaselessly flew about our heads, sometimes even pecking at caps and hats.

Not being a birdwatcher, I had come for a quite different reason. Here to Inner Farne, in the last quarter of the seventh century, there came one of the great figures of early English Christianity. His name was Cuthbert. He lived here for two separate periods.

We know a great deal about Cuthbert because his memory has been treasured in Northumbria down the centuries. We know that the last decade of his life was a struggle to preserve his health. For some years he had served as prior at both Melrose and Lindisfarne. While he discharged these duties faithfully, Cuthbert was at heart a hermit. Public and political life simply did not interest him; in fact, they caused him almost unbearable stress. In 676 he left Holy Island and retreated to Inner Farne to find peace in a solitary hermit's cell. After eight years in retirement, the King of Northumbria forced him to accept the position of bishop. Cuthbert endured the strain less than two years, until it became unbearable. Returning to Inner Farne in 686, he died within a year.

There are stories of his radically austere existence here. They say he would stand all night in the frigid waters of the North Sea, praying. The day of our visit was, by local standards, a pleasant day. The air had that wonderfully bracing quality of the sea. There was a light breeze under a blue sky. I found a spot on the small hill at the center of the island and sat for a while. At some point, I began to recall periods of stress over the course of my own ministry, as I struggled with the responsibility of senior clerical appointments during times of immense and relentless change in society and in the Church. Inevitably, there were periods of anxiety, sleep problems from time to time, occasional bouts of depression. However, I was under no illusion that I was a latter day Cuthbert. I knew that neither isolation nor asceticism were ways I would have chosen.

Thoughts of Cuthbert brought to mind stories of the self-denying habits of other early leaders of Christian communities. This severe path to Christian spirituality was particularly true of the Irish church. I thought of the legends of Kevin in Glendalough, standing for hours in that frigid lake in the valley. One story has it that a bird came and rested on his upraised palm, eventually built a nest and reared its young, all the time supported by the saintly hand. Not a performance for the fainthearted, to put it mildly.

I was not worried about missing the boats for the homeward trip. From where I sat, I could see the dock. So I began to reflect about prayer and the ways in which many of us—myself included—wrestle with it. I suspect that for a lot of people, the word prayer can often induce guilt, especially if we have been brought up on stories of the great saints: Cuthbert, Kevin, Brigid at her well in Kildare, unrelenting in prayer. And there is Patrick shivering on the slopes of Slemish Mountain in County Antrim, praying, so he tells us, a hundred times a day.

Where do you and I stand in all this high-stakes praying? I don't know about you, but I, for one, can feel defeated before I even start. Most of us consider ourselves, quite rightly, to fall so short of this kind of standard as to not even be in the race. On the other hand, could it be that these hagiographic images are woven from many different kinds of cloth? Perhaps the folk who were the contemporaries of these towering spiritual figures of the past, who knew them or knew of them, admired, respected, even loved them, were groping for ways to fitly capture how highly they thought of them. Then consider how the stories of their sanctity were told again and again, down through the ages. It would be strange, indeed, if there were not at least a few exaggerations as time passed.

I don't say this to lessen the greatness of our saints. I am merely trying to root them in the kind of reality you and I have to live in—the same kind of reality they experienced in their day. I would wager that a lot of their prayer was done on the fly, just like ours. After all, Cuthbert had a monastery to run at a time when things were pretty rough and dangerous in Northumbria. Brigid was always out and about visiting the sick and the poor. Patrick had to keep a weather eye on all those wandering sheep on the mountain slope, not to speak of having to watch his back in his adult years when he had enemies. I suspect they did what we all do: they prayed on the fly, or when life temporarily slowed down enough to let them snatch a moment of serenity. All of which should help to lift some of our guilt about our prayer life. I saw the boats returning to take us home. I recall realizing that in an ironic way, Cuthbert and his island had given me a taste of the solitariness he had once sought. For him, it had been a hard-fought and long-lasting solitude, for me a mere interlude. But that interlude was enough to move me into a meditative mood, and for that I was grateful.

## 5. THE SWANS AT MOUNT STEWART
### County Down, Northern Ireland, 2006

It is midafternoon on a lovely summer's day. I am with a friend, one of four of us visiting from Canada. This large estate was once the property of Lord Londonderry, a prominent public figure in English political life in the thirties and forties of the last century. On the eastern shore of Strangford Lough, the estate is now the property of the National Trust. Behind us is the large mansion that we have just viewed. We are walking along a wooded pathway that leads from the house toward a small lake.

The lake is at the top of a slight rise and reveals itself as we approach, its surface utterly still. To our right and across the lake we see two swans. There is something about swans—a dignity, a gracefulness, a beauty—that makes it quite impossible to regard them casually. We watch them gliding slowly on the glassy surface of the lake, every movement dispersing silent ripples. One knows that under the surface the steady strokes of the powerful webbed feet make this stately progress possible. Wonderfully, other than an inclination of the head to this side and that, there is no other movement of the body. All is deliberate, unhurried, almost mesmerizing.

All the more startling, then, is the sudden change that occurs. In a moment, as if a silent agreement has passed between them, their stillness is transformed into rapid movement. Huge wings stretch, lashing at the water around them, rising and falling as they seek the air. Long, curved necks extend. Every aspect of these two lovely creatures is transformed. They rise from the surface not to any great height, but enough to be just clear of the lake. There are moments when their webbed feet seem almost to touch the surface of the water. Their powerful wings beat the air with a kind of thunder as they head down the length of the small body of water, the sound echoing along the canopy of the trees like a vast organ in a great cathedral. Reaching the other end of the lake, they wheel and sink again to the surface. Once again there is the stillness, the slow grace of drifting together, almost as if what we have just seen never happened.

It all happens far too quickly for any attempt to capture the glory of it with a camera lens. Yet it remains imprinted on the eye of my memory. And there is good reason why it could hardly be otherwise. In my generation, there would hardly have been a child in Ireland who would not have been told the story of the Children of Lir. Set deeply in Irish mythology, it tells of the four children of King Lir, of whom the eldest is a girl named Fionnuala. She has three brothers. Their mother dies and their father marries again. The stepmother casts an evil spell on the children. Transformed into four magnificent white swans, they are cursed to travel the seas of Ireland for nine hundred years.

Through the long centuries Fionnuala becomes guide and mentor to her three younger brothers. The four share a wonderful gift, the gift of song. It is said that their singing became known and loved all over Ireland. Time passes and the swans turn for home. All is gone. Their father's royal castle is a ruin in the long grasses beside the lake. Sadly, the four swim toward the shore. As they touch the grassy bank, they are instantly transformed into four incredibly old people.

Word spreads quickly among the locals that the great swans have come home. Everyone knows the ancient story, passed on down the generations. Saint Patrick is called from his journeys around Ireland. He comes and listens kindly as Fionnuala and her brothers tell him of the old world and the old faith. The saint then tells them of the new faith, the story of the One who suffers, dies, and rises. He asks Fionnuala if she and her brothers wish to be baptized into this new resurrection faith. She accepts. Gently the local people carry the old ones, supporting them in the water as the saint baptizes them, then bringing them to where they can lie on the green grass. There they die.

It is said that when storms sweep over Ireland and the ocean thunders against the Cliffs of Moher, the singing of the Children of Lir can be heard on the wind. Perhaps it was because I had known that legend since my childhood that the flight of the swans at Mount Stewart moved me so deeply.

## 6. A FIRE NEVER QUENCHED
### St. Brigid's Well, Kildare, Ireland, 2007

The place where the well is situated is part of a larger field owned by a local farmer. In all, the area is about twenty-five yards wide and about a hundred yards long, and is enclosed by a simple wire fence. From the upper end, originating in the well, a stream flows underground until it emerges near the entrance to the enclosure and forms a small pool now outlined in cut stone. The visitor enters at the lower end of the area by a tiny bridge across the stream. There within a few yards is the pool.

Beyond the pool stands Brigid. The life-sized statue is made of bronze. She is young and vibrant. She wears a plain but flattering homespun robe. Her stance shows her stepping forward, reaching out eagerly, and holding aloft a flame. The effect is to communicate a vibrant, graceful woman. She could be a sister of a working order of nuns in the slums or barrios of this century, or the founder of an order in her own long ago fifth century, as, in fact, she was. She radiates life, purpose, dignity, and resolution.

Born in a brutal and dangerous world, Brigid grew up in an atmosphere of power and leadership. Her father ruled over a large extended family and its tract of countryside. Much was expected of this vivacious daughter. There would be a suitable marriage, an alliance that would add to her father's authority and influence. Brigid absolutely refused to live up to any of these conventional expectations. She wished to become a woman of the new Christian faith, and so she did. She proved to be an extraordinary human being, able to claim the allegiance of other women, ceaselessly active and adventurous herself, a tireless champion of the poor and downtrodden.

For centuries, perhaps even millennia before her, there had been a pagan fire temple in the area of Kildare, about forty miles southeast of today's Dublin. The name Kildare means "the Church of the Oak Tree." Brigid took over the ancient tradition and she and her sisters preserved the flame. To this day, there is a small group of Brigidine Sisters in the town of Kildare who keep a flame alive in their residence. So powerful is the memory of Brigid's life and ministry that her human life became interwoven, in medieval times, with that of the pagan goddess of the same name. Legends abound about Brigid's works of charity and powers of healing. Proof of her undying influence is the way in which in modern Ireland her name graces such activities as reconciliation and social action.

On a day of mingled showers and sunshine, we enter her shrine. Some of us kneel by the pool, dipping our hands in the clear water and touching it to our foreheads. We gather around the well and say prayers for our own time and world. Beside us is a living testimony to the power of faith—both Christian and pagan. By the fence there is a hawthorn tree. Each branch has prayers attached to it. They move silently on the gentle breeze: slips of paper, bits of cardboard, pieces of brightly colored cloth, anything on which a prayer can be written and hung on the tree.

The prayers are for the full spectrum of human need and hope. "For my friend who has cancer." "For peace in our country." "For the crops and the harvest." Every few weeks, the local sisters take down the worn artefacts of prayer to make room for new ones. The branches are always filled. "Prayer goes on." "The flame never goes out." "Brigid lives." "Christ is Risen."

# 7. THE CROSS OF MUIREDACH

## Monasterboice, County Louth, Ireland, 2016

In the late ninth century in Western Europe, an art form developed that has lasted for more than a thousand years. The skills of gifted stone carvers came together with the needs and resources of the many monastic settlements that had grown up across the west. Together they brought into being what today we call high crosses. These skills flowered particularly in Ireland. In their size and in the elaboration of their carving, the Irish high crosses became a wonder of the Christian world.

We came to Monasterboice as a family: two grandparents, our son Niall, and two of his sons. I had brought many groups of people here before. This time, however, because of the two boys, I realized that the way I presented the cross would have to be different. I was used to showing it to people who had an informed background acquaintance with the faith, the history of the church, and holy scripture. The boys were creatures of their generation. Their education in public school had included almost nothing that would serve me in this situation. I realized I would have to start from bedrock to tell the story of this wonderful cross. So I began that story as simply as possible without selling it short.

Imagine an Ireland a thousand years ago, heavily forested. There are no towns or villages. People tend to cluster for security and community around the monastic settlements that have formed since the still comparatively new religion of Christianity has arrived. These settlements, often isolated and set in the midst of a dangerous and violent world, are really fortified communities where a reasonably human quality of life is possible.

The monks wish to tell the Christian story to those around them, so they hit on a device. They will offer something impressive, even mysterious. They hire stone carvers to cut a set of five pieces of stone, three of them massive and two smaller. The first piece is a heavy broad base about two feet high and four feet wide. The second is a long narrow stone about seven feet long and a foot thick. The third, the most elaborate, is a crosspiece of stone around which a stone circle is formed. The fourth block of granite, about two feet high, is fixed in place above the circle and is crowned by the fifth and smallest piece of the cross. This is shaped like a small dwelling. It is an essential part of the design, because those looking up at it will be told that it is a model of the Ark of the Covenant that once held the tablets of the law given by God to Moses on Mount Sinai.

The cutting of the stone blocks, though laborious, is the easy part. The hard part is the years of carving that lie ahead to decorate and adorn the cross. And, of course, money has to be found to pay the stonecutters and carvers. A thousand years ago, the then abbot of the community—his name was Muiredach—must have decided to go all out, in spite of the expense. He gave the carvers a list of episodes from the Christian story. Each image would be set in a square etched into the cross. Figures would be carved to tell people that particular story, since almost all the onlookers would be illiterate.

I think it was at this point that I remembered our grandsons' iPads. I pointed out that it was interesting that each of the squares on the high cross was about the size of an iPad, and that both of these surfaces, in spite of being separated by a thousand years, were devices that could show images for teaching. At that moment, to my immense satisfaction, I could tell that I had caught their attention.

For years the carving would have continued. Then, when all the small squares were filled with scenes, it was time for the heavy lifting. The place for the cross would have been selected. Assembling the cross would then have begun: first the base, then the long stem, then the huge heavy circle of stone and the crosspiece, then the short upper stem, then the small house-like carving on top.

One thing more was needed: to paint the whole cross in vivid colors. It is easy for us to forget this part. By the time we arrive on the scene a thousand years later, all those vivid colors are long gone, and we are looking at dark gray granite mottled with the wear and tear of a thousand years of weather.

When the work was complete, all nineteen feet of it, there would have been a great celebration. The cross must have been simply magnificent, looming above the onlookers, blazing with color, solid, powerful, and beautiful. My guess is that it would have been dedicated by Muiredach on some feast day of the church's year—maybe Good Friday when Jesus was crucified, or Easter, the day of Christ's resurrection.

I wonder at what point the carvers showed the surprise they had prepared for their benefactor. On the base they had inscribed a text that is still legible after all the centuries. It says simply (in Latin), "Pray for Muiredach who had this cross erected."

At that point I stopped. Teenaged grandsons can only take so much history, and even less religion. I got them to move around all four sides of the cross as I pointed out that there are no less than twenty-two carved panels, including scenes from the Old Testament, stories from the life of Jesus, one hundred and twenty-four figures in all. Almost as if they didn't want to finish, the carvers even included two lions, two cats, two birds, a group of serpents, the sun and the moon, and, for good measure, the signs of the zodiac.

I then tried to link the boys with those who would have stood here all those centuries ago, listening and looking as they were told stories of the faith. Reaching again for their love of their modern technology, I ended by saying, "Come to think of it, they were looking at stone screens blazing with color." My reward was to receive the ultimate accolade of their generation: "Cool, Grandpa. Thanks."

# 8. RISKING THE TIDE

## Iona, Scotland, Fall 2008 / Spring 802 CE

With a group of friends, all of us travelling as pilgrims interested in the history of what has come to be called Celtic Christianity, my wife, Paula, and I had been visiting Iona. The day we were to leave the island (happily, not for the last time), the weather happened to be very stormy. At such times, the narrow stretch of water that separates Iona from the larger Isle of Mull can become quite a formidable barrier.

Even at the best of times, the tidal race is very powerful—so much so that the car and passenger ferry, substantial as it is, cannot just head straight across the sound from one dock to the other, but must make for a point far upstream, so as to allow itself to be swept down again by the tide to arrive safely on the far side.

As we left Iona that day, the thought occurred to me that the crossing of that stretch of water must have been a serious, sometimes even impossible, challenge to the small craft available to the early monastic community on the island. From that thought came this imagined voyage of the still-unknown poet who composed the verses we know as "Saint Patrick's Breastplate."

The coming of the Vikings is not imagined. Indeed, that terrible coming has never been forgotten in the coastal communities of these northern islands, and further south in Ireland. Early in the sailing season of the year 802, two small groups of Viking warships slid out of the harbors of Avaldsnes and Skiringssair in southern Norway. One of those squadrons headed due west for the Shetlands and the Orkneys, then sailed around the north coast of Scotland, through the Hebrides, until it reached Iona. The other set its course southwest for Lindisfarne, on the east coast of Northumberland. As they terrorized the small coastal communities, the news of their cruelty travelled ahead of them.

Thinking back to the ninth century, I find myself imagining a young monk of Iona traversing the storm-tossed channel between his island and the west coast of Mull—the same crossing I am making some twelve centuries later. He has to work hard to keep the small craft steady against the powerful pull of the tide. It occurs to him that he isn't getting any younger. He's been hearing recently how the atmosphere in the small communities up and down the coast is changing. Up to a few years ago, life had been vibrant and on the whole joyous. Now the first of the Viking long ships has begun to appear among the western isles, bringing rape and pillage and slavery, destruction and devastation and death.

His thoughts turn to the project he has recently begun, probably because he knows well his own life could be in danger at any time. He has begun to feel the need to express in some way what he has come to believe as a Christian Celt. His abbot, who often spoke about the faith, teaching and explaining it, was fond of expounding the concept of the Trinity: God as Father, Son, and Holy Spirit. But somehow the abbot's words were never sufficiently exciting or moving to capture and engage young minds. And so the idea had come to his student to write a poem.

Because he knew his superior would have to approve his work, he had begun with language he knew the abbot would like: "I bind unto myself today the strong name of the Trinity." A few days later, he had added two verses about Jesus, his life and the things that had happened to him. There were a few lines he was particularly proud of: "His death on cross for my salvation, his bursting from the spicèd tomb, his riding up the heavenly way, his coming at the day of doom." That last line made him shudder, thinking again of the Viking ships.

A sudden squall blows the tiny craft off course, but instead of fear he suddenly finds himself challenged, even elated, by the roar of the wind, the heaving of the sea, and the shriek of the gulls. He realizes that lines are coming to him that capture the awesome beauty and natural grandeur of God's world all around him. Suddenly, risking himself, he stands up and shouts his new words into the rising gale:

I bind unto myself today
the virtues of the starlit heaven,
the glorious sun's life-giving ray,
the whiteness of the moon at even,
the flashing of the lightning free,
the whirling wind's tempestuous shocks,
the stable earth, the deep salt sea
around the old eternal rocks.

He feels himself filled with gratitude for the inspiration that has come. All he wants now is to beach his small craft safely on the far shore, get to the community, find a bit of manuscript and something to write with, and capture the new lines before they fade from his mind.

He knows that he will always remember this moment in the storm, the feeling of an intense sense of oneness with the ocean, the wind, the birds, the clouds, the sun, the distant hills—with creation itself. The wonderful thing is that he has never before felt more secure, more at peace, and is sure he never will again.

Perhaps that is the reason for what would happen a few weeks later, just before he was due to return to his own community on the island. He was working in the small scriptorium his host abbot had lent him. He had just finished copying his newly completed verses, when he realized that something more was demanding to be written. He felt almost as if his hand were being guided. He knew with absolute certainty that these unexpected new lines expressed his own deepest faith: "Christ be with me." He continued to write.

All of this was long, long ago. We will never know who he was, though there must have been many young men like him. Doubtless he would have returned to his island, again pulling against the current, hearing the screams of the gulls, and seeing the surfacing of the odd curious seal. The community must have accepted and preserved his verses. At some stage, someone would have dedicated them to the long dead but much revered saint of their northern world, and the song became known as "Saint Patrick's Breastplate."

One other thing we know. The Vikings did, indeed, come to Iona, pulling ashore on the beach at the north end of the island. There on the white sands, they slaughtered forty monks from the community who wished only to welcome them.

We also know that the words of our unknown poet would continue to be sung for more than a thousand years. We know this because ours are the voices that sing them.

Christ be with me, Christ within me,
Christ behind me, Christ before me,
Christ beside me, Christ to win me,
Christ to comfort and restore me.

# A Spiritual Geography

## VICTORIA, BC, MAY 2020

I wonder why ancient people drew on their cave walls? Was it to give themselves images for reflection as the fire flickered at night, throwing shadows that gave life and movement to their drawings? Perhaps they drew to make this particular cave like no other, marking it as distinctively their cave and their home, a refuge where there could be rest and some sense of security in a harsh and fearful world.

Thoughts like this come because I have been spending a lot of time lately in my study, preparing this book of memoirs. Recently, it came to me what I have done here in this room. On all four walls, covering almost every square inch of available space, there are images—some photographs, some paintings, some line drawings—all evoking, indeed embodying, places and people that mean much in my life, and for which I feel an abiding sense of gratitude.

Come with me on a tour so modest that it can be accomplished by simply standing in the center of my study and turning as we gaze.

Look there, underneath the skylight: that huge outcrop of rock, crowned by an outer wall; within the wall nothing less than a cathedral, an abbey, and a round tower, all of them poised to overlook the Golden Vale, the pastureland of southern Tipperary. This is Cashel of the Kings, for millennia in ancient Ireland a fortress. Its most recent role, beginning in the Middle Ages, was as an ecclesiastical complex so magnificent that for centuries it was referred to as the Acropolis of the West.

Beside the Cashel frame hangs a photograph of one of the world's most graceful libraries, the Long Room in Trinity College Dublin. Today it houses the priceless manuscript of the Book of

Kells. I can remember studying for exams under that noble roof. Fifteen centuries before I pored over my books, watching my breath ascend in the frigid winter air of the library, others pored over the vellum pages that would survive many threats to their existence. With infinite care, they gave us the beauty of this manuscript, many layered, blazing with color.

Now, look slightly to the right. Ruined walls again. An abbey in Sligo, once the pride of the newly arrived Benedictines, coming under the protection of the Norman invaders in the twelfth century, intent on reforming what they saw as a corrupt and fading Irish church tradition.

Immediately under this hangs a haunting photograph of another church: a modern one this time, built on ancient foundations. You are standing within the church called *Dominus Flevit*, built on the slopes of the Mount of Olives to recall where Jesus once wept as he looked across at Jerusalem.

Continue to turn. Here is the picturesque fishing village of Roundstone in western Galway, in the distance the mountains that cradle Connemara, Ireland's west country, from which has come some of its loveliest poetry and drama.

Beside this, we look at the seventh-century Gallarus Oratory on the Dingle Peninsula in Kerry, a small, stone, beehive-shaped chapel that has faced the Atlantic winds and rain for at least thirteen centuries.

Turn slightly again and you are in the cavernous mouth of Fingal's Cave on the uninhabited island of Staffa in the Inner Hebrides, made famous first in eighteenth-century Scottish poet James Macpherson's epic verses, and even more so by nineteenth-century composer Felix Mendelssohn's majestic musical evocation of this place.

Move to the left and there is the Abbey of Iona itself. Once more we see a Benedictine foundation, damaged by King Henry's greed in the sixteenth century, and lovingly reconstructed by George MacLeod's Iona community in the twentieth.

Here by my favorite chair is a reproduction of a figure in stained glass: tall, strong, young, roughly clad. He holds a staff that is both a shepherd's crook and a bishop's crozier. This is Patrick, the great

Apostle of Ireland. The original window stands above the altar in Saul (or Sawel) Church in Downpatrick, south of Belfast, the site where, newly arrived in Ireland with his companions in the summer of 432, he was given the gift of a barn to begin his work. "Sawel" (or *sabhal*) is the Gaelic word for a barn.

Here on the wall beside the piano is Brigid in her shrine near Kildare, a generation after Patrick. Daughter of a chieftain, she founded her order. The very word "Kildare" evokes Cill Dara, meaning the Church of the Oak Tree, reminding me of the thousand years of Druidic spirituality that preceded the coming of Irish Christianity. To this day in Kildare, a small group of Brigidine sisters tend a flame in their modest residence, witnessing to the reality that Brigid's fire has never been quenched.

Now, take a great leap into a different world. We are gazing out across a frozen lake. Mountains rise steeply on either side. At the end of the lake is a vast glacier. We are in Lake Louise in the Rockies of southern Alberta. It is the depth of winter, with all the terrible beauty of that season in Western Canada.

Above me where I sit to write, the great Orthodox icon of our Lord—*Christos Pantocrator*, Christ the King—looks down on my labors, his face stern, his deep eyes probing but not unkindly. Beside him is a large image of Le Mont San-Michel, ancient outpost of Celtic Christianity on the Normandy coast, the tide far out, allowing a long line of pilgrims to approach across the wet sands.

Then something precious and personal: an old print of Carrick-fergus Castle in County Antrim, on the north shore of Belfast Lough. It's a memento of where I became betrothed to someone beloved who, in spite of my many shortcomings and idiosyncrasies, has remained with me for some sixty-five years as I write.

Beside it, a line-drawn print of the now about to be restored College of Preachers on the close of the National Cathedral in Washington, where in two years of residence and in many subsequent occasions as visiting lecturer, I learned much about the deep and subtle relationship between clergy and their ministry of preaching, both its joys and its stresses.

Images continue to gather as life goes on. If I mention some only briefly, it does not mean they have any lesser significance. Here beneath a wall lamp, a handshake with the Dalai Lama as I welcome him to Christ Church Cathedral in Vancouver. The farmyard of my grandfather's farm in Donaguile, a place of many childhood memories. Above the study door a simple plaque, the words those of Carl Jung, a great mind to whom I owe many insights about my own life and those of others: "Bidden or not bidden, God is present."

Such are the images around this study—images of people and places, images of experiences and memories, images of a life. I am certain such images exist for you too. Gather them and treasure them. They will continue to speak to you, continue to remind you of how much there is in your life for which to be grateful.